IAN MCIA.

The Tyndale New Testament Commentaries

General Editor:
THE REV. CANON LEON MORRIS, M.Sc., M.Th., Ph.D.

THE LETTER OF PAUL TO THE ROMANS

TO ELLA
IN MEMORY OF ATHOL

THE LETTER OF PAUL TO THE ROMANS

AN INTRODUCTION AND COMMENTARY

by

F. F. BRUCE, D.D., F.B.A.

Emeritus Professor, University of Manchester

Inter-Varsity Press
Leicester, England

William B. Eerdmans Publishing Company
Grand Rapids, Michigan

Inter-Varsity Press
38 De Montfort Street, Leicester LE1 7GP, England
Wm. B. Eerdmans Publishing Company
255 Jefferson S.E., Grand Rapids, MI 49503

Published and sold in the USA and Canada only by
Wm. B. Eerdmans Publishing Co.

British Library Cataloguing in Publication Data

Bruce, F. F.
    The letter of Paul to the Romans: an
    introduction and commentary.—2nd ed.—
    (The Tyndale New Testament commentaries)
    1. Bible. N.T. Romans—Commentaries
    I. Title   II. Bruce, F. F. Epistle of Paul to
    the Romans   III. Series
    227'.107   BS2665.3
    IVP EDITION 0–85111–875–5

Library of Congress Cataloging in Publication Data

Bruce, F. F. (Frederick Fyvie), 1910-
    The letter of Paul the Apostle to the Romans.

    (The Tyndale New Testament commentaries)
    Rev. ed. of: The Epistle of Paul to the Romans.
    1st ed. 1963.
    Bibliography: p.
    1. Bible.   N.T. Romans — Commentaries.   I. Bruce,
    F. F. (Frederick Fyvie),   1910-   .   The Epistle of
    Paul to the Romans.   II. Title.   III. Series.
    BS2665.3.B694   1985   227'.107   85-1506
    ISBN 0-8028-0062-9 (Eerdmans)

Phototypeset in Linotron Palatino 10/11pt
in Great Britain by Input Typesetting Ltd,
London
Printed in USA by Eerdmans Printing Company,
Grand Rapids, Michigan

Inter-Varsity Press is the publishing division of the Universities and Colleges Christian Fellowship (formerly the Inter-Varsity Fellowship), a student movement linking Christian Unions in universities and colleges throughout the United Kingdom and the Republic of Ireland, and a member movement of the International Fellowship of Evangelical Students. For information about local and national activities write to UCCF, 38 De Montfort Street, Leicester LE1 7GP.

GENERAL PREFACE

The original *Tyndale Commentaries* aimed at providing help for the general reader of the Bible. They concentrated on the meaning of the text without going into scholarly technicalities. They sought to avoid 'the extremes of being unduly technical or unhelpfully brief'. Most who have used the books agree that there has been a fair measure of success in reaching that aim.

Times, however, change. A series that has served so well for so long is perhaps not quite as relevant as when it was first launched. New knowledge has come to light. The discussion of critical questions has moved on. Bible-reading habits have changed. When the original series was commenced it could be presumed that most readers used the Authorized Version and one could make one's comments accordingly, but this situation no longer obtains.

The decision to revise and up-date the whole series was not reached lightly, but in the end it was thought that this is what is required in the present situation. There are new needs, and they will be better served by new books or by a thorough updating of the old books. The aims of the original series remain. The new commentaries are neither minuscule nor unduly long. They are exegetical rather than homiletic. They do not discuss all the critical questions, but none is written without an awareness of the problems that engage the attention of New Testament scholars. Where it is felt that formal consideration should be given to such questions, they are discussed in the Introduction and sometimes in Additional Notes.

But the main thrust of these commentaries is not critical. These books are written to help the non-technical reader to understand his Bible better. They do not presume a knowledge of Greek, and all Greek words discussed are transliterated; but the authors have the Greek text before them and their comments are made on the basis of the originals. The authors are free to choose their own modern translation, but are asked to bear in mind the variety of translations in current use.

The new series of *Tyndale Commentaries* goes forth, as the former series did, in the hope that God will graciously use these books to help the general reader to understand as fully and clearly as possible the meaning of the New Testament.

LEON MORRIS

CONTENTS

The sustained argument of this letter makes it impossible to bring out its meaning adequately on a verse-by-verse basis. The procedure adopted, accordingly, is to present an exposition of the successive divisions of the argument, each section of the exposition being followed by more detailed verse-by-verse comments on the division just expounded. The student who wishes to consult this work for help on a particular verse should therefore read the exposition of the passage within which that verse falls as well as any comment that may be provided expressly on the verse itself.

AUTHOR'S PREFACE

It is fitting, at the outset of this Tyndale Commentary on Romans, to remind ourselves of William Tyndale's own estimate of the letter as 'the principal and most excellent part of the New Testament' and 'a light and a way in unto the whole scripture' He goes on:

'No man verily can read it too oft or study it too well; for the more it is studied the easier it is, the more it is chewed the pleasanter it is, and the more groundly it is searched the preciouser things are found in it, so great treasure of spiritual things lieth hid therein.'[1]

Readers or interpreters of Paul, especially when they find themselves strongly attracted by his personality and reasoning power, are frequently tempted to tone down those features in his writings which are felt to be uncongenial, not to say scandalous, to modern tastes. It is possible to go along with Paul so far, and then try to go farther, not by accepting more of his teaching, but by unconsciously modifying his concepts so as to bring them into closer conformity with current thought. But a man of Paul's calibre must be allowed to be himself and to speak his own language. Well-meant attempts to make him prophesy a little more smoothly than in fact he does can but diminish his stature, not enhance it. We of the twentieth century shall grasp his abiding message all the more intelligently as we permit him to deliver it in his own uncompromising first-century terms.

---

[1] From the prologue to Romans in Tyndale's English New Testament (1534 edition).

I have used the opportunity provided by this revised edition not only to replace the AV by the RSV as the basis of the commentary, but also to incorporate the results of twenty years' further thought and study. I am greatly indebted to the excellent commentaries which have appeared since my first edition was published in 1963; among these the works of Ernst Käsemann and C. E. B. Cranfield call for specially honourable mention.

F.F.B.

CHIEF ABBREVIATIONS

ad loc.	At the place (under discussion).
AV	Authorized (King James') Version, 1611.
BAGD	W. Bauer, *Greek-English Lexicon of the New Testament*, translated by W. F. Arndt and F. W. Gingrich, second edn. rev. and augmented by F. W. Gingrich and F. W. Danker (Chicago, 1979).
BJRL	*Bulletin of the John Rylands (University) Library, Manchester.*
EQ	*Evangelical Quarterly.*
E.T.	English Translation.
ExT	*Expository Times.*
GNB	Good News Bible (Today's English Version), 1976.
JBL	*Journal of Biblical Literature.*
JTS	*Journal of Theological Studies.*
LXX	Septuagint (pre-Christian Greek version of the Old Testament).
mg.	Margin.
MT	Massoretic Text (of the Hebrew Bible).
NEB	New English Bible, 1970.
NIDNTT	*New International Dictionary of New Testament Theology*, edited by Colin Brown (Exeter, 1975–78).
NIV	The Holy Bible, New International Version, 1978.
NTS	*New Testament Studies.*
RGG	*Religion in Geschichte und Gegenwart.*
RSV	American Revised Standard Version, Old Testament, 1952; New Testament, [2]1971.
RV	Revised Version, 1885.
SJT	*Scottish Journal of Theology.*
s.v.	Under the word (being discussed).

TB   Babylonian Talmud.
TDNT   *Theological Dictionary of the New Testament*, edited by
     G. Kittel and G. Friedrich, translated by G. W.
     Bromiley, 10 vols. (Grand Rapids, 1964–76).
ZNW   *Zeitschrift für die neutestamentliche Wissenschaft.*

INTRODUCTION

I. THE OCCASION OF THE LETTER

Paul spent the ten years from AD 47 to 57 in intensive evangelization of the territories east and west of the Aegean Sea. During those years he concentrated in succession on the Roman provinces of Galatia, Macedonia, Achaia and Asia. Along the main roads of these provinces and in their principal cities the gospel had been preached and churches had been planted. Paul took with proper seriousness his commission as Christ's apostle among the Gentiles, and now he might well contemplate with grateful praise not (he would have said) what he had done, but what Christ had done through him. His first great plan of campaign was concluded. The churches he had planted in Iconium, Philippi, Thessalonica, Corinth, Ephesus and many another city in those four provinces could be left to the care of their spiritual leaders, under the overruling direction of the Holy Spirit.

But Paul's task was by no means finished. During the winter of AD 56–57, which he spent at Corinth in the home of his friend and convert Gaius, he looked forward (with some misgivings) to a visit which had to be paid to Jerusalem in the immediate future – for he had to see to the handing over to the elders of the church there of a gift of money which he had been organizing for some time past among his Gentile converts, a gift which he hoped would strengthen the bond of Christian love between the mother church in Judaea and the churches of the Gentiles.[1]

---

[1] See comments on Rom. 15:25–32 (pp. 248–251).

When that business had been transacted, Paul looked forward to the launching of a plan which had been taking shape in his mind over the past few years. With the conclusion of his apostolic mission in the Aegean lands, he must find fresh fields to conquer for Christ. In making choice of a new sphere of activity, he determined to go on being a pioneer; he would not settle down as an apostle in any place to which the gospel had already been brought; he would not 'build on another man's foundation' (Rom. 15:20). His choice fell on Spain, the oldest Roman province in the west and the chief bastion of Roman civilization in that part of the world.

But a journey to Spain would afford him the opportunity of gratifying a long-standing ambition – the ambition to see Rome. Although he was a Roman citizen by birth,[1] he had never seen the city whose freeman he was. How wonderful it would be to visit Rome and spend some time there! All the more wonderful because there was a flourishing church in Rome, and several Christians whom Paul had met elsewhere in his travels were now resident in Rome and members of that church. The very fact that the gospel had reached Rome long before Paul himself ruled out Rome as a place where he could settle for pioneer evangelism; but he knew that he would continue his journey to Spain with all the more zest if he could first of all refresh his spirit by some weeks of fellowship with the Christians in Rome and then, perhaps, be provided by them with a base for his advance into Spain.

During the early days of AD 57, therefore, he dictated to his friend Tertius – a Christian secretary possibly placed at his disposal by his host Gaius – a letter destined for the Roman Christians. This letter was to prepare them for his visit to their city and to explain the purpose of his visit; and he judged it wise while writing it to set before them a full statement of the gospel as he understood and proclaimed it.[2]

One reason for his setting this full statement before them may have been his awareness that his message was being misrepresented by his opponents in various places; he seizes

---

[1] See Acts 22:28, 'I was born a citizen.'
[2] Other suggestions of the purpose of the letter are made by some contributors to *The Romans Debate*, ed. K. P. Donfried (1977).

the opportunity to set the record straight. But more than that: he probably wishes to involve the Roman Christians in his ministry. He bespeaks their prayers for his safety in Judaea; but if it turned out that he was 'not only to be imprisoned but even to die at Jerusalem for the name of the Lord Jesus' (Acts 21:13), he would like to know that the continuation of his witness – especially its western extension to Spain – could confidently be entrusted to such a faithful body of people as the Christian community of Rome.

II. CHRISTIANITY AT ROME

It is plain from the terms in which Paul addresses the Christians in Rome that the church of that city was no recent development. But when we try to ascertain something about the origin and early history of Roman Christianity, we find very little direct evidence to help us, and have to reconstruct the situation as far as possible from various literary and archaeological references.

According to Acts 2:10 the crowd of pilgrims who were present in Jerusalem for the Pentecost festival of AD 30, and heard Peter preach the gospel, included 'visitors from Rome, both Jews and proselytes'. We are not told if any of these were among the three thousand who believed Peter's message and were baptized. It may be significant that these Roman visitors are the only contingent from the continent of Europe to receive express mention among the pilgrims.

In any case, all roads led to Rome, and once Christianity had been securely established in Judaea and the neighbouring territories, it was inevitable that it should be carried to Rome. Within two or three years, if not (as Foakes-Jackson thought) 'by the autumn following the Crucifixion, it is quite as possible that Jesus was honoured in the Jewish community at Rome as that He was at Damascus'.[1] The fourth-century Latin Father who is called Ambrosiaster says in the preface to his commentary on this letter that the Romans 'had embraced the faith of Christ, albeit according to the Jewish rite, without seeing any

---

[1] F. J. Foakes-Jackson, *Peter, Prince of Apostles* (1927), p. 195.

sign of mighty works or any of the apostles'. It was evidently members of the Christian rank and file who first carried the gospel to Rome and planted it there – probably in the Jewish community of the capital.

There was a Jewish community in Rome as early as the second century BC. It was considerably augmented in consequence of Pompey's conquest of Judaea in 63 BC and his 'triumph' in Rome two years later, when many Jewish prisoners of war graced his procession, and were later given their freedom. In 59 BC Cicero makes reference to the size and influence of the Jewish colony in Rome.[1] In AD 19 the Jews of Rome were expelled from the city by decree of the Emperor Tiberius (see p. 88), but in a few years they were back in as great numbers as ever. In the time of Claudius (AD 41–54) we have the record of another mass–expulsion of Jews from Rome. This expulsion is briefly referred to in Acts 18:2, where Paul, on his arrival in Corinth (probably in the late summer of AD 50), is said to have met 'a Jew named Aquila, . . . lately come from Italy with his wife Priscilla, because Claudius had commanded all the Jews to leave Rome'. The date of this edict of expulsion is uncertain, although Orosius may well be right in placing it in AD 49.[2] Other references to it appear in ancient literature, the most interesting of which is a remark by Suetonius in his *Life of Claudius* (25.2), that Claudius 'expelled the Jews from Rome because they were constantly rioting at the instigation of Chrestus (*impulsore Chresto*)'. This Chrestus may conceivably have been a Jewish agitator in Rome at the time; but the way in which Suetonius introduces his name makes it much more likely that the rioting was a sequel to the introduction of Christianity into the Jewish community of the capital. Suetonius, writing some seventy years later, may have known a contemporary record of the expulsion order which mentioned Chrestus as the leader of one of the parties involved, and inferred that he was actually in Rome

[1] *Pro Flacco* 66.

[2] *History* 7.6.15 f. According to Dio Cassius (*History* 60.6), Claudius had already imposed some restrictions on the Roman Jews at the beginning of his principate: 'As the Jews had again increased in numbers, but could not easily be expelled from the city because there were so many of them, he did not actually drive them out but forbade them to meet in accordance with their ancestral customs.' See F. F. Bruce, *New Testament History* (1971), pp. 279–282.

at the time. He would know that Chrestus (a variant Gentile spelling of *Christus*) was the founder of the Christians, whom he elsewhere describes as 'a pernicious and baneful class of people',[1] and it would seem quite a reasonable inference to him that Chrestus had taken an active part in stirring up these riots.

Priscilla and Aquila appear to have been Christians before they met Paul, and were probably members of the original Roman group of believers in Jesus. We do not know where or when they first heard the gospel; Paul himself never suggests that they were his children in the faith. We may be sure that the original group of believers in Rome consisted predominantly, if not entirely, of Jewish Christians, whose departure and dispersal followed Claudius's expulsion order.

The effects of the expulsion order, however, were short-lived. Before long the Jewish community was flourishing in Rome once more, and so was the Christian community. Less than three years after the death of Claudius Paul can write to the Christians of Rome and speak of their faith as a matter of universal knowledge. The expulsion edict would have lapsed with Claudius's death (AD 54), if not indeed earlier.[2] But in AD 57 the Christians in Rome included not only Jewish but Gentile believers. Some of the latter may have stayed on in the city after the expulsion of their Jewish brethren; if so, their numbers were greatly augmented by the time Jewish Christians were able to return. Paul indeed has to remind the Gentile Christians that, even if they are now in the majority, the base of the community is Jewish, and that they must not despise their Jewish brethren just because they outnumber them (Rom. 11:18).

In fact, the Jewish basis of Roman Christianity was not soon forgotten. As late as the time of Hippolytus (died AD 235) some features of Christian religious practice at Rome continued to proclaim their Jewish origin – an origin, moreover, which should be sought in sectarian or nonconformist Judaism rather than in the main stream.[3]

---

[1] *Life of Nero* 16.2.

[2] *Cf.* G. Edmundson, *The Church in Rome in the First Century* (1913), pp. 80, 84; T. W. Manson, *Studies in the Gospels and Epistles* (1962), pp. 37–40.

[3] Hippolytus, *Apostolic Tradition* 20.5. *Cf.* M. Black, *The Scrolls and Christian Origins* (1961), pp. 114 f.

If the greetings in Romans 16:3–16 were addressed to Rome (see pp. 253–257), then we may find in them some interesting information about members of the Roman church in AD 57. The people to whom greetings are sent by name included Christians whom Paul had met in other places during his missionary activities and who were at this time resident in Rome. Some of them were very early Christians, like Andronicus and Junias (or rather Junia), who, as Paul says, were 'in Christ' before himself and were well known in apostolic circles and may, indeed, have been reckoned as apostles themselves (16:7). The Rufus to whom greetings are sent in 16:13 has been tentatively identified with the son of Simon of Cyrene mentioned in Mark 15:21; Paul may have known him and his mother at Syrian Antioch. Priscilla and Aquila, who had been compelled to leave Rome eight years previously, were now back in th✔ capital, and their house was one of the meeting-places for church members there. (The fact that the basilica, the regular style of early church edifice, preserves the outline of a private Roman house, reminds us that the house-church was the regular Christian meeting in primitive times.)

By AD 57, the year in which Paul wrote to the Romans, Christianity may already have begun to make some impact in the higher reaches of Roman society. In that year Pomponia Graecina, the wife of Aulus Plautius (who conquered the province of Britain for the Roman Empire in AD 43), was tried and acquitted by a domestic court on a charge of embracing a 'foreign superstition', which could have been Christianity.[1] But, to the majority of Romans who knew anything about it, Christianity was simply another disgusting oriental superstition, the sort of thing that the satirist Juvenal had in mind sixty years later when he complained of the way in which the sewage of the Orontes was discharging itself into the Tiber.[2] (Since Antioch on the Orontes was the home of Gentile Christianity, Juvenal probably thought of Gentile Christianity as one of the ingredients in that sewage.)

When, seven years after the writing of this letter, Rome was devastated by a great fire, and the Emperor Nero looked around

---

[1] Tacitus, *Annals* 13.32.3–5. [2] *Satire* 3.62.

for scapegoats against which he could divert the popular
suspicion which (quite unjustly, it may be) was directed against
himself, he found them ready to hand. The Christians of Rome
were unpopular – reputed to be 'enemies of the human race'[1]
and credited with such vices as incest and cannibalism. In large
numbers, then, they became the victims of the imperial malevolence – and it is this persecution of Christians under Nero that
traditionally forms the setting for Paul's martyrdom.

Three years after he sent this letter, Paul at last realized his
hope of seeing Rome. He realized it in a way which he had not
expected when he wrote. The misgivings which he expressed
in the letter (15:31) about his reception in Jerusalem proved to
be well founded. Not many days after his arrival in Jerusalem
he was charged before the Roman governor of Judaea with a
serious offence against the sanctity of the temple. His trial
dragged on inconclusively until Paul at last exercised his right
as a Roman citizen and appealed to have his case transferred
to the jurisdiction of the emperor in Rome. To Rome, then, he
was sent, and after shipwreck and wintering in Malta he
reached the capital early in AD 60. As he was conducted north
along the Appian Way by the courier force in whose custody
he was, Christians in Rome who heard of his approach walked
out to meet him at points thirty or forty miles south of the city
and gave him something like a triumphal escort for the
remainder of his journey. The sight of these friends proved a
source of great encouragement to him. For the next two years
he remained in Rome, kept under guard in his private lodgings,
with permission to receive visitors and to propagate the gospel
at the heart of the empire.

What happened at the end of these two years is a matter of
conjecture. It is not at all certain if he ever fulfilled his plan of
visiting Spain and preaching the gospel there. What is reasonably certain is that, a few years later at most, he was sentenced
to death at Rome as a leader of the Christians, led out of the
city along the Ostian Way and beheaded at the place then called
Aquae Salviae (modern Tre Fontane). His tomb lies beneath the

[1] Tacitus, *Annals* 15.44.5.

high altar of the basilica of *San Paolo fuori le Mura* ('St Paul Outside the Walls').

The blood of the martyrs, however, in Tertullian's words, proved to be seed.[1] Persecution and martyrdom did not extinguish Christianity in Rome. The church in that city continued to flourish in increasing vigour and to enjoy the esteem of Christians throughout the world as a church 'worthy of God, worthy of honour, worthy of congratulation, worthy of praise, worthy of success, worthy in purity, pre-eminent in love, walking in the law of Christ and bearing the Father's name'.[2]

III. ROMANS AND THE PAULINE CORPUS

'St. Paul's letter to the Romans – and others' was a title suggested for this letter by T. W. Manson.[3] He believed (not without good reason) that, in addition to the copy of the letter which was taken to Rome, further copies were made and sent to other churches. One pointer to this is the textual evidence at the end of chapter 15 (see pp. 28, 252), which might indicate that there was in circulation in antiquity an edition of the letter which lacked chapter 16 – a chapter which, with its personal greetings, would have been relevant only to one church.[4]

This one church, as is argued below (pp. 255–257), was the Roman church. It was for the Roman church that the letter was specifically designed. The copy received by that church was certainly treasured, copied and recopied. About AD 96 Clement,

---

[1] Tertullian, *Apology* 50.

[2] This description comes from the preface of Ignatius's *Letter to the Romans* (*c*. AD 110).

[3] The title of a lecture first published in *BJRL* 31 (1948), pp. 224–240, reprinted in T. W. Manson, *Studies in the Gospels and Epistles* (1962), pp. 225–241, and in K. P. Donfried (ed.), *The Romans Debate* (1977), pp. 1–16.

[4] This one church, in Manson's view, was Ephesus: Paul designed Romans 1 – 15 for Rome, but added chapter 16 to a copy which he sent to Ephesus. This I find improbable (see pp. 253–255). Much more improbable is the theory that the letter to the Romans, as we know it, is the expansion of an earlier general letter 'written by St. Paul, at the same time as Galatians, to the mixed Churches which had sprung up round Antioch and further on in Asia Minor' (K. Lake, *The Earlier Epistles of St. Paul*, 1914, p. 363; *cf.* F. C. Burkitt, *Christian Beginnings*, 1924, pp. 126–128).

'foreign secretary' of the Roman church, shows himself well acquainted with the letter to the Romans; he echoes its language time and again in the letter which he himself sent in that year on behalf of the Roman church to the church of Corinth. The way in which he echoes its language suggests that he knew it by heart; it could well be that it was read regularly at meetings of the Roman church from the time of its reception onwards.

It is clear from Clement's letter that by AD 96 some of Paul's letters had begun to circulate in other quarters than those to which they were sent in the first instance;[1] Clement, for example, knows and quotes from 1 Corinthians. And not many years after, an unknown benefactor of all succeeding ages copied at least ten Pauline letters into a codex from which copies were made for use in many parts of the Christian world.[2] From the beginning of the second century Paul's letters circulated as a collection – the *corpus Paulinum* – and not singly. The second-century writers, both 'orthodox' and 'heterodox', who refer to the Pauline letters knew them in the form of a corpus.

One of these writers, of the 'heterodox' variety, was Marcion, a native of Pontus in Asia Minor, who came to Rome about AD 140 and a few years later published an edition of Holy Scripture. Marcion repudiated the authority of the Old Testament and

---

[1] Paul himself took some initial steps to secure a wider circulation of some of his letters; *cf.* his directions in Colossians 4:16 that the Colossian and Laodicean churches should exchange letters received from him. His letter to the Galatians was sent to several churches. It is implied in Galatians 6:11 that originally the one MS was taken from church to church, rather than that one was sent to each church; but some of the Galatian churches would make copies for themselves before passing it on. The letter to the 'Ephesians' was probably composed as an encyclical, and may have been despatched in a number of copies, with blanks left in verse 1 for the address to be supplied – in one early copy the address supplied in the blank space was evidently 'Laodicea'. Between the original reception of Paul's letters and the publication of the *corpus Paulinum* there may have been smaller, regional collections, such as a collection of the letters sent to the churches of Macedonia (1 and 2 Thessalonians and Philippians) and one of those sent to the province of Asia (Philemon, Colossians and Ephesians).

[2] G. Zuntz thinks that the corpus was compiled and published at Alexandria; it was evidently a critical edition, showing signs of 'dependence upon the scholarly Alexandrian methods of editorship' (*The Text of the Epistles*, 1954, pp. 14–17, 276–279). This is at least more probable than the once popular view that it was compiled in Ephesus (*cf.* E. J. Goodspeed, *Introduction to the New Testament*, 1937, pp. 217–219; C. L. Mitton, *The Formation of the Pauline Corpus of Letters*, 1955, pp. 44–49), a romantic embellishment of which was J. Knox's thesis that the prime mover in the compilation of the corpus was Onesimus, bishop of Ephesus *c.* AD 100 and former slave to Philemon (*Philemon among the Letters of Paul*, 1935, ³1960).

held that Paul was the only faithful apostle of Jesus, the earlier apostles having corrupted his teaching with judaizing admixtures. Marcion's canon reflected his distinctive views. It consisted of two parts: the *Euangelion*, an edition of the Gospel of Luke which began with the words, 'In the fifteenth year of Tiberius Caesar Jesus came down to Capernaum, a city of Galilee' (*cf.* Lk. 3:1; 4:31), and the *Apostolikon*, comprising ten Pauline letters (excluding those to Timothy and Titus).

Galatians, for which Marcion had a natural predilection on account of its anti-judaizing emphasis, stood first in his *Apostolikon*. The other letters followed in descending order of length, the 'double' letters (*i.e.* the two to the Corinthians and the two to the Thessalonians) being reckoned for this purpose as one for each pair. Romans thus came after 'Corinthians'. To each of the letters a Marcionite preface was attached in due course.[1] The Marcionite preface to Romans runs thus:

> 'The Romans are in the region of Italy. These had been visited already by false apostles and seduced into recognizing the authority of the law and the prophets, under pretext of the name of our Lord Jesus Christ. The apostle calls them back to the true faith of the gospel, writing to them from Athens.'

This is not the inference which a reader would naturally draw from Paul's argument in this letter, but Marcion and his followers approached the apostolic writings with firmly held presuppositions. Where they found statements in Paul's letters running counter to these presuppositions, they concluded that the text had been tampered with by judaizing scribes, and emended it accordingly (see pp. 27–30). But such was the influence of Marcion's edition, well beyond the limits of his own following, that many 'orthodox' MSS of the Pauline letters contain the Marcionite prefaces.

Our oldest surviving MS of the Pauline letters, dating from the end of the second century, contains the shorter corpus of ten letters together with the letter to the Hebrews. This MS (Papyrus 46, one of the Chester Beatty biblical papyri) comes

---

[1] This is said in awareness of the view about the Marcionite prefaces expressed by J. Regul, *Die antimarcionitischen Evangelienprologe* (1969), pp. 13, 85, 88–94.

from Egypt, and in Egypt (unlike Rome) Hebrews was regarded as Pauline as early as AD 180. In P46 (as this MS will henceforth be called) Romans comes first.

Romans comes last among the Pauline letters sent to churches in another document from the closing years of the second century, the 'Muratorian Canon' or fragmentary list of New Testament books recognized at Rome. This list includes the longer Pauline corpus of thirteen letters, for after the letters to churches it adds those addressed to individuals – not only Philemon but also Timothy and Titus.

In the order which ultimately became established Romans takes pride of place among the Pauline letters. Historically, this is because it is the longest letter, but there is an innate fitness in the accordance of this position of primacy to a letter which, above all others, deserves to be called 'The Gospel according to Paul'.

IV. THE TEXT OF ROMANS

a. English Versions
This commentary is designed as a companion to the study of the text of Romans; it cannot be used without constant reference to the letter which it endeavours to expound and annotate.

The text on which the commentary is based is that of the RSV (1971 edition); but it can be used equally well with the NEB (1970) or the NIV (1978). In all three of these the English translation is based on what is called an 'eclectic' Greek text. That is to say, in each place where existing witnesses to the Greek text differ in the readings they present, the translators have chosen that reading which, in their judgment, corresponds most closely to the wording of the biblical author. They have not given their preference to a single 'best' MS or group of MSS, as had been done in some earlier versions of the New Testament.

b. The early Pauline text
How many copies of the letter to the Romans were in circulation between AD 57 and the end of the first century cannot be known. But, from the time that the *corpus Paulinum* was

compiled at the beginning of the second century, Romans, like each of the other Pauline letters, no longer circulated separately but as a component part of the corpus.

The question naturally arises whether some evidence may not have survived in the textual tradition of the letters which goes back to a time before the corpus. The quotations in 1 Clement (AD 96) probably represent the pre-corpus text; but nearly all the other elements in the extant textual tradition are derived from the text of the corpus. Sir Frederic Kenyon's statistics showing the measure of agreement and disagreement between P[46] and other principal MSS reveal significant variations in this regard from one letter to another; Romans, in particular, stands apart from the others – a state of affairs which Kenyon thought could best be explained if the textual tradition goes back to a time when the individual letters circulated separately.[1] Professor Zuntz mentions a few examples of 'primitive corruption' and marginal annotation which the compiler of the corpus probably found already present in one or another of the MSS which he used, and copied into his edition.[2] But the first edition of the *corpus Paulinum* is the archetype which textual criticism of the letter, as its primary task, must try to recover, because it is the archetype from which the common text of the second century and the main text-types of the following centuries are derived.

From the end of the second century onwards two main text-types can be distinguished for the Pauline letters – an eastern type and a western. In addition to P[46] (our oldest surviving witness), early witnesses to the eastern text-type include B (the fourth-century *Codex Vaticanus*), *Aleph* (the fourth-century *Codex Sinaiticus*), 1739 (a tenth-century Athos minuscule) or rather the very ancient and excellent MS (no longer extant) from which its text of the thirteen Pauline letters and Hebrews was copied,[3] citations in Clement of Alexandria (*c.* AD 180) and Origen (died AD 254), and the two main Coptic versions (Sahidic and

---

[1] F. G. Kenyon (ed.), *The Chester Beatty Biblical Papyri*, fasc. 3, Supplement (1936), pp. xv ff.

[2] G. Zuntz, *The Text of the Epistles*, pp. 15, 278–280.

[3] The text of this ancient MS (the ancestor of 1739) agrees with that known to Origen, especially in Romans; the MS may have belonged to the great library of Pamphilus in Palestinian Caesarea.

Bohairic).[1] The western text of the Pauline letters is attested chiefly by citations in Tertullian (c. AD 200), by other authorities for the Old Latin version (other patristic citations and the text of d),[2] and by the common ancestor of the codices D, F and G.[3] This western text goes back to the popular and rather corrupt text of the second century; the relative purity of the eastern text is due, Zuntz thinks, to the constant application to it of the editorial techniques of Alexandrian textual scholarship.[4]

c. Early recensions of Romans
There are a number of indications in the textual history of Romans that it circulated not only in the form in which we know it but in one or even two shorter editions. These indications appear mainly towards the end of the letter, but there are two pieces of possibly relevant evidence at the beginning.

1. *The beginning of the letter.* (i) Romans 1:7. In this verse the words 'in Rome' were absent from the text on which Origen's commentary on Romans was based, and also, probably, from the text on which Ambrosiaster's commentary was based (although in the MS tradition of both commentaries the basic text has been conformed to that in common use). The margins of 1739 and 1908[5] attest the omission of the words from Origen's text and commentary.

The Graeco-Latin codex G, one of the western witnesses to the Pauline text, also lacks the reference to Rome in this verse, presenting the reading 'to all who are in the love of God' where the common text has 'to all God's beloved in Rome, who are called to be saints'. Other western witnesses, all of them Latin, exhibit the shorter reading of G adapted to the common text by the addition of the words 'in Rome'; thus: 'to all who are in

[1] It is noteworthy that nearly all these witnesses (including P[46]) are of Egyptian provenance.

[2] *d* is the Latin text of the bilingual codex D (see next note); it is independent of the accompanying Greek text.

[3] D is the sixth-century Graeco-Latin *Codex Claromontanus*. It was closely related to the common ancestor of F (*Augiensis*) and G (*Boernerianus*), ninth-century Graeco-Latin codices (their Latin texts, *f* and *g*, unlike *d*, have no independent value). See H. J. Frede, *Altlateinische Paulus-Handschriften* (1964).

[4] *The Text of the Epistles*, pp. 269–283.

[5] An eleventh-century MS in the Bodleian Library, related to 1739.

Rome in the love of God' (so *d*, the Vulgate codices *Amiatinus*, *Ardmachanus* and two others, Pelagius and possibly Ambrosiaster).

(ii) Romans 1:15. The words 'who are in Rome' are absent from G, while some of the companions of this codex show attempts to adapt this abridged form to the common text.

It looks as if the ancestor of the codices D and FG lacked 'in Rome' in 1:7 and 1:15 alike.[1] That the omission was not exclusively western is indicated by the fact that Origen's text also lacked 'in Rome' in 1:7.

2. *The end of the letter.* Some phenomena towards the end of the letter suggest that various recensions of it ended at different points. A suitable conclusion might have been provided by any one of the benedictions or quasi-benedictions of 15:5–6; 15:13; 15:33; 16:20b (repeated by western and Byzantine witnesses in 16:24). But the most interesting textual phenomenon at the end of the letter concerns the position of the final doxology (16:25–27 in the common text).

(i) In *Amiatinus* and a few other Vulgate codices the Pauline letters are supplied with 'chapter-summaries' (Lat. *breues*) taken over from a pre-Vulgate Latin version. In them Romans is divided into fifty-one 'chapters' or sections. For the last two of these the summaries are as follows:

'50. Concerning the danger of grieving one's brother with one's food, and showing that the kingdom of God is not food and drink but righteousness and peace and joy in the Holy Spirit.

'51. Concerning the mystery of God, which was kept in silence before the passion but has been revealed after his passion.'

The summary of section 50 corresponds to the substance of 14:1–23; that of section 51 corresponds to the doxology of 16:25–27. This suggests that a shorter edition of the letter existed in which the concluding doxology followed immediately after

---

[1] G's sister-codex F lacks Rom. 1:1 – 3:19, so its evidence is not available for 1:7, 15.

14:23. There are some other indications that such a shorter edition was known and used.[1]

(ii) The *Book of Testimonies* ascribed to Cyprian (died AD 258) includes a collection of biblical texts which enjoin withdrawal from heretics; this collection does not include Romans 16:17, which might have been thought an apt text for his purpose. This argument from silence, which would have little weight if it stood alone, must be taken along with other pieces of evidence.

(iii) Although Romans 15 and 16 are so full of potential anti-Marcionite ammunition,[2] Tertullian nowhere quotes from these chapters in his five books *Against Marcion*. In the fifth book of that treatise, however (chapter 13), he does quote Romans 14:10, and says that it comes in the concluding section (Lat. *clausula*) of the letter.

(iv) Rufinus (*c.* AD 400), in his Latin abridgement of Origen's commentary on Romans, says on 16:25–27: 'Marcion, who introduced alterations into the evangelic and apostolic writings, removed this section completely from this letter, and not only so, but he cut out everything from that place where it is written, "whatever does not proceed from faith is sin" (14:23), right to the end.' There is no reason to doubt that here Rufinus has given a straightforward rendering of Origen's own words.

(v) In the Byzantine textual tradition the doxology of 16:25–27 comes after 14:23 and before 15:1. Origen knew of MSS which put the doxology in this position, but he also knew of others which put it after 16:24, and believed (not unnaturally) that the latter was the proper place for it. But those MSS which place the doxology between chapters 14 and 15 are probably witnesses to an edition of the letter which ended with 14:23, followed by the doxology (this truncated edition being later completed by the addition of chapters 15 and 16).

(vi) G (with some codices known to Jerome) lacks the doxology altogether. It is probable, indeed, that it was lacking in the ancestor of D and FG. Moreover, from the fact that this ancestor apparently had a western text in chapters 1 – 14 but a

---

[1] In the Vulgate MSS 1648, 1792 and 2089 the letter ends at 14:23, followed by a benediction and the doxology.

[2] For Marcion's point of view, see pp. 21–22.

text with several peculiar readings in chapters 15 and 16, it has been inferred that behind it lay a text which came to an end with 14:23 (omitting the doxology).[1] It is more than a coincidence that this is how Marcion is said to have brought the letter to an end.

(vii) A few witnesses (A P 33 104, and some Armenian codices) have the doxology both after 14:23 and again after 16:24.

(viii) In P[46] the doxology comes between chapters 15 and 16. This has been regarded as evidence for an edition of Romans which came to an end at 15:33.

We thus appear to have evidence for two shorter editions of Romans – one ending at 15:33 and the other ending at 14:23 (with or without an added doxology). We also have evidence for an edition which lacked the words 'in Rome' in 1:7, 15; this edition may or may not have been identical with one or other of the two shorter editions just mentioned.

There is no difficulty in understanding why an edition should have circulated without chapter 16. If copies of the letter were sent to a number of churches, because of the general interest and relevance of its contents, all but one of these copies would very naturally have lacked chapter 16, which with its many personal messages would have been applicable to one church only.[2]

But why should an edition have circulated without chapter 15? The argument which begins with 14:1 continues into chapter 15 and leads on naturally to Paul's personal statement in 15:15–33.[3] We have, however, Origen's testimony that Marcion omitted everything after 14:23 and brought the letter to an end at that point. Why Marcion should have done so will be apparent to anyone who looks at the series of Old Testament

---

[1] Cf. P. Corssen, 'Zur Überlieferung des Römerbriefes', ZNW 10 (1909), p. 9.

[2] Alternatively, in an edition intended for liturgical purposes, chapter 16 with its many personal messages might have been omitted as superfluous. Certainly no other letter of Paul ends as chapter 15 does.

[3] F. C. Burkitt curiously held that 14:23 'is a real conclusion: nothing but a Doxology is really in place after it', and supposed that 15:1–13 was 'a weld, a join, an adaptation', by means of which Paul attached the following personal details when he expanded his earlier circular letter (see p. 20, n. 4) and sent the expanded form to Rome (Christian Beginnings, p. 127).

quotations in 15:9–12, or at the statement in 15:4 that 'whatever was written in former days was written for our instruction', or at the description of Christ in 15:8 as 'a servant to the circumcised to show God's truthfulness, to confirm the promises given to the patriarchs'. Such a concentration of material offensive to Marcion can scarcely be paralleled in the Pauline writings.

To Marcion, then, we may assign the edition which ended at 14:23.[1] But such was the influence of Marcion's edition that his text, like his disciples' prefaces, was reproduced in greater or lesser degree in several orthodox lines of transmission, especially in western (and, more particularly, Latin) copies.[2]

What now can be said of the omission of the references to Rome in 1:7, 15? It might have been expected that this omission would belong to the more generalized edition of the letter which supposedly came to an end with 15:33. But in the textual history of Romans the witnesses to the omission of the Roman reference in 1:7, 15 belong to the tradition which attests the fourteen-chapter edition, not the fifteen-chapter edition. Was Marcion, then, responsible for the omission of the reference to Rome at the beginning of the letter, as well as for the omission of everything after 14:23 at the end? But why should he have struck out the twofold reference to Rome? When the Roman church repudiated Marcion and his teaching, he might have judged it unworthy to be mentioned in the text of his *Apostolikon*. 'This is no more than a conjecture',[3] and against it must be set the

---

[1] For Harnack's view that the doxology was composed by later Marcionites to round off this edition, see pp. 267f.

[2] It has been argued that Marcion's text lacked also Romans 1:19 – 2:1 and 3:31 – 4:25 (*cf.* T. Zahn, *Geschichte des neutestamentlichen Kanons*, ii, 1892, p. 516; A. Harnack, *Marcion*, ²1924, pp. 48, 103*, 104*).

[3] So says T. W. Manson (*Studies in the Gospels and Epistles*, p. 230), whose conjecture it is. He would explain the omission of 'in Ephesus' from Ephesians 1:1 in the same way, since it was 'at Rome and Ephesus that Marcion received his two great and humiliating rebuffs'; but this explanation is much less probable for Eph. 1:1 than it is for Rom. 1:7, 15. The context in Romans, as he says, 'imperatively demands a particular reference to a well-known community not founded by Paul or hitherto visited by him' (*op. cit.*, p. 229), and indeed this could only be Rome. But almost any other place-name within Paul's Gentile mission-field could stand in place of Ephesus in Eph. 1:1 without doing violence to the context. Ephesians was evidently designed from the first as a circular letter, a blank being left in the opening salutation which could be filled in with any appropriate place-name. Marcion evidently knew it in an edition which read 'in Laodicea' where the majority text has 'in Ephesus'. *Some* place-name, preceded by the preposition 'in', had to be supplied, as the construction is not Greek otherwise.

fact (as it appears to be) that in his canon the letter retained the title 'To the Romans'.[1]

V. ROMANS AND THE PAULINE GOSPEL

Romans was Paul's last letter written before his prolonged period of detention, first in Caesarea and then in Rome. It is thus later than his letters to the Thessalonians, Corinthians and Galatians, and earlier than those to Philemon, the Colossians, Ephesians and Philippians (not to speak of the Pastorals). This is a conclusion which can be reached not only by external evidence and incidental chronological indications in the letters, but also by a study of their subject-matter.

Some of the themes of Paul's Corinthian correspondence recur in Romans. We may compare what is said about the food question in 1 Corinthians 8:1–13; 10:14 – 11:1 with what is said in Romans 14:1 – 15:6; we may compare what is said about the members of the body and their respective functions in 1 Corinthians 12:12–31 with what is said in Romans 12:3–8; we may compare the antithesis between Adam and Christ in 1 Corinthians 15:21–22, 45–50 with that in Romans 5:12–19; we may compare the references to the collection for Jerusalem in 1 Corinthians 16:1–4 and 2 Corinthians 8:1 – 9:15 with Paul's account of it in Romans 15:25–32. In some of these instances the Romans passage is self-evidently later than the parallel in 1 or 2 Corinthians. More particularly, Romans 8:2–25 reproduces much of the argument of 2 Corinthians 3:17 – 5:10 (combined with part of the argument of Galatians 4 – 5) in a manner which has been described as 'the free creation, on two separate occasions, of verbal clothing for familiar logical outlines'.[2]

Of all the Pauline letters, however, the one which has the closest affinity with Romans is Galatians. In both of these letters Paul's gospel of justification by faith is most clearly expounded. A comparison of the two leaves no doubt that Galatians is the earlier; the arguments which are pressed on the churches of Galatia in an urgent and *ad hoc* manner are set forth more

---

[1] See H. Gamble, *The Textual History of the Letter to the Romans* (1977).

[2] C. H. Buck, Jr., 'The Date of Galatians', *JBL* 70 (1951), p. 116.

systematically in Romans. Galatians, according to J. B. Light-foot, is related to Romans 'as the rough model to the finished statue'.[1]

There is indeed a marked difference in tone between Galatians and Romans. Galatians is, in the main, a polemical document, addressed to Paul's Gentile converts who were in danger of abandoning the message of salvation by grace which he had taught them and slipping into legalism. Romans is not polemical: Paul writes to gain the good-will and co-operation of a flourishing church not personally known to him. The Roman church comprised a variety of groups, some more liberal and some more conservative, and Paul deals with both tendencies in conciliatory and understanding terms. The liberal Christian must not despise his conservative fellow-believer; the conservative must not sit in judgment on his liberal brother. If Paul expostulates with the Galatian Christians for observing 'days, and months, and seasons, and years' (Gal. 4:10), he contemplates with equanimity the situation in which some Roman Christians observe certain days religiously, while others set apart no special days: 'Let every one', he says, 'be fully convinced in his own mind' (14:5). His teaching about the role of the law is essentially the same in both letters, but he treats it more dismissively in Galatians than in Romans.

The letter to the Galatians was sent to churches in the Roman province of Galatia (most probably to churches in South Galatia) to warn them against relapsing from the gospel of free grace under the persuasion of teachers who insisted that their salvation depended on their submitting to circumcision and certain other requirements of the law of Moses, over and above their faith in Christ. Those teachers believed and taught that Jesus was the Messiah of Israel, but the Messiah was for *Israel*. The true Israel, the 'Israel of God', comprised those Israelites who acknowledged him as Messiah and Lord, but the only way in which non-Israelites could share the saving blessings which he brought was by incorporation into the true Israel, and this involved circumcision (for men) and the fulfilment of some other legal requirements. In Paul's eyes those other require-

---

[1] 'Or rather', he goes on, '. . . it is the first study of a single figure, which is worked into a group in the latter writing' (*Saint Paul's Epistle to the Galatians*, 1865, p. 49).

31

ments were not so much an addition to the pure gospel as a perversion of it. The teaching to which his Galatian converts were being exposed nullified the principle that God's salvation is bestowed by his sheer grace and received by faith alone; it gave human beings a contributory share in that saving glory which, according to the gospel, belongs to God alone. It implied, moreover, that the age of law was still running its course; if so, then the age of the Messiah had not yet arrived, and Jesus, accordingly, was not the Messiah. The 'agitators' (as Paul calls them) who pressed their teaching on the Galatian churches were far from drawing this conclusion from it, but Paul drew it for them, and pronounced an anathema on them.[1] Their whole scheme was a different gospel from that which Paul and the other apostles preached;[2] it was, in fact, no gospel at all.

In his endeavour to show his Galatian friends where the truth of the matter lies, Paul raises the fundamental question of men and women's justification in the sight of God. That God was the supreme judge of the world was common Jewish doctrine, as was also the belief that a day would come when he would pronounce final judgment on all mankind. Paul, however, taught that, thanks to the work of Christ, the verdict of the great day could by anticipation be known and accepted in this present life – that those whose hearts were right with God could have the assurance of acquittal in his court here and now. But how in fact could human beings know themselves to be 'in the right' so far as God's assessment of them was concerned? If it was possible to be justified before God by observing the requirements of the Jewish law, as the Galatian Christians were now being taught, then what was the point of the death of Christ, which was central to the gospel? According to the gospel, his death procured his people's redemption and set them right with God; but there was no need for his death if this end could have been attained by the law. But we know, says Paul, that one 'is not justified by works of the law but through faith in Jesus Christ' – and his converts had proved

---

[1] Cf. F. F. Bruce, The Epistle to the Galatians (1982), pp. 83 f., 176.
[2] Cf. 1 Cor. 15:11 for Paul's witness that he and the Jerusalem apostles preached the same basic message.

this to be true in their own experience. So, he continues, 'we have believed in Christ Jesus, in order to be justified by faith in Christ, and not by works of the law, because by works of the law shall no one be justified' (Gal. 2:16).[1]

Faith in Christ, not legal works: that is one antithesis which Paul emphasizes to the Galatians. A companion antithesis in his argument is *Spirit, not flesh*. The new life which they had received when they believed the gospel was a life imparted and maintained by the Holy Spirit; it was unthinkable that the work of the Spirit, which belongs to a new order, should require to be supplemented by ordinances which were so completely bound as were circumcision and all that went with it to the old order of the 'flesh'.[2] The attempt to live partly 'according to the Spirit' and partly 'according to the flesh' was foredoomed to failure, because the two orders were in sharp opposition the one to the other: 'the desires of the flesh are against the Spirit, and the desires of the Spirit are against the flesh' (Gal. 5:17).

Both these antitheses – 'faith in Christ *versus* legal works' and 'Spirit *versus* flesh' – recur in Romans in their logical sequence, the former antithesis in chapters 3 and 4, where the way of righteousness is under discussion, and the latter in chapters 6 – 8, where the subject is the way of holiness.

Another *motif* of Galatians which appears also in Romans is the appeal to the precedent of Abraham. Since the Jewish ordinance of circumcision was based on the covenant made by God with Abraham (Gn. 15:10–14), those who insisted that Gentile converts to Christianity ought to be circumcised argued that otherwise they could claim no share in the blessings promised to Abraham and his descendants. To this Paul replies that the basis of Abraham's acceptance by God was not his circumcision, or any comparable 'work', but his *faith*: 'Abraham "believed God, and it was reckoned to him as righteousness" ' (Gal. 3:6).[3] So the children of Abraham, who inherit the blessings promised to Abraham, are those who, like him, have faith in God and are accordingly justified by his grace. The gospel, in short, is the fulfilment of the promises made by God to

[1] An echo of Ps. 143:2; *cf.* Rom. 3:20 (p. 94).
[2] On the two orders see pp. 39–50, below.
[3] Quoted from Gn. 15:6; *cf.* Rom. 4:3 (pp. 104–106).

Abraham and his posterity – promises which have not been annulled or modified by anything, such as the Mosaic law, which was instituted since they were made.

Moreover, Paul assures the Galatian Christians, those who submit to circumcision as a legal obligation put themselves under an obligation to observe the whole law of Moses, and become liable to the curse which the law pronounces on those who fail to keep it in its entirety.[1] But the liberating message of the gospel tells how 'Christ redeemed us from the curse of the law, . . . that in Christ Jesus the blessing of Abraham might come upon the Gentiles, that we might receive the promise of the Spirit through faith' (Gal. 3:13–14).

The principle of righteousness by law-keeping belongs to a stage of spiritual immaturity. But now that the gospel has come, those who obey it and believe in Jesus attain their spiritual majority as full-grown sons and daughters of God. The Spirit of God who has taken up his abode in the hearts of believers is also the Spirit of his Son, and at his prompting they address God spontaneously as Father in the same way as Jesus himself did.[2]

Again, the gospel is a message of liberty in place of the yoke of bondage carried by those who rely on the law to secure their acceptance by God. Why should those who have been emancipated by Christ give up their freedom and submit to servitude afresh? On the other hand, the freedom brought by the gospel has no affinity with anarchic licence. The faith of which the gospel speaks is a faith which manifests itself in a life of love, and thus fulfils 'the law of Christ' (Gal. 5:6; 6:2).[3]

So Paul reasons with the churches of Galatia, arguing *ad hominem* as well as *ad hoc*. He recalls them to faith in the gospel which first brought them salvation. It has been said, indeed, that 'justification by faith, while not necessarily incompatible with Paul's earlier doctrine, was actually formulated and expressed by him for the first time when he found it necessary to answer the arguments of the Judaizers in Galatia. It seems not at all unlikely that the term justification, which takes on its familiar Pauline meaning and importance only in Galatians and

[1] Gal. 3:10, quoting Dt. 27:26.   [2] Gal. 4:6; *cf.* Rom. 8:15 (see pp. 156–158).
[3] *Cf.* Rom. 12:9–21; 13:8–10 (pp. 215–218, 226f.).

Romans, derived this importance and at least a part of this meaning not from Paul's regular theological vocabulary but from that of his opponents.'[1]

But the gospel which Paul sets forth in the letter to the Galatians is not only the gospel which he preached to its readers when he presented the message of the cross so vividly that it was as if 'Jesus Christ crucified' were publicly placarded before their very eyes (Gal. 3:1); it was the gospel which had revolutionized Paul's own life.[2] Justification by faith was implicit in his Damascus-road experience. Paul, as we know, was suddenly converted to the service of Christ from a life in which the law had been the centre around which everything else was organized. In his previous system of thought and practice there was no room to entertain even the possibility that the disciples' claim about Jesus might be true. His teacher Gamaliel might concede the possibility, if only for the sake of argument, but not so Paul. The disciples' claim that Jesus was the Messiah undermined the law, and could not be tolerated. If one thing more than another disproved that claim, it was the fact of Jesus' crucifixion. Whether he merited such a death or not was of secondary importance; what was of primary importance was the affirmation of the law: 'a hanged man is accursed by God' (Dt. 21:23). The idea that one who died under the curse of God could be the Messiah was blasphemous and scandalous.

When Paul, in mid-career as a persecutor of the church, was compelled to recognize that the crucified Jesus was alive, risen

---

[1] C. H. Buck, Jr., 'The Date of Galatians', pp. 121 f.: this conclusion, he says, 'seems inescapable' after a comparison of 2 Cor. 1 – 9, where only the 'flesh/spirit' antithesis appears, with Galatians, where Paul uses both this and the 'works/faith' antithesis. Galatians is accordingly later than 2 Cor. 1 – 9, he finds, because if Paul had already formulated the 'works/faith' antithesis in his mind before he wrote 2 Cor. 1 – 9, he could scarcely have avoided using it there at least once in view of the 'vehement anti-legal position' he takes up in those chapters. I have tried to show elsewhere (*The Epistle to the Galatians*, pp. 48 f.) that this conclusion is not so inescapable as is claimed. For earlier statements on the polemical origin of Paul's message of justification by faith see W. Wrede, *Paul*, E.T. (1907), p. 123; W. Heitmüller, *Luthers Stellung in der Religionsgeschichte des Christentums* (1917), pp. 19 f.; *cf.* the discussion in K. Holl, *Gesammelte Aufsätze* ii (1928), pp. 18 f.

[2] *Cf.* S. Kim, *The Origin of Paul's Gospel* (²1984); R. Y. K. Fung, 'The Relationship between Righteousness and Faith in the Thought of Paul, as expressed in the Letters to the Galatians and the Romans', unpublished Ph.D. thesis, University of Manchester (1975); 'Justification by Faith in 1 & 2 Corinthians', in *Pauline Studies*, ed. D. A. Hagner and M. J. Harris (1980), pp. 246–261.

from the dead, and that he was all that his disciples claimed him to be – Messiah, Lord, Son of God – his whole system of thought and life, previously organized around the law, must have been shaken to pieces. The confident judgment which he had formed about Jesus in accordance with that system was shown to be utterly wrong. But the fragments of the broken system quickly began to reorganize themselves in a completely different pattern, around a new centre, the crucified and exalted Jesus. Henceforth, for Paul, to live was – Christ.

But what of the old argument – that the crucified one died under the curse of the law? Was it no longer valid? It was still valid, but received a new significance. By raising Jesus from the dead, God had reversed that curse. But why should Jesus have undergone the curse in the first place? Sooner rather than later, Paul must have reached the conclusion set out in Galatians 3:10–13, that Jesus submitted to the death of the cross in order to take on himself the curse which the law pronounced on all who failed to keep it completely (Dt. 27:26). The *form* of this argument – interpreting two texts in the light of a common term which they shared (here, the term 'cursed' or 'accursed' in Dt. 21:23 and 27:26, LXX) – was such as Paul was quite familiar with in the rabbinical schools, but no rabbi had ever formulated the *substance* of this bold argument: that, by voluntarily undergoing the curse of the law in one form, the Messiah should neutralize that curse on behalf of those who had incurred it in another form. But in this way the doctrine of a crucified Messiah, which had once been such a stone of stumbling to Paul, became the corner-stone of his faith and preaching.[1]

We cannot say how soon this reinterpretation took shape in Paul's mind, but it must have been sooner rather than later. It could perhaps have been assisted at an early stage by consideration of the portrayal of the Suffering Servant who, in Isaiah 53:10–12, gives his life as a guilt-offering for others and, by bearing the sin of many, procures righteousness for them.[2] But it cannot be too strongly emphasized that Paul's theology was not based primarily on study or speculation. It was based

---

[1] See Rom. 9:32–33 (pp. 186–188).
[2] See Rom. 4:25 (pp. 112f.).

primarily on the Damascus-road revelation of Jesus Christ (Gal. 1:12, 16)[1] and the flooding of his inner being with divine love through the impartation of the Spirit (Rom. 5:5). All that Paul had sought so long by painstaking observance of the law was now his by God's gift – all that and much more. For now he could do the will of God with a glad spontaneity such as he had never known under the law; he knew himself accepted by God, justified by his grace, blessed with a new power within, and called to a service which for ever thereafter gave purpose and zest to life.

'The just shall live by faith' – or, as Paul expounds it, 'it is the one who is righteous by faith that will live'[2] – is not only the kernel of Galatians and the text of Romans, but it was a foundation-principle in Paul's own life. Time and again he reverts to it, and not only in these two letters. When he reminds the Corinthians how Christ was 'made . . . sin' for us 'so that in him we might become the righteousness of God' (2 Cor. 5:21), or tells the Philippians of his ambition to 'gain Christ and be found in him, not having a righteousness of my own, based on law, but that which is through faith in Christ, the righteousness from God that depends on faith' (Phil. 3:8–9), he shows quite plainly what was the ground of his hope and the motive-power of his apostolic ministry. The very contrast between his former activity as a persecutor and his new life as a bond-slave of Jesus Christ magnified the grace of God which had been lavished so abundantly on him, wiping the slate clean and making him what he now was.

The way of righteousness, then, which he sets forth to the Romans was a way which was well-known to him, ever since his feet were planted on it outside the walls of Damascus. A doctrine inherent in his conversion experience cannot be adequately explained as a polemical response to the arguments of judaizers. Whatever may be said about Galatians, there was no need to introduce a polemical note into the argument of Romans. There is more autobiography in this letter than meets

[1] See G. Bornkamm, 'The Revelation of Christ to Paul on the Damascus Road and Paul's Doctrine of Justification and Reconciliation', in *Reconciliation and Hope: Essays presented to L. L. Morris*, ed. R. J. Banks (1974), pp. 90–103.

[2] Habakkuk 2:4b, quoted in Gal. 3:11 and Rom. 1:17 (see pp. 75–77).

the eye – the autobiography of a man who has been justified by faith.[1]

The gospel of justification by faith sets human beings by themselves as individuals before God. If it humbles them to the dust before God, it is that God may raise them up and set them on their feet. One who has had such personal dealings with God, and been made to stand erect in his presence by almighty power and grace, can never be enslaved in spirit to any other man or woman. Justification by faith is a bastion of true freedom. Luther was charged with 'inciting revolution by putting little people in mind of their prodigious dignity before God'. How could he deny the charge? The gospel, as he had learnt it from Paul, does precisely that.

Yet, crucial as the justification of sinners by faith alone is to the Pauline gospel, it does not exhaust that gospel. It is not, as Albert Schweitzer called it, 'a subsidiary crater',[2] but in itself it

---

[1] See J. Buchanan, *The Doctrine of Justification* (1867, reprinted 1951); J. A. Ziesler, *The Meaning of Righteousness in Paul* (1972). Paul whole-heartedly believed in the implanting of a righteous character, but as something logically subsequent to, and distinguished from, the conferment of a righteous status. Reformed theology has generally distinguished the two by calling the latter 'justification' (the subject of Rom. 1:17; 3:19 – 5:21) and the former 'sanctification' (the subject of Rom. 6 – 8). Failure to observe this distinction leads to confusion in the interpretation of Paul. While the distinction – between justification by faith as the initial act of God's grace and sanctification as the following and continuous work of his grace – is commonly viewed as characteristically Lutheran and Reformed doctrine, there is ample evidence that justification by faith alone was understood and held before and alongside Luther and the Reformers. The Reformed doctrine had been antici-pated at almost every point by the Lady Julian of Norwich in the fourteenth century. In the first half of the sixteenth century it was expounded by several theologians in the papal camp (especially in Italy). When Cardinal Gaspare Contarini wrote a treatise on justification by faith alone, the English Cardinal Reginald Pole congratulated him on being the first to bring to light 'that holy, fruitful, indispensable truth'. It was the Council of Trent that checked this trend on the papal side. Despite Pole's exhortation 'not to reject an opinion simply because it was held by Luther', the Council in 1546 defined justification in terms which confused it with sanctification and made it dependent on works as well as faith, and anathematized point by point those who affirmed the Reformed – or rather the Pauline – doctrine. See *Acta Concilii Tridentini*, Sessio VI ('De iustificatione'); also L. von Ranke, *History of the Popes*, E.T., I.ii (1908), pp. 109, 113, 158–160. More recently it has been argued, *e.g.* by the Roman Catholic theologians W. H. van der Pol and Hans Küng (*cf.* especially the latter's *Justification*, E.T., 1964, with introduction by Karl Barth), that it was not the biblical doctrine of justification 'by faith alone' that the Council condemned, but the Reformers' 'external' interpretation of that doctrine, and that the Tridentine formulations (conditioned as they were by the polemical situation) have been misunderstood by Prot-estants as teaching a synergistic soteriology. There is a concise (pre-Vatican II) critique of this account of the matter in G. C. Berkouwer, *Recent Developments in Roman Catholic Thought* (1958), pp. 56–63.

[2] A. Schweitzer, *The Mysticism of Paul the Apostle*, E.T. (1931), pp. 220 f.

is not the centre of Paul's teaching. Various attempts have been made to say what the centre is, and some writers on Paul have been criticized for failing to define it. But it is probably a mistake to think in terms of one centre for his theology. Reconciliation, union with Christ, the indwelling Spirit, instatement as sons and daughters of God, joint-membership of the one body, sanctification, the hope of glory – these are all interrelated in Paul's thought; none occupies a position of centrality in relation to the others.

Paul himself speaks of the gospel as 'the power of God for salvation to every one who has faith' (Rom. 1:16), and in so speaking he provides us with a term which, if not central to his message, certainly comprehends everything that it contained. The term 'salvation' includes, as Anderson Scott has pointed out, 'all the chief factors in Christianity, whether in theory or in practice'. Not only so, but in the term 'salvation' Paul's message 'found a point of attachment to the religious needs both of the Jewish and of the pagan world'.[1] Jews and Gentiles alike were conscious of their deep need for salvation, even if they did not mean the same thing by that word. Certainly in Paul's preaching of salvation God's act of grace in justifying the sinner played a basic part.

Paul's doctrine of justification, together with his other doctrines, is set in the context of the new creation that has come into being with and in Christ. That the acquittal of the day of judgment is pronounced in advance here and now on those who believe in Jesus is part and parcel of the truth that for them 'the old order has gone, and a new order has already begun' (2 Cor. 5:17, NEB) – a truth made real in their present experience by the advent and activity of the Spirit.

VI. 'FLESH' AND 'SPIRIT' IN ROMANS

To readers of this letter Tyndale's prologue to Romans gives the following wise advice: 'First we must mark diligently the manner of speaking of the apostle, and above all things know

---

[1] C. A. A. Scott, *Christianity according to St. Paul* (1927), pp. 17 f.

what Paul meaneth by these words – the Law, Sin, Grace, Faith, Righteousness, Flesh, Spirit and such like – or else, read thou it never so often, thou shalt but lose thy labour.'

Of these words two of the most important are the opposed terms 'flesh' and 'spirit', which in their distinctive Pauline usage relate respectively to the old order superseded by Christ and the new order inaugurated by him. Flesh and spirit wage incessant warfare one against the other within the citadel of Mansoul. This warfare, as described in Paul's writing, is not the conflict between matter and mind, between the physical and rational elements in humanity, which we meet in other schools of ancient thought. The background of the Pauline usage of these terms is the Old Testament, although their Old Testament usage is extended by Paul along lines peculiarly his own.[1]

a. 'Flesh'

In the Old Testament 'flesh' (Heb. *bāśār*, *šeʾēr*)[2] is the basic material of human (and animal) life. Leaving aside the frequent occurrences of 'flesh' in the sense of animal life (*e.g.* Gn. 6:19) or the meat of animals which may be eaten (*e.g.* Ex. 12:8), we observe that, as 'flesh', human beings are distinguished from 'the gods, whose dwelling is not with flesh' (Dn. 2:11). When God announces that he will limit the duration of human life, he says, 'My spirit shall not abide in man for ever, for he is flesh' (Gn. 6:3). Man, in fact, is animated flesh; 'all flesh' (*e.g.* Gn. 6:12; Is. 40:5–6; Joel 2:28) means 'all mankind' (when the context does not indicate the wider sense of 'all animal life'). 'Flesh' may denote human nature in its weakness and mortality: 'he remembered that they were but flesh' (Ps. 78:39). It can be used of the human body, as when a man is instructed to 'bathe his flesh in water' (*e.g.* Lv. 14:9, RV); or of the man himself in a more general sense, as in Psalm 63:1, where 'my flesh faints for thee' stands in synonymous parallelism with the preceding clause, 'my soul (Heb. *nepeš*) thirsts for thee' (here both 'my

[1] Excellent treatments of these terms are given by E. Schweizer and others in *TDNT* VI, pp. 332–455 (article *pneuma*, 'spirit'); VII, pp. 98–151 (article *sarx*, 'flesh'); also pp. 1024–1094 (article *sōma*, 'body').

[2] Because RSV (like NEB and NIV) sometimes renders these terms (and their Greek equivalent *sarx*) on a 'meaning-for-meaning' basis, some references below (as indicated) are to RV, which renders them uniformly by the literal 'flesh'.

soul' and 'my flesh' are little more than alternative ways of saying 'I').

It is against this Old Testament background, then, that we are to understand the Pauline use of the term (Gk. *sarx*), with more particular reference to the letter to the Romans.

1. 'Flesh' is used in the ordinary sense of *bodily flesh* in Romans 2:28 (*cf.* Gn. 17:11), where the literal 'circumcision, which is outward in the flesh' (RV), is contrasted with the spiritual 'circumcision' of the heart.

2. 'Flesh' is used of *natural human descent or relationship*. Thus Christ is said in 1:3 to be David's descendant 'according to the flesh', as in 9:5 he is said to belong to the nation of Israel 'according to the flesh'.[1] In 4:1 Abraham is called 'our forefather according to the flesh' (*i.e.* the ancestor of those of us who are Jews by birth), whereas spiritually he is the father of all believers (4:11–12, 16); his descendants by physical propagation are 'the children of the flesh' by contrast with 'the children of the promise' (9:8). People of Jewish birth are Paul's 'kinsmen according to the flesh' (9:3, RV) or simply his 'flesh' (11:14, RV).[2]

3. 'Flesh' is used in the sense of *mankind* in Romans 3:20, 'by the works of the law shall no flesh be justified' (RV). This is a common Hebrew usage: Old Testament examples are 'To thee shall all flesh come' (Ps. 65:2) and 'no flesh has peace' (Je. 12:12). We may compare our Lord's words: 'except the Lord had shortened the days, no flesh would have been saved' (Mk. 13:20, RV). Paul appears to have been fond of this usage: in Romans 3:20 he quotes Psalm 143:2, where the word 'flesh' does not appear in the Old Testament text, yet he introduces it into his quotation both here and in Galatians 2:16. (*Cf.* 1 Cor. 1:29, RV, 'that no flesh should glory before God.') Sometimes the same idea is expressed by 'flesh and blood' (*e.g.* Gal. 1:16,

---

[1] In these two places 'flesh' denotes not only natural descent but also the state of our Lord's earthly existence before he was glorified (see pp. 68f., 175f.).

[2] 'Flesh' appears in this sense in the Old Testament as, for example, when Abimelech says to his Shechemite kinsmen, 'Remember also that I am your bone and your flesh' (Jdg. 9:2).

'I did not confer with flesh and blood', *i.e.* with any human being).

4. 'Flesh' is used variously in the sense of *human nature*, as follows:

(i) *Weak human nature*. In Romans 6:19 Paul explains his argument by the aid of an analogy from everyday life 'because of the infirmity of your flesh' (RV); by 'flesh' here he refers more particularly to his readers' *intelligence*. Again, in 8:3 he speaks of the law as being unable to produce righteousness because it was 'weakened by the flesh', *i.e.* the frail human nature with which it had to work. (A good example of this sense of 'flesh' is provided by the saying of Jesus in Mt. 26:41, 'the spirit indeed is willing, but the flesh is weak.')

(ii) *The human nature of Christ*. The humanity of Christ is something he shares with all mankind. But our flesh is 'sinful flesh', because sin has established a bridgehead in *our* life from which it dominates the situation. Christ came in real flesh, but not in 'sinful flesh'; sin was unable to gain a foothold in *his* life. Therefore he is said to have come 'in the *likeness* of sinful flesh' (Rom. 8:3). Having come thus, he dealt effectively with sin in his humanity: he repelled its attempts to secure an entrance into his life, and when in death he presented his sinless life to God as a sin-offering, God by this means 'condemned sin in the flesh' (Rom. 8:3) – the territory ruled by sin was redeemed from its domination through the incarnation, sacrifice and victory of the man Christ Jesus.

(iii) *The 'old nature' in the believer*. When Paul speaks of 'my flesh', he most often means his sinful propensity inherited from Adam. There is nothing good in it (7:18); with it, he says, 'I serve the law of sin' (7:25).[1] It is still present with him, even if progressively disabled – and this in spite of its having been 'crucified' (*cf.* Gal. 5:24, 'those who belong to Christ Jesus have crucified the flesh with its passions and desires').[2] This apparent paradox is met repeatedly in the Pauline writings: believers are

[1] The Corinthian Christians, though they were indwelt corporately and individually by the Spirit of God (1 Cor. 3:16; 6:19), were not spiritual but 'men of the flesh' (1 Cor. 3:1, 3).

[2] *Cf.* also Rom. 6:6, 'our old self was crucified with him', which has a somewhat different meaning (see pp. 130f.).

enjoined time and again to be what they are – to be in actual practice what they are as members of Christ. Thus they are said to have 'put off the old nature' and 'put on the new nature' (Col. 3:9–10), while elsewhere they are exhorted to 'put off' their 'old nature' and 'put on the new nature' (Eph. 4:22, 24). The 'old nature' is what they were 'in Adam'; the 'new nature' is what they are 'in Christ'. Therefore to put on the new nature is to put on Christ; and while Paul tells the Galatians that 'as many . . . as were baptized into Christ have put on Christ' (Gal. 3:27), he bids the Romans 'put on the Lord Jesus Christ' (Rom. 13:14).

(iv) *Unregenerate human nature.* Though 'my flesh' is still present with me, I am no longer 'in the flesh'.[1] To be 'in the flesh' is to be unregenerate, to be still 'in Adam', in a state in which one 'cannot please God' (Rom. 8:8). Believers were formerly 'in the flesh' (7:5), but now they 'are not in the flesh' but 'in the Spirit', if indeed the Spirit of God dwells within them – and if he does not, they do not yet belong to Christ (8:9).

5. Since, then, believers are no longer 'in the flesh' but 'in the Spirit', they should no longer live 'according to the flesh' – according to the pattern of their old unregenerate life[2] – but 'according to the Spirit' (see 8:4–5, 12–13). They have exchanged their unregenerate outlook ('the mind that is set on the flesh') for one which properly belongs to the children of God (who

---

[1] In Gal. 2:20 ('the life I now live in the flesh'), 'in the flesh' means 'in mortal body'. The phrase (*en sarki*) is the same as in Rom. 8:8, but it has no such pejorative force in Gal. 2:20 as it has there.

[2] One important occurrence of the phrase 'according to the flesh' (*kata sarka*) is in 2 Cor. 5:16, 'Wherefore we henceforth know no man after the flesh: even though we have known Christ after the flesh, yet now we know him so no more' (RV; RSV renders the phrase 'from a human point of view'). These words have been so regularly misapplied that it is worth emphasizing here that Paul does not deprecate any interest in the earthly life of Christ, or suggest that the other apostles' companionship with him during his ministry was now irrelevant, and of no religious advantage; he contrasts rather his own present estimate of Christ with his estimate before his conversion, as NEB makes clear: 'With us therefore worldly standards have ceased to count in our estimate of any man; even if once they counted in our understanding of Christ, they do so now no longer.' It is in the light of Christ's exaltation, and of the new creation inaugurated by his triumph over death, that his earthly ministry must be evaluated; but in this light the importance of his earthly ministry is enhanced, not diminished.

'set the mind on the Spirit'), and it is for them now to 'make no provision for the flesh, to gratify its desires' (8:5–7; 13:14).[1]

6. The flesh is subject to the principle of 'sin and death' (Rom. 7:23; 8:2), and so is under sentence of death, for 'in Adam all die' (1 Cor. 15:22). 'To set the mind on the flesh is death' (Rom. 8:6); 'if you live according to the flesh you will die' (8:13). As it is put in Galatians 6:8, 'he who sows to his own flesh will from the flesh reap corruption' – or, in the NEB rendering, 'if he sows seed in the field of his lower nature, he will reap from it a harvest of corruption'.

The flesh, the human nature which is ours 'in Adam', is corrupted by sin; but the sins of the flesh have a much wider range in Paul's thought than they have tended to have in Christian moral theology. They include the sins that are specially associated with the body, but they also include sins which might more naturally be classified by us as sins of the mind. Thus, Paul's catalogue of 'the works of the flesh' in Galatians 5:19–21 comprises not only fornication and related forms of sexual vice, with drunkenness and carousing, but also sorcery, envy, quarrelsomeness, selfish ambition and idolatry. Sin of any kind, in fact, is a 'work of the flesh'.

Sometimes the term 'body' is used instead of 'flesh'. Thus what are called 'the works of the flesh' in Galatians 5:19 are called 'the deeds of the body' in the same comprehensive sense in Romans 8:13. We may compare 'the sinful body', lit. 'the body of sin' (Rom. 6:6), with 'sinful flesh', lit. 'flesh of sin' (Rom. 8:3); cf. also 'this body of death' (Rom. 7:24). (On the other hand, the 'body' of Rom. 8:10, which is 'dead because of sin', is more simply the mortal body of flesh and blood.) We may also compare 'your members which are upon the earth' (Col. 3:5, RV; RSV renders 'what is earthly in you'), which are to be treated as dead.[2]

---

[1] Cf. Gal. 5:16, 'walk by the Spirit, and you will by no means fulfil the desire of the flesh' (see p. 148, n. 2).

[2] What Paul says about the 'flesh' in the sense of unregenerate human nature must not be taken as applying to the physical body. Of the 'flesh' in that sense he has nothing good to say; but the believer's body, while formerly used by the master-power of sin as an instrument of unrighteousness (Rom. 6:13), can be presented to God as a 'living sacrifice' for the doing of his will (Rom. 12:1), is indwelt by his Spirit (Rom. 8:11; cf. 1 Cor. 6:19–20),

b. 'Spirit'

In the Old Testament, 'flesh' is set over against 'spirit' (Heb. *rûaḥ*, primarily 'wind', then 'vital vigour'). A classic text is Isaiah 31:3, 'The Egyptians are men, and not God; and their horses are flesh, and not spirit.' God, by implication, is Spirit (*cf.* Jn. 4:24); not only so, but the Spirit of God can energize men and impart to them physical power, mental skill, or spiritual insight that they would not otherwise have. The spirit in man is his breath, his disposition, his vitality.[1]

Similarly in the Pauline writings 'flesh' and 'spirit' are opposed terms. Believers in Christ are no longer 'in the flesh' but 'in the Spirit' (Rom. 8:9); they 'walk not according to the flesh but according to the Spirit' (Rom. 8:4); they do not produce 'the works of the flesh' but 'the fruit of the Spirit' (Gal. 5:19, 22).

We are under the embarrassment of having to choose between a capital 'S' and a minuscule 's' each time we write the word; Paul was subject to no such embarrassment when he pronounced the Greek work *pneuma* during his dictation of this letter, and neither was Tertius as he wrote it down. (The distinctive use of capital initials to denote nouns referring to divine persons is of relatively recent date.)

The following principal usages of 'spirit' can be distinguished in Paul:[2]

1. *The 'spiritual' part of the human constitution.* 'I serve' God 'with my spirit', says Paul (Rom. 1:9); with this we may compare Romans 7:6, where believers, being no longer under law but under grace, 'serve not under the old written code but in the new life of the Spirit' (which, however, goes beyond 1:9 in its

---

and will one day be redeemed from mortality and invested with glory (Rom. 8:23; *cf.* Phil. 3:21). Paul does not share the Greek depreciation of the body as the fetter or prison-house of the soul. See also W. D. Stacey, *The Pauline View of Man* (1956); R. Jewett, *Paul's Anthropological Terms* (1971).

[1] *Cf.* A. R. Johnson, *The Vitality of the Individual in the Thought of Ancient Israel* (1949), pp. 26–39.

[2] Among other usages, not listed above, there are a few occurrences of the word to denote 'spirit-beings' or 'spiritual powers' such as 'the spirit of the world' (1 Cor. 2:12), 'the spirit that is now at work in the sons of disobedience' (Eph. 2:2) or the spirits (not always the Spirit of God) by whose inspiration prophets speak (1 Cor. 12:10); or to denote a personal disposition, *e.g.* 'a spirit of stupor' (Rom. 11:8).

implications).[1] Circumcision which is 'spiritual and not literal' – *i.e.* the inward purification of the heart, of which the prophets spoke (Je. 4:4; *cf.* Dt. 10:16) – is contrasted with the external circumcision of the flesh (Rom. 2:28–29). The spirit of believers moves in harmony with the Spirit of God (Rom. 8:16).[2]

The other New Testament writers use 'spirit' more or less as a synonym of 'soul'. This appears, for example, in the opening words of the *Magnificat*: 'My soul magnifies the Lord, and my spirit rejoices in God my Saviour' (Lk. 1:46–47). Again, our Lord's words in John 12:27, 'Now is my soul troubled', may be compared with the Evangelist's statement in John 13:21 that 'he was troubled in spirit'. Paul himself uses 'spirit' in this more general sense when he asks, 'what person knows a man's thoughts except the spirit of the man which is in him?' (1 Cor. 2:11). But for the most part 'spirit' and 'soul' – especially in the adjectives derived from the two nouns – are distinguished in Paul, and indeed set in contrast: the 'unspiritual man' of 1 Corinthians 2:14 (AV 'natural man') is literally the 'soulish' man (*psychikos*, from *psychē*, 'soul'), in contrast to the 'spiritual man' of verse 15 (*pneumatikos*, from *pneuma*, 'spirit').[3] In Paul the human spirit may perhaps be described as the God-conscious element, which is dormant, if not dead, until it is stirred into life by the Spirit of God. Or it may be thought of as the 'Christian personality' of those 'who, if we may put it so, are not only alive, but "Christianly" alive'.[4]

2. *The Spirit of God, or the Holy Spirit.* He is called 'the Spirit of holiness' in Romans 1:4, in relation to the resurrection of Christ; *cf.* 8:11, where he is called 'the Spirit of him who raised

[1] Lit. 'in newness of spirit and not in oldness of letter'. *Cf.* 2 Cor. 3:6, where Paul and his colleagues are 'ministers of a new covenant; not of the letter, but of the spirit: for the letter killeth, but the spirit giveth life' (RV). The allusion to the new covenant of Je. 31:31–34, explicit in 2 Cor. 3:6, is implicit in other places where 'letter' and 'spirit' are thus contrasted. The antithesis Spirit/letter is common to Romans and 2 Corinthians, as the antithesis Spirit/ flesh is common to Romans and Galatians. See pp. 139, 153 f.

[2] The 'spirit' of Rom. 12:11 is the human spirit in AV ('fervent in spirit'), NEB ('in ardour of spirit'), and probably NIV ('keep your spiritual fervour'), but the Spirit of God in RSV ('be aglow with the Spirit').

[3] Compare the distinction in 1 Cor. 15:44–46 between the present mortal body, which is a 'physical body' (*sōma psychikon*, lit. 'soulish body', AV 'natural body'), and the resurrection body, which is a 'spiritual body' (*sōma pneumatikon*).

[4] W. Barclay, *Flesh and Spirit* (1962), p. 14.

Jesus from the dead'. Under his enlightenment the human conscience bears true witness (9:1). In the proclamation of the gospel he supplies the power to make the message effective in the hearers (15:19); those who are thus brought to faith in Christ are 'sanctified' by the Holy Spirit' (15:16). Into the hearts of those who believe the gospel he comes pouring out the love of God (5:5; cf. 15:30), and by his power they are filled with peace, joy and hope (14:17; 15:13).

Since God has revealed himself in Christ, the Spirit of God is the Spirit of Christ (8:9). So completely does the Spirit convey to believers the life and power of the risen and exalted Christ that *in practice* the two seem frequently to be identified (although in principle they are distinguished).[1] For example, the expressions 'if in fact the Spirit of God dwells in you' (8:9) and 'if Christ is in you' (8:10) are practically synonymous.

It is in chapter 8 that the nature and implications of the Holy Spirit's indwelling and operation in the believer are most clearly set forth.[2]

(i) *The Spirit imparts life*. His law is the law of life; to 'walk . . . according to the Spirit' and so 'set the mind on the Spirit' is to live (8:4, 5, 6, 10),[3] for he enables the believer to treat 'the deeds of the body' – the practices of the old unregenerate existence – as dead things, with no further power in life. There can be no true life without him. To be 'in the Spirit' (*en pneumati*) is the opposite of being 'in the flesh' (*en sarki*); and all believers are regarded as being 'in the Spirit' (8:9). In practice, then, to be 'in the Spirit' is to be 'in Christ' (or 'in Christ Jesus'); to be in the Spirit is thus no individualist matter. The life which he imparts is the common life in the body of Christ: it is 'by one Spirit', says Paul in another letter, that 'we were all baptized into one body' (1 Cor. 12:13). To be 'in Christ' is to be incorporated into Christ, to be a member of Christ, and so to be a fellow-

---

[1] *Cf.* 1 Cor. 15:45b; 2 Cor. 3:17a. N. Q. Hamilton speaks of this identification of the Spirit with the ascended Lord as 'dynamic' but not 'ontological' (*The Holy Spirit and Eschatology in Paul*, 1957, p. 6). E. Käsemann describes the Spirit as 'the earthly *praesentia* of the ascended Lord' (*RGG*³ ii, 1958, col. 1274, *s.v.* 'Geist'). See F. F. Bruce, 'Christ and Spirit in Paul', *BJRL* 59 (1976–77), pp. 259–285.

[2] See G. Smeaton, *The Doctrine of the Holy Spirit* (1882, reprinted 1958), pp. 71–77; E. F. Kevan, *The Saving Work of the Holy Spirit* (1953).

[3] *Cf.* Gal. 6:8b, 'he who sows to the Spirit will from the Spirit reap eternal life.'

member of all others who are similarly incorporated into Christ (Rom. 12:5). The new solidarity which believers share 'in Christ Jesus' (8:1) is elsewhere described by Paul as 'the fellowship of the Holy Spirit' (2 Cor. 13:14; *cf.* Phil. 2:1) or 'the unity of the Spirit' (Eph. 4:3); the Spirit is the animating principle of the body of Christ.

(ii) *The Spirit bestows freedom*. However spiritual bondage be viewed – as bondage to sin, bondage to the law, bondage to death – it is the Spirit who brings liberation. It is he who conveys to believers the power of the risen Christ, by which they are 'set free from sin' (Rom. 6:18, 22); it is he who releases them from legal bondage, so that they now serve God 'in the new life of the Spirit' (7:6); it is he who imparts the new principle of 'life in Christ Jesus' which sets them free from 'the law of sin and death' (8:2). All these aspects of his ministry illustrate the principle concisely stated in 2 Corinthians 3:17b, 'where the Spirit of the Lord is, there is freedom.'

(iii) *The Spirit supplies directive power in the lives of the children of God*. It is those who are led by him that are God's sons and daughters; he is 'the Spirit of sonship' by whose prompting believers approach God as his children and call him by the same familiar name of 'Father' as Jesus used when speaking to him (Rom. 8:14–15). To the same effect Paul tells the Galatians, 'because you are sons, God has sent the Spirit of his Son into our hearts, crying, "Abba! Father!" ' (Gal. 4:6).

(iv) *The Spirit intercedes for the people of God*. While Christ intercedes for his people in his place of exaltation in the presence of God (Rom. 8:34), the Spirit makes intercession from within the lives of the believers whom he indwells (8:26–27).[1]

(v) *The Spirit is the sanctifying agency in the lives of believers*. 'Spirit' and 'flesh' are in unremitting opposition, and wage perpetual warfare the one with the other. But the Spirit is divinely powerful, and can put the 'flesh' progressively out of action in those lives which are yielded to his control and

[1] This ascription of an intercessory ministry both to the exalted Christ and to the indwelling Spirit is paralleled by the twofold use of 'paraclete' or 'advocate' in the Johannine writings: 'Jesus Christ the righteous' is his people's 'advocate with the Father' (1 Jn. 2:1), and the Spirit is 'another . . . Advocate' (Jn. 14:16, NEB), sent by the Father to remain with and in believers.

enabling grace. It is no quietist doctrine that Paul propounds: he knew his own spiritual life to involve constant self-discipline (1 Cor. 9:24–27), but he knew that victory and final glory were assured by the Spirit (Rom. 8:15b–17). And in the lives of those whom the Spirit is preparing for final glory his congenial work here and now is to reproduce in increasing measure the likeness of Christ (*cf.* 2 Cor. 3:18).

(vi) *The Spirit is the pledge of coming glory.* According to Old Testament prophecy, the outpouring of the Spirit of God would be a sign of the approaching day of the Lord (Joel 2:28–32). Joel's prophecy was quoted by Peter when the Spirit came down on the disciples of Jesus on the day of Pentecost: 'this', he said, 'is what was spoken by the prophet Joel' (Acts 2:16). The present interval 'between the times' is in a peculiar sense the age of the Spirit; in this age he not only makes effective in believers what Christ has accomplished for them, he not only communicates to them the power of the living and exalted Lord, but he enables them to live in the present enjoyment of the glory that is yet to be revealed.

Not only does the Spirit supply life here and now; his presence guarantees entry into resurrection life on a day yet to dawn. Thus the life of the age to come, 'eternal life', is conveyed to believers as the present 'free gift of God . . . in Christ Jesus our Lord' (Rom. 6:23) – as an advance instalment, so to speak, of the coming resurrection life which accompanies the redemption of the body (8:23).[1]

Not only does the Spirit enable believers here and now to realize their prerogative as 'the Lord's free-born children in the way of holiness'[2]; this too is an advance instalment of that 'liberty of the glory of the children of God' (Rom. 8:21, RV) which is eagerly awaited not only by themselves but by all creation. The deliverance from bondage which they have already begun to enjoy in the Spirit will be consummated then; the 'adoption' (8:23) on which they will enter fully at the resurrection is anticipated already by the Spirit's aid (8:15), and the

---

[1] The redeemed body of the resurrection is a 'spiritual body' (1 Cor. 15:44, 46). In 2 Cor. 5:4–5 the present gift of the Spirit is the 'guarantee' of the time when believers will be 'clothed' with their 'heavenly dwelling', when mortality will be 'swallowed up by life'.

[2] *Memoir of Anthony Norris Groves*, ed. H. Groves (1869), p. 418.

glory of full conformity to the image of God's Son, for which they were predestined (8:29), will be the full flowering of that sanctifying work on which the Spirit is even now engaged in their lives. The gift of the Spirit is thus presented in terms of 'proleptic eschatology'.[1] He is the 'first fruits' of the final salvation (8:23),[2] the immediate 'down-payment' of that inconceivably rich heritage which God has prepared for those who love him.

VII. 'LAW' IN ROMANS

The term 'law' (*nomos*) occurs over seventy times in this letter, not always in the same sense. Most often it means the law of God in one form or another, but there are some places where it means something else. Here are its principal meanings, in order more or less from the less frequent to the more frequent.

1. *Law in general.* When Paul says in Romans 4:15 that 'where there is no law there is no transgression', or in 5:13 that 'sin is not counted where there is no law', he may be echoing a general legal maxim, even if he is thinking more particularly of the Mosaic law. Again, when he says in 7:1, 'speaking to those who have some knowledge of law' (NEB), that 'the law is binding on a person only during his life', it makes no difference to the sense of his words whether he or his readers took them to refer to Jewish law or to Roman law. Theologically, however, he ignores the presence of non-Jewish codes of law before or alongside the law of Moses. Gentiles are said to 'have no law' (2:14, NEB) in the sense that they do not live under the Mosaic law; indeed, before the Mosaic law was given there was 'no law' (5:13). Had Paul known of the laws of Hammurabi or other pre-Mosaic codes, these would have been as irrelevant to his theological argument as was contemporary Roman law.

[1] See G. Vos, 'The Eschatological Aspect of the Pauline Conception of the Spirit', in *Princeton Seminary Biblical and Theological Studies* (1912), pp. 209–259; *The Pauline Eschatology* (1952), pp. 58–61.

[2] *Cf.* Gal. 5:5, 'Through the Spirit, by faith, we wait for the hope of righteousness.' So, in Eph. 1:13–14, believers are said to have been 'sealed with the promised Holy Spirit, which is the guarantee of our inheritance until we acquire possession of it' (*cf.* Eph. 4:30).

2. *A principle.* In Romans 3:27 Paul, having established that the grace of God justifies men and women through faith, says that, this being so, there is no room for boasting. 'By what manner of law? of works? Nay: but by a law of faith' (RV). These two occurrences of 'law' rightly appear as 'principle' in RSV. The law of works (not the same thing as 'the works of the law') and the law of faith are two contrasted principles by which human beings seek to secure God's acceptance.

In 7:21 Paul, considering the moral conflict that rages in the soul of one who lives under law, discovers 'a law' – that is, a principle or an observed regularity – 'that when I want to do right, evil lies close at hand'.[1] In the same context the moral conflict itself is viewed as a conflict between two laws or principles: first, the law or principle which hands one over bound to the domination of sin (7:23, 25b), and second, 'the law of my mind' which acknowledges the goodness of God's law and desires to do it, but lacks the power to enforce what it acknowledges and desires (7:23). But when yet another principle begins to operate in the soul – 'the law of the Spirit of life in Christ Jesus' – this proves stronger than 'the law (principle) of sin and death' and sets one free from the thraldom of the latter (8:2).

3. *The Pentateuch.* When it is said that God's way of righteousness through faith is attested by 'the law and the prophets' (Rom. 3:21b), 'the law' means the first five books of the Old Testament, as 'the prophets' is a comprehensive designation for the remaining books. This is a common New Testament usage, and reflects the Jewish application of the Hebrew word *Tōrāh* not only to the law in the stricter sense, but also to the five books which pre-eminently contain the law.

4. *The Old Testament as a whole.* In Romans 3:19 Paul says, 'we know that whatever the law says it speaks to those who are under the law.' The clause 'whatever the law says' refers to the

---

[1] But even here C. K. Barrett (*The Epistle to the Romans,* 1957, p. 149) sees, as elsewhere throughout chapter 7, the law of Moses: he quotes J. Denney's paraphrase (*ad loc.*): 'This is what I find the law – a life under the law – to amount to in my experience: when I wish to do good, evil is present with me.'

catena of biblical quotations in the preceding verses (10–18); but of these quotations five are from the Psalms and one from Isaiah. If it is 'the law' that says these things, 'the law' can mean only the Hebrew Bible – our Old Testament.

5. *The law of God.* To a man of Paul's heritage and training it was most natural to equate the law of God with the law of Moses – in other words, with the law as God gave it to Israel through Moses (not to speak of the oral amplification of the written law, which in rabbinical tradition was received by Moses at Sinai as truly – in theory, at least – as the written law itself). This was the form in which Paul had come to know the law of God in his own experience. Whether Romans 7:7–13 be regarded as a fragment of Paul's spiritual autobiography or not, the person whose experience is there described tells how it was his first awareness of the law that gave him his first consciousness of sin. That the Mosaic law is in view there is evident from the fact that the particular commandment selected to illustrate the point is the last one in the Decalogue: 'You shall not covet.'

When Paul deals with the situation of the Jews, who rejoiced in being the people of the law (2:17–27) and set themselves to attain the standard of righteousness which it prescribed (9:31; 10:3), it is naturally the Mosaic law that he has in mind. When he speaks in 5:13–14, 20a, of 'law' being unknown in the ages between Adam and Moses – that is, until God spoke at Sinai – the same equation of the law of Moses with the law of God can be recognized. Indeed, when he shows how Christians ought to live, and stresses the supremacy of the law of love, he formulates the law of love (as Jesus had done before him) in a commandment from the Pentateuch: 'You shall love your neighbour as yourself' (13:9, quoting Lv. 19:18). Similarly, when he goes on to say that 'love is the fulfilling of the law' (13:10), he explains what he means by 'law' by quoting a selection of commandments from the Decalogue.

Paul does not mean that the revelation of God's will was confined to the Mosaic legislation, but that in the Mosaic legislation his will was given the form of law. When he argues that Jews and Gentiles are on an equal footing before God as regards their failure to do his will, he points out that, while Jews had a special revelation of God's will in the Mosaic law, Gentiles were not deprived of all knowledge of his will, for 'when Gentiles who have not the law do by nature what the law requires . . . they show that what the law requires is written on their hearts, while their conscience also bears witness' (2:14–15). That is to say, the Gentiles had not been given the Tōrāh, or even the Ten Commandments, but they did have a sense of right and wrong: they had a built-in awareness of the essence of God's law. So, when Paul says (3:20) that through law comes our knowledge of sin, he says something that is true in principle of Jews and Gentiles alike; and when he says in the same context that by works of law no human being will be justified in God's sight, this too is equally valid for Jew and Gentile. Whether the 'works of law' are performed in accordance with a code promulgated by express divine authority, or in accordance with the dictates of conscience, the moral law within, Wordsworth's 'stern daughter of the voice of God', or in accordance with an accepted standard of decent behaviour – no matter, these are not the grounds on which men and women are accepted by God. Whichever of these forms 'law' may take, it is right to keep it; it is wrong, and indeed disastrous, to break or defy or ignore it; but it is vain to imagine that by keeping it one can accumulate a store of merit in the heavenly treasure-house. God has given law for a variety of purposes, and it has many uses; but when it is a question of his *justifying* human beings, he proceeds by a more excellent way.

The law, then, whether spelt out in a code or implanted in the conscience, is God's law, 'holy and just and good' (7:12). If, as Paul insists, it was not given as the means of justification, why was it given? To this question the letter to the Romans provides a variety of answers, which may be arranged under four principal heads.[1]

(i) *It was given to be a revelation of God and his will.* The distinc-

---

[1] To the second, third and fourth of these correspond the three uses of the law in Lutheran tradition: as a means of preservation, as a summons to repentance, as guidance for the church (*Formula of Concord*, 1576, article 6). Luther himself, in contrast to his followers, taught only two uses of the law – the 'theological' or 'spiritual' use (*usus theologicus* or *spiritualis*) and the 'political' or 'civil' use (*usus politicus* or *civilis*).

tion between right and wrong is not simply a matter of social convention: it is rooted in the being and character of God, and is written into the constitution of man, created as he has been in the image of God. Because the law is God's law, it is, like God himself, 'true, and righteous altogether' (Ps. 19:9).

(ii) *It was given for the health and preservation of the human race.* This particular purpose is served mainly by civil government, which (as is clearly stated in Rom. 13:1–7) is a ministry instituted by God to protect and encourage well-doing and to curb and punish wrong-doing.[1]

(iii) *It was given to bring sin to light, and to lead sinners to cast themselves on the pardoning grace of God.* While in theory the person who keeps the law will live by it (10:5), in practice no-one is justified by the works of the law, because of universal failure to keep it perfectly (3:20a, 23). The innate human tendency to go contrary to the will of God manifests itself in concrete acts of disobedience when his will is revealed in the form of specific commandments (5:13), so that 'through the law comes knowledge of sin' (3:20b; *cf.* 7:7). But those who have experienced the law's power to bring their sin to light, together with its inability to procure for them a righteous standing in God's sight, are the more ready to cast themselves in faith on the grace of God brought near in Christ as the sole means of their justification. Thus, as Paul puts it in another letter, 'the law was our custodian until Christ came, that we might be justified by faith' (Gal. 3:24). But now that Christ has come, he 'is the end of the law, that every one who has faith may be justified' (Rom. 10:4). Not only has he fulfilled the law himself, by his perfect obedience to the will of God, but since God's way of righteousness has been opened up in him, he marks the supersession or 'end' of the law as even a theoretical means of justification. Those who are justified by faith in him are 'not under law but under grace' (Rom. 6:14–15).

(iv) *It was given to provide guidance for the believer's life.* Thanks to the indwelling of the Spirit in those who are 'in Christ Jesus', the righteous requirements of the law are fulfilled in them by

[1] 'Pray for the welfare of the government', said Rabbi Hanina, deputy high priest (Paul's contemporary), 'since were it not for their fear of it men would swallow one another alive' (*Pirqe Aboth* 3.2).

a divine spontaneity as they live 'according to the Spirit' (Rom. 8:3–4). But even so Paul finds it proper at a later point in the letter to lay down fairly detailed guide-lines for the lives of Christians, so that by experience they may 'prove what is the will of God, what is good and acceptable and perfect' (Rom. 12:1–2). These guide-lines coincide with what Paul elsewhere calls 'the law of Christ' (Gal. 6:2). While he himself was 'not under law but under grace', while he rejoiced in being 'discharged from the law' so as to 'serve not under the old written code but in the new life of the Spirit' (Rom. 7:6), yet he could speak of himself as 'not being without law toward God but under the law of Christ' (1 Cor. 9:21). But this law of Christ is the law of love which he himself embodied and which he bequeathed as a 'new commandment' to his disciples. Moreover, the law of love sums up and brings to perfection all the commandments of the Mosaic law (Rom. 13:8–10; Gal. 5:14).

Paul's gospel is thus fully absolved from the charge of antinomianism. When men and women have been justified by faith, right is still right, wrong is still wrong, and the will of God is still the rule of life. But for them the will of God is not simply enshrined in an external code of regulations: it is implanted within their hearts as a new principle of life. Like Paul, they are for evermore subject to 'the law of Christ'. The detailed resemblance between the ethical directions of Romans 12:1 – 15:4 and our Lord's Sermon on the Mount (Mt. 5 – 7) amply entitles those directions to be described as 'the law of Christ'. The law of Christ is no more able to justify the sinner than the law of Moses was; whether expressed in the ethical directions of Romans 12:1 – 15:4 or in the Sermon on the Mount, Christ's law of love sets a higher standard than even the Ten Commandments. 'The Sermon on the Mount is not, as many people fondly imagine nowadays, the fulfilment or essence of the Gospel, but it is the fulfilment of the Law.'[1] It presents the standard by which the disciples of Christ – those who have been justified by faith in him – ought to live. Those into whose hearts the love of God has been 'poured' by the Holy Spirit are empowered by the same Spirit to fulfil the law of Christ by that

---

[1] A. R. Vidler, *Christ's Strange Work* (1944), p. 14.

love to God and mankind which is the reflection of God's own love, and their proper response to it.[1]

VIII. THE INFLUENCE OF ROMANS

In the summer of AD 386 Aurelius Augustinus, native of Tagaste in North Africa, and now for two years Professor of Rhetoric at Milan, sat weeping in the garden of his friend Alypius, almost persuaded to begin a new life, yet lacking the final resolution to break with the old. As he sat, he heard a child singing in a neighbouring house, *Tolle, lege! tolle, lege!* ('Take up and read! take up and read!').[2] Picking up a scroll which lay at his friend's side, he let his eyes rest on the words: 'not in revelling and drunkenness, not in debauchery and licentiousness, not in quarrelling and jealousy. But put on the Lord Jesus Christ, and make no provision for the flesh, to gratify its desires' (Rom. 13:13b–14). 'No further would I read', he tells us, 'nor had I any need; instantly, at the end of this sentence, a clear light flooded my heart and all the darkness of doubt vanished away.'[3] What the church and the world owe to this influx of light which illuminated Augustine's mind as he read these words of Paul is something beyond our power to compute.

In August 1513, Martin Luther, Augustinian monk and Professor of Biblical Theology in the University of Wittenberg, began to deliver a course of lectures on the Psalms. His mind at the time was preoccupied with the agonizing endeavour to 'find a gracious God'. He was struck by the prayer of Psalm 31:1, 'in thy righteousness deliver me!' But how could God's

---

[1] See also P. Fairbairn, *The Revelation of Law in Scripture* (1869, reprinted 1957); C. H. Dodd, *Gospel and Law* (1951); T. W. Manson, *Ethics and the Gospel* (1960); G. A. F. Knight, *Law and Grace* (1962); E. F. Kevan, *The Grace of Law* (1964); C. E. B. Cranfield, 'St. Paul and the Law', *SJT* 17 (1964), pp. 43–68; C. F. D. Moule, 'Obligation in the Ethic of Paul', in *Christian History and Interpretation: Studies presented to John Knox*, ed. W. R. Farmer, C. F. D. Moule, R. R. Niebuhr (1967), pp. 389–406; H. Hübner, *Law in Paul's Thought*, E. T. (1985); H. Räisänen, *Paul and the Law* (1983); E. P. Sanders, *Paul, the Law and the Jewish People* (1983); W. D. Davies, 'Paul and the Law', *Jewish and Pauline Studies* (1984), pp. 91–122.

[2] On the child's lips these words may have been part of a game, meaning something like 'Pick up and choose'; but they conveyed another message to Augustine.

[3] Augustine, *Confessions* 8.29.

righteousness deliver him? Was it not calculated to condemn the sinner and not to save him? As he pondered this question, his attention was more and more attracted to Paul's statement in Romans 1:17, that in the gospel 'the righteousness of God is revealed through faith for faith; as it is written, "He who through faith is righteous shall live" ' (Hab. 2:4b). The outcome of his study is best told in his own words:

'I had greatly longed to understand Paul's letter to the Romans, and nothing stood in the way but that one expression, "the righteousness of God", because I took it to mean that righteousness whereby God is righteous and acts righteously in punishing the unrighteous. . . . Night and day I pondered until . . . I grasped the truth that the righteousness of God is that righteousness whereby, through grace and sheer mercy, he justifies us by faith.[1] Thereupon I felt myself to be reborn and to have gone through open doors into paradise. The whole of scripture took on a new meaning, and whereas before "the righteousness of God" had filled me with hate, now it became to me inexpressibly sweet in greater love. This passage of Paul became to me a gateway into heaven.'[2]

The consequences of Luther's new insight into the liberating gospel according to Paul are writ large in history.[3]

In the evening of 24 May 1738 John Wesley 'went very unwillingly to a society in Aldersgate Street [London], where one was reading Luther's Preface to the Epistle to the Romans. About a

---

[1] Here Luther shows signs of help received from Augustine (*On the Spirit and the Letter*, 15).

[2] From the preface to the Wittenberg edition of his Latin works (1545); *cf. Luther's Works*, American edition, 34 (1960), pp. 336 f.

[3] Earlier still, in 1496, John Colet (later Dean of St Paul's) returned from Italy to his own University of Oxford and (though he had no theological degree and was not even in deacon's orders) delivered a course of lectures on the letters of Paul, and primarily on Romans, which deeply impressed many of his hearers. He made a clean break with the exegetical methods of the mediaeval schoolmen and expounded the text in accordance with the plain sense of the words, viewed in relation to their historical situation. Erasmus and More were both influenced by Colet; to him Erasmus owed much of his insight into the true principles of biblical interpretation.

quarter before nine', as he records in his journal, 'while he was describing the change which God works in the heart through faith in Christ, I felt my heart strangely warmed. I felt I did trust in Christ, Christ alone, for my salvation; and an assurance was given me that he had taken *my* sins away, even *mine*; and saved me from the law of sin and death.'[1] That critical moment in John Wesley's life provided the spark which kindled the 'inextinguishable blaze' of the eighteenth-century Evangelical Revival.

In August 1918 Karl Barth, pastor of Safenwil in Canton Aargau, Switzerland, published an exposition of the letter to the Romans. 'The reader', he said in his preface, 'will detect for himself that is has been written with a joyful sense of discovery. The mighty voice of Paul was new to me, and if to me, no doubt to many others also. And yet, now that my work is finished, I perceive that much remains which I have not yet heard . . .'[2] But what he had heard he wrote down, and others heard it too. He compared himself to a man who, clutching in the dark at a rope for guidance, finds that he has pulled on a bell-rope and made a sound fit to wake the dead.[3] That first edition of his *Römerbrief* fell, it was said, 'like a bombshell on the theologians' playground'.[4] The repercussions of the explosion are with us still.

There is no saying what may happen when people begin to study the letter to the Romans. What happened to Augustine, Luther, Wesley and Barth launched great spiritual movements which have left their mark in world history. But similar things have happened, much more frequently, to very ordinary men and women as the words of this letter came home to them with power. So, let those who have read thus far be prepared for the consequences of reading farther: you have been warned!

---

[1] J. Wesley, *Journal*, i (1872 edition), p. 103. See p. 159, below (on 8:17) for his own assessment (in Pauline terms) of what was involved in his 'conversion' experience.

[2] K. Barth, *The Epistle to the Romans*, E. T. (1933), p. 2.

[3] K. Barth, *Die Lehre vom Worte Gottes* (1927), preface.

[4] Karl Adam, in *Das Hochland*, June 1926, as quoted by J. McConnachie, 'The Teaching of Karl Barth', *Hibbert Journal* 25 (1926–27), pp. 385 f.

IX. ARGUMENT

Prologue

Greetings from me, Paul, to the Christians in Rome. I thank God for all that I hear about your faith, and I remember to pray for you constantly. I have often longed to pay you a visit, and now at last I am to have an opportunity to do so. To preach the gospel in Rome is a long-standing ambition of mine.

A

I. I am in no way ashamed of the gospel: no indeed, it is the message which God uses effectively for the salvation of all who believe. This is the message which reveals God's way of putting men and women right with himself by the exercise of faith, in accordance with the statement of Scripture: 'It is the one who is righteous through faith that will live.'

II. The need for such a message becomes clear as we contemplate the world of mankind. Not only do we see divine retribution working itself out among pagans, whose wrong way of life is the fruit of wrong ideas about God; we see the Jewish nation too, in spite of their knowing the law of God and enjoying so many other privileges, failing to keep the law they know. In fact all human beings, Jews and Gentiles alike, are morally bankrupt before God; no-one can hope to be pronounced righteous by God on the basis of any work or merit of his own.

III. If men and women are to be pronounced righteous by God, then, it must be by his grace. And God in his grace has made it possible for them to be put in the right with him, thanks to the redemptive work of Christ. On the ground of his sacrificial death, Christ is set before us as the one who makes full atonement for our sins; and we may, by faith, appropriate the benefits of his atoning work. Thus God maintains his own righteousness, and at the same time bestows righteousness on all believers in Jesus, regardless of whether they are Jews or

Gentiles. The law of God is thus vindicated, and the sacred Scriptures are fulfilled.

If you consider Abraham, for example, you will find that this was the way in which he found acceptance with God: 'Abraham believed God', says the Scripture, 'and it was reckoned to him as righteousness.' (Nor is he an isolated case; the same principle can be seen at work in the testimony of David.) Mark this too: these words about Abraham were spoken while he was still uncircumcised, showing that this way of righteousness by faith is for Gentiles as well as for Jews. Abraham is thus the spiritual father of all believers, irrespective of their racial origin. And the statement that Abraham's faith was reckoned to him as righteousness means that if we believe in God, whose saving power has been revealed in the death and resurrection of Christ, it will similarly be reckoned to us as righteousness.

So then, by faith we receive God's gift of righteousness, and with that we receive also peace, joy and the hope of glory. Thus we can endure affliction cheerfully, for God himself is our joy. If his love, demonstrated in the sacrifice of Christ, has reconciled us to himself, much more will the risen life of Christ procure our final salvation on the day of judgment.

Once we formed part of an old solidarity of sin and death, when we lived 'in Adam' and shared the fruits of his disobedience. But now that old solidarity has been dissolved, to be replaced by the new solidarity of righteousness and life which is ours 'in Christ', the fruits of whose perfect obedience are shared by many. The law of Moses has nothing to do with this change of status; it was introduced simply so that human sinfulness might be brought into the open. But God's grace has triumphed over human sinfulness and now reigns supreme.

IV. Do I hear someone say, 'Let our sinfulness increase, then, so that God's grace may be glorified yet more'? Perish the thought! For 'in Christ' we have entered on a new life; we are dead so far as our old relation to sin is concerned. That, surely, was the meaning of our baptism. You may think of sin as a slave-owner, whose slaves we used to be. A slave is bound to obey his master's orders, but when he dies, or passes into the ownership of another, his former master has no further authority over him. So sin no longer has any authority over you, for now you belong to God, who has liberated you from your former slavery. Sin was a harsh master who dealt out death as his wages; God, by contrast, bestows on his servants the free gift of eternal life in Christ.

So, too, as regards the old bond of legal obligation. Those who lived under the law were as much bound to it as a wife is bound to her husband. But as death breaks the marriage-bond, so the believer's death-with-Christ has broken the bond that once bound him to the law, and has set him free to be united to Christ. The law stimulated the very sins it forbade; those who are united to Christ produce the fruits of righteousness and life.

I know what I am talking about when I say that the law stimulates the sins it forbids; it was the commandment 'You shall not covet' that first brought the sin of covetousness to my attention and tempted me to commit it.

It is not the law that is at fault; it is my corrupt nature that reacts in this way to the law. And that nature is still present, in league with indwelling sin and waging war against those elements in me that recognize the nobility of the law of God and desire to obey it. But my own strength is insufficient to win the victory over indwelling sin, or to prevent it from forcing me to do its bidding. I remain divided at heart and defeated in life until I gratefully appropriate the victory that is mine through Jesus Christ my Lord.

Those who are in Christ receive his Spirit, and the Spirit of Christ sets in operation a new principle – the principle of life – which counteracts the old principle of sin and death. And those whose life is directed by the Spirit are able to fulfil the requirements of God as the law never enabled them to do. The Spirit enables the new nature to triumph over the old; the Spirit keeps the new life in being and action here and now, as one day he will transform our mortal bodies into immortal ones. The Spirit, thus directing our lives, enables us to live as the freeborn children of God: it is he who prompts us spontaneously to call God 'Father'. The day is coming when the sons and daughters of God, liberated from all that is mortal, will be manifested to the universe in the glory for which they were created; and on that day all creation will be liberated from its present frustration and share their glorious freedom.

For that day creation longs, and so do we, but amid our present restrictions we have the aid and intercession of the Spirit, and the assurance that he co-operates in all things for our good, since our good is God's purpose. His purpose, which cannot fail, is to invest with glory all those whom he chose, predestined, called and justified.

Let us therefore take courage. God is on our side; Christ is our almighty Saviour, and from his love no power in the universe, here or hereafter, can separate his people.

V. In all this, however, I have one unceasing sorrow. My own kith and kin, the nation specially prepared for the coming of the Saviour, the nation into which he was born, have failed to accept him.

This does not mean that God's promises to Israel have been frustrated. Throughout the course of history he has set his choice on some and passed others by. And my kinsfolk have refused the way of righteousness through faith presented to them by God, preferring their own way of righteousness through law-keeping. The Gentiles have chosen God's way, while Israel has refused it.

Israel has refused it, I say, but not *all* Israel. As God had his faithful remnant in earlier days, so he has in our day a remnant chosen by his grace. And as then, so now the remnant is a promise of better things to come; Israel's refusal of the gospel and consequent setting aside by God are only temporary. The Gentiles' enjoyment of gospel blessings will stimulate my kinsfolk to jealousy; they will turn and embrace the gospel for themselves, and all Israel will rejoice in God's salvation.

You see, God's ultimate purpose for the human family is that all without distinction, Israel and the Gentiles together, should enjoy his blessings in Christ. How wonderfully and wisely God works his purpose out! To him be eternal glory!

B

In view of all that God has done for you in Christ, your lives should be lived out in his service. You are fellow-members of the body of Christ: see that you discharge your respective functions for the well-being of the whole body corporate. And in all your relations with others, show the forgiving mercy of Christ.

Render all due obedience to the civil authorities. They in their way are servants of God. Let your one continuing debt be the debt of love. And in the ominous times that impend, keep alert in spirit and live as Christians should.

Show great gentleness and consideration to your fellow-Christians. There are matters such as special days and certain kinds of food on which Christians do not all agree. Christian liberty is a fine thing, but it should not be asserted at the expense of Christian charity. Remember the example of Christ, how he always considered other people's interests before his own.

Epilogue

I write to you as the apostle to the Gentiles. I attach the highest importance to this ministry of mine; it serves the divine purpose of blessing for all nations, a purpose disclosed in the ancient Scriptures. I have fulfilled this ministry from Jerusalem to Illyricum, and now I propose to take it up in Spain, and pay you a visit on my way there. First I must go to Jerusalem with a gift which the Gentile churches have contributed for the relief of their brethren there. Pray that all may go well in this respect.

Give a warm welcome to Phoebe, the bearer of this letter. Give my greetings to all my friends who are with you. Beware of those who bring divisive teachings; preserve the fine reputation you enjoy throughout the churches. My friends here send you their greetings. The grace of Christ be with you, and all glory be to God.

ANALYSIS

PROLOGUE (1:1–15)
a. *Salutation* (1:1–7)
b. *Introduction* (1:8–15)

A. THE GOSPEL ACCORDING TO PAUL (1:16 – 11:36)

I. THE THEME OF THE GOSPEL: THE RIGHTEOUSNESS OF GOD REVEALED (1:16–17)

II. SIN AND RETRIBUTION: THE UNIVERSAL NEED DIAGNOSED (1:18 – 3:20)
a. *The pagan world* (1:18–32)
b. *The moralist* (2:1–16)
c. *The Jew* (2:17 – 3:8)
   1. *Privilege brings responsibility* (2:17–29)
   2. *Objections answered* (3:1–8)
d. *All mankind found guilty* (3:9–20)

III. THE WAY OF RIGHTEOUSNESS: THE UNIVERSAL NEED MET (3:21 – 5:21)
a. *God's provision* (3:21–31)
b. *Two Old Testament precedents* (4:1–8)
c. *The faith of Abraham* (4:9–25)
d. *The blessings which accompany justification: peace, joy, hope, love* (5:1–11)
e. *The old and the new solidarity* (5:12–21)

IV. THE WAY OF HOLINESS (6:1 – 8:39)
   a. *Freedom from sin* (6:1–23)
      1. *A supposed objection* (6:1–2)
      2. *The meaning of baptism* (6:3–14)
      3. *The slave-market analogy* (6:15–23)
   b. *Freedom from law* (7:1–25)
      1. *The marriage analogy* (7:1–6)
      2. *The dawn of conscience* (7:7–13)
      3. *The conflict within* (7:14–25)
   c. *Freedom from death* (8:1–39)
      1. *Life in the Spirit* (8:1–17)
      2. *The glory to come* (8:18–30)
      3. *The triumph of faith* (8:31–39)

V. HUMAN UNBELIEF AND DIVINE GRACE (9:1 – 11:36)
   a. *The problem of Israel's unbelief* (9:1–5)
   b. *God's sovereign choice* (9:6–29)
   c. *Human responsibility* (9:30 – 10:21)
      1. *The stumbling-stone* (9:30–33)
      2. *The two ways of righteousness* (10:1–13)
      3. *The world-wide proclamation* (10:14–21)
   d. *God's purpose for Israel* (11:1–29)
      1. *Israel's alienation not final* (11:1–12)
      2. *Admonition to Gentile Christians* (11:13–24)
      3. *The restoration of Israel* (11:25–29)
   e. *God's purpose for the world* (11:30–36)

B. THE CHRISTIAN WAY OF LIFE (12:1 – 15:13)

I. THE LIVING SACRIFICE (12:1–2)

II. THE COMMON LIFE OF CHRISTIANS (12:3–8)

III. THE LAW OF CHRIST (12:9–21)

IV. THE CHRISTIAN AND THE STATE (13:1–7)

V. LOVE AND DUTY (13:8–10)

COMMENTARY

PROLOGUE (1:1–15)

A. SALUTATION (1:1–7)

An ancient letter began with a simple salutation: 'X to Y, greetings.' Such a greeting forms the skeleton of the prescripts of most of the New Testament Epistles, variously expanded and given a Christian emphasis.

The salutation at the beginning of this letter takes a similar form: 'Paul . . . to all God's beloved in Rome . . . grace . . . and peace.' But each part of the greeting is expanded: the sender's name, the recipient's name, and even the greetings.

1. *Paul, a servant of Jesus Christ, called to be an apostle.* The word translated 'servant' is Greek *doulos*, 'slave'. Paul is completely at his Master's disposal. His summons to be an apostle, a special commissioner of Christ, came directly, he claims, from 'Jesus Christ and God the Father' (Gal. 1:1), who laid on him the responsibility of proclaiming the gospel in the Gentile world on the occasion when he revealed his Son to him on the Damascus road (Gal. 1:16).

Set apart for the gospel of God, that is, for the ministry of the gospel, long before his conversion; *cf.* Galatians 1:15, where he says that he was divinely set apart for this purpose before his birth. All the rich and diversified gifts of Paul's heritage (Jewish, Greek and Roman), together with his upbringing, were foreordained by God with a view to his apostolic service. *Cf.* the risen Lord's description of Paul as 'a chosen instrument of mine to carry my name before the Gentiles . . .' (Acts 9:15). The 'gospel of God', his *euangelion*, is the joyful proclamation of the death and resurrection of his Son, and of the consequent amnesty and liberation which men and women may enjoy through faith in him. The Old Testament background of the New Testament use of *euangelion* is found in the LXX of Isaiah 40 – 66 (especially Is. 40:9; 52:7; 60:6; 61:1), where this noun or its cognate verb *euangelizomai* is used of the proclamation of Zion's impending release from exile. The New Testament writers treat this proclamation as foreshadowing the proclamation of release from spiritual estrangement and bondage procured by the death and resurrection of Christ (see p. 196).

2. *Which he promised beforehand through his prophets in the holy scriptures.* This statement is amplified in 1:17; 3:21; 4:3, 6–25; 10:5–20; 15:9–12, 21.

3. *Concerning his Son.* This phrase, which expresses the subject-matter of 'the gospel of God', introduces a short confessional summary (verses 3–4) which may have been as familiar to the Roman Christians as to Paul himself; it is likely, however, that Paul has recast its wording so as to bring out certain necessary emphases.

Who was descended from David according to the flesh. The Davidic descent of Jesus was clearly an element in early Christian preaching and confession. Jesus himself appears to have laid no weight on it, but he did not refuse the designation 'Son of David' when it was applied to him, as by blind Bartimaeus (Mk. 10:47–48). His question about the scribal exegesis of Psalm 110:1 (Mk. 12:35–37) should not be construed as a repudiation of Davidic descent.

The phrase 'according to the flesh' (*i.e.* 'by natural descent') is used of Christ again in 9:5.

4. *Designated Son of God in power.* The word rendered 'designated' (*horizō*) is used in Acts 10:42; 17:31 of Christ's appointment as judge of all. Paul does not mean that Jesus *became* the Son of God by the resurrection, but that he who during his earthly ministry 'was the Son of God in weakness and lowliness' became by the resurrection 'the Son of God in power' (A. Nygren, *ad loc.*). Similarly Peter at Pentecost concludes his proclamation of the resurrection and exaltation of Christ by calling on 'all the house of Israel' to 'know assuredly' that God has made the crucified Jesus 'both Lord and Christ' (Acts 2:36). The phrase 'with power' (*en dynamei*, as here) appears also in Mark 9:1, where the coming of the kingdom of God 'with power' (by contrast with the limitations under which it was manifested during Jesus' ministry) is probably the direct sequel to Jesus' death and vindication.

According to the Spirit of holiness. There is an obvious antithesis between 'according to the flesh' and 'according to the Spirit'. But when Paul states the second member of this antithesis, he makes its meaning plain by adding the genitive 'of holiness'. *The Spirit of holiness* is the regular Hebrew way of saying 'the Holy Spirit'; Paul here reproduces the Hebrew idiom in Greek. By the antithesis of 'flesh' and 'Spirit' here he 'plainly . . . does not allude to the two natures of our Lord, but to *the two states* of humiliation and exaltation'.[1] It is one and the same Son of God who appears as the earthly Jesus and as the heavenly Christ; but his Davidic descent, a matter of glory 'according to the flesh', is now seen nevertheless to belong to the phase of his humiliation, and to be absorbed and transcended by the surpassing glory of his exaltation, by which he has inaugurated the age of the Spirit. The outpouring and ministry of the Spirit attest the enthronement of Jesus as 'Son of God in power'.[2]

By his resurrection from the dead. The phrase is literally 'in consequence of the resurrection of dead ones'; the plural 'dead ones' is an instance of what grammarians call the 'generalizing plural'. Exactly the same phrase is used in Acts 26:23 of the resurrection of Christ. So here it is Christ's own resurrection that is referred to, and not (as some have thought) his raising of Lazarus and others – still less the phenomenon described in Matthew 27:52–53. But Christ's resurrection is denoted by a phrase which hints at the future resurrection of his people; his

---

[1] G. Smeaton, *The Doctrine of the Holy Spirit* (1882), p. 72.
[2] See M. Hengel, *The Son of God*, E.T. (1976).

resurrection is the first instalment of 'the resurrection of the dead', as is made clear in 8:11 (where those who are indwelt by 'the Spirit of him who raised Jesus from the dead' have through that Spirit the assurance of their own resurrection). (*Cf.* 1 Cor. 15:20–23, 44–49.)

5. *Grace and apostleship.* This is probably a hendiadys, meaning 'the grace (or divine gift) of apostleship'; *cf.* the references in 12:6 to the 'gifts that differ according to the grace given to us', and in 15:15–16 to the 'grace' given to Paul by God 'to be a minister of Christ Jesus to the Gentiles'.

To bring about the obedience of faith, i.e. the obedience that is based on faith in Christ. The 'faith' here is not the gospel or the body of doctrine presented for belief, but the belief itself. (*Cf.* 15:18; 16:26.)

Among all the nations. This phrase indicates Paul's special vocation to be the apostle to the Gentiles (*cf.* 11:13). The Greek noun *ethnē* (like its Hebrew equivalent *gōyîm*) is variously rendered 'nations', 'Gentiles' or 'heathen' (for this last *cf.* 1 Cor. 12:2; 1 Thes. 4:5).

6. *Including yourselves.* This probably means not only that the Roman church was situated in the Gentile world but also that its membership was now predominantly Gentile.

Who are called to belong to Jesus Christ. Cf. 8:28, 30 for the divine calling.

7. *To all God's beloved in Rome, who are called to be saints.* Because they are the well-loved people of God, they are called to be holy as he is holy (Lv. 19:2, *etc.*; 1 Pet. 1:15–16). He has summoned them to be set apart for himself; they are saints by divine vocation. There are hints here and there in the New Testament that 'the saints' was a designation (possibly a self-designation) of those Jewish believers (*cf.* 15:25; Eph. 2:19) who looked on themselves as 'the saints of the Most High' who were destined to receive royal and judicial authority from God (Dn. 7:18, 22, 27). Paul insists on applying the same designation to Gentile believers, concorporate with their brethren of Jewish race.

For the phrase 'in Rome' see the textual note on pp. 25–26.

Grace to you and peace. The Greek greeting was *Chaire*, which literally means 'Rejoice!'. The Jew said *Shālōm*,[1] 'Peace!' This was sometimes amplified to 'Mercy and peace' (as in 2 Baruch 78:2). Paul takes over the amplified form, but in place of 'mercy' he habitually uses his favourite word 'grace' (Gk. *charis*). The *grace* of God is his free love and unmerited favour to men and women, imparted through Christ; the *peace* of God is the well-being which they enjoy through his grace.

From God our Father and the Lord Jesus Christ. This spontaneous and repeated collocation of Christ with God bears witness to the place which Christ held in the thought and worship of Paul and other early Christians.

B. INTRODUCTION (1:8–15)

Having thus introduced himself and his theme, Paul explains his present purpose in writing. News that he has received about the high and renowned quality of their faith calls forth deep thanksgiving from Paul, and he assures them of their constant place in his prayers. The churches for which he had primary responsibility – those which he himself had founded – made heavy and continual demands on his time and attention, but he could remember before God other churches too, and not least the church of the capital. He tells them of his long-standing desire and prayer for the opportunity of visiting them; and now, after earlier hindrances, it appeared that his prayer was about to be answered. He hopes not only to impart a blessing to the Roman Christians, but to receive one for himself through his fellowship with them. And while he has no thought of asserting his apostolic authority in Rome, he looks forward to preaching the gospel there and making some converts in Rome as in the rest of the Gentile world. The preaching of the gospel is in his blood, and he cannot refrain from it; he is never off duty but must constantly be at it, discharging a little more of that obligation which he owes to the whole human family – an

---

[1] Compare the Arabic *salaam*, which has the same meaning.

obligation which he will never fully discharge so long as he lives.

8. *I thank my God through Jesus Christ.* As it is through Christ that God's grace is conveyed to human beings (verse 5), so it is through Christ that their gratitude is conveyed to God. The mediatorship of Christ is exercised both towards God and towards humanity. (See p. 213, n. 1.)

Your faith is proclaimed in all the world. Cf. 1 Thessalonians 1:8, 'your faith in God has gone forth everywhere.' In both passages Paul thinks more particularly of all the places where Christianity has been established (see also note on 10:18, p. 197).

9. *Whom I serve with my spirit.* NEB, 'to whom I offer the humble service of my spirit'.

Without ceasing I mention you always in my prayers. (Cf. Eph. 1:16; Phil. 1:3–4; Col. 1:3; 1 Thes. 1:2; 2 Thes. 1:3; Phm. 4.) That Paul should pray regularly for his own converts is what one might expect, but it is evident from this passage that his prayers went beyond his immediate circle of personal acquaintance and apostolic responsibility.

10. *At last.* (Cf. 'often', verse 13.) Of these earlier occasions when Paul had hoped or planned to visit Rome we have no direct information.

12. *That we may be mutually encouraged.* This would correct any impression given by verse 11 that he would be the benefactor and they the beneficiaries. He hopes to receive help as well as to give it during his purposed visit to Rome.

13. *I want you to know, brethren.* A favourite Pauline expression, literally 'I do not want you to be ignorant' (*cf.* 11:25; 1 Cor. 10:1; 12:1; 2 Cor. 1:8; 1 Thes. 4:13).

Thus far have been prevented. One obstacle could have been the imperial edict of AD 49 expelling Jews from Rome (*cf.* Acts 18:2; see p. 16).

14. *Both to Greeks and to barbarians.* To the Greeks, all non-

Greeks were 'barbarians' (*barbaroi*, a word which probably imitated the unintelligible sound of foreign languages). *Cf.* Acts 28:2; 1 Corinthians 14:11.

15. *In Rome.* See textual note on p. 26.

A. The Gospel according to Paul (1:16 – 11:36)

I. THE THEME OF THE GOSPEL: THE RIGHTEOUSNESS OF GOD REVEALED (1:16–17)

'Believe me,' Paul goes on, 'I have no reason to be ashamed of the gospel I preach. No indeed; it is the powerful means which God employs for the salvation of all who believe – the Jew first, and the Gentile also. And why is this so? Because in this gospel there is a revelation of God's way of righteousness – a way of righteousness based on the principle of faith and presented to men and women for their acceptance by faith. It was of this righteousness that the prophet said, "He who through faith is righteous shall live." '

To understand the sense in which the gospel is said to reveal God's righteousness it is necessary to bear in mind some facts about the concept of righteousness in the Old Testament, which forms the chief background of Paul's thought and language.

'The ideas of right and wrong among the Hebrews are forensic ideas; that is, the Hebrew always thinks of the right and the wrong as if they were to be settled before a judge. Righteousness is to the Hebrew not so much a moral quality as a legal status. The word "righteous" (*ṣaddîq*) means simply "in the right", and the word "wicked" (*rasha'*) means "in the wrong". "I have sinned this time", says Pharaoh, "Jehovah is in the right (A.V. righteous), and I and my people are in the wrong (A.V. wicked)", Exod. ix.27. Jehovah is always in

73

the right, for He is not only sovereign but self-consistent. He is the fountain of righteousness . . . the consistent will of Jehovah is the law of Israel.'[1]

God is himself righteous, and those men and women are righteous who are 'in the right'[2] in relation to God and his law. When, therefore, the righteousness of God is revealed in the gospel, it is revealed in a twofold manner. The gospel tells us first how men and women, sinners as they are, can come to be 'in the right' with God and second how God's personal righteousness is vindicated in the very act of declaring sinful men and women 'righteous'. This second aspect of the matter is not dealt with immediately, but the former is expanded sufficiently to show that the principle on which God brings people into the right with himself is the principle of faith, and for this statement Old Testament authority is adduced in the words of Habakkuk 2:4b, 'the righteous shall live by his faith'. Habakkuk 2:4b may be called the 'text' of this Epistle; what follows is in large measure an exposition of the prophet's words.

16. *I am not ashamed of the gospel.* This is an instance of the figure of speech called litotes: Paul means that he glories in the gospel and counts it a high honour to proclaim it. *Cf.* C. K. Barrett, *New Testament Essays* (1972), pp. 116–143.

17. *For in it the righteousness of God is revealed.* A remarkable anticipation of this twofold sense of 'the righteousness of God' – (*a*) his personal righteousness and (*b*) the righteousness with

---

[1] W. R. Smith, *The Prophets of Israel* (1882), pp. 71 f. So, when Isaiah condemns the corrupt judges who 'acquit the guilty for a bribe, and deprive the innocent of his right' (Is. 5:23), he refers to legal decisions; he does not mean that the righteous man is made intrinsically unrighteous. But God's word is a self-fulfilling word: when *he* declares someone to be in the right, that person *is* in the right. See G. Quell and G. Schrenk, *TDNT* II, pp. 174–225 (*s.v. dikē, dikaios, etc.*).

[2] Or, to use a modern expression, 'in the clear' – with which may be compared God's insistence in the Old Testament that he 'will by no means clear the guilty' (Ex. 34:7; see also note on Rom. 4:5, p. 106). Discussing a Neo-Melanesian ('Pidgin') version of the new Testament for Papua New Guinea, H. K. Moulton says, 'We salute strokes of genius such as the translation of "Justification": "God e spik em olrite"' (*The Bible in the World*, Jan.–Feb. 1963, p. 10; Sept. 1967, p. 15).

which he justifies sinners on the ground of faith – appears in the Qumran literature.

'By his righteousness my sin is blotted out . . . If I stumble because of fleshly iniquity, my justification is in the righteousness of God which shall stand for ever. . . . By his mercy he has caused me to approach and by his loving kindness he brings my justification near. By his true righteousness he justifies me and by his abundant goodness he makes atonement for all my iniquities. By his righteousness he cleanses me from the impurity of mortal man and from the sin of the sons of men, that I may praise God for his righteousness and the Most High for his glory.'[1]

Through faith for faith. 'It is based on faith and addressed to faith' (NEB mg., which is preferable to NEB text, 'a way that starts from faith and ends in faith'). According to J. Murray, Paul's purpose in the repetition here and in 3:22 ('through faith in Jesus Christ for all who believe') is 'to accent the fact that not only does the righteousness of God bear savingly upon us *through faith* but also that it bears savingly upon *every one* who believes'.[2]

'He who through faith is righteous shall live.'[3] These words from Habakkuk 2:4b have already been quoted by Paul in Galatians 3:11 to prove that it is not by the law that people are justified before God. They appear again, together with part of their context, in Hebrews 10:38 to encourage the readers of that Epistle to press on and not lose heart. Hebrew *'emûnâ*, translated 'faith' in Habakkuk 2:4 (LXX *pistis*), means 'steadfastness' or 'fidelity'; in the Habakkuk passage this steadfastness or fidelity is based on a firm belief in God and his word, and it is this firm belief that Paul understands by the term.

Habakkuk, crying out to God against the oppression under which his people groaned (late in the seventh century BC),

---

[1] From the 'Hymn of the Initiants'; *cf.* also the translation of G. Vermes, *The Dead Sea Scrolls in English* (1962), pp. 89–94.

[2] *The Epistle to the Romans*, I, p. 32, with Excursus, 'From Faith to Faith', pp. 363–374.

[3] MT 'the righteous one shall live by his faith(fulness)'; LXX ' . . . by my faithfulness' (or 'by faith in me'). One group of LXX MSS attaches the pronoun 'my' to 'righteous one', whence Heb. 10:38, 'my righteous one shall live by faith.'

received the divine assurance that wickedness would not triumph indefinitely, that righteousness would ultimately be vindicated, and the earth would 'be filled with the knowledge of the glory of the LORD, as the waters cover the sea' (Hab. 2:14). This vision might be slow in being realized, but it would certainly be fulfilled. Meanwhile, the righteous would endure to the end, directing their lives by a loyalty to God inspired by faith in his promise.

In the Qumran commentary on Habakkuk this oracle is applied to 'all the doers of the law in the house of Judah, whom God will save from the place of judgment because of their toil and their fidelity to the Teacher of Righteousness'.[1] In the Talmud (TB *Makkoth* 24a) the same oracle is quoted alongside Amos 5:4, 'Seek me and live', as an example of how the whole law may be summed up in one sentence. 'Perhaps "seek" (in Amos 5:4) means "seek the whole Torah"?' asked Rabbi Nachman ben Isaac. 'No', was the reply of Rabbi Shimlai; 'Habakkuk came after him and reduced it to one sentence, as it is written, "The righteous shall live by his faith".'

When Paul takes up Habakkuk's words and sees in them the foundation truth of the gospel, he gives them the sense, 'it is he who is righteous (justified) through faith that will live.' The terms of Habakkuk's oracle are sufficiently general to make room for Paul's application of them – an application which, far from doing violence to the prophet's intention, expresses the abiding validity of his message.

For Paul, as for many other Jews, 'life' (especially eternal life) and 'salvation' were practically synonymous. If Paul's self-designation as 'a Hebrew born of Hebrews' (Phil. 3:5) means (as is probable) that he was the Aramaic-speaking child of Aramaic-speaking parents, he would very likely, when speaking his native tongue, employ the same word *ḥayyē* [2] for both 'life' and 'salvation'. 'It is he who is righteous (justified) by faith that will live' means, therefore, 'it is he who is righteous (justified) by faith that will be saved'. For Paul, life in the sense of salvation begins with justification but goes beyond it (*cf.* 5:9–10); it

---

[1] *Cf.* G. Vermes, *The Dead Sea Scrolls in English*, p. 237.

[2] In the Syriac New Testament this is the term used in the two phrases 'the words of this Life' (Acts 5:20) and 'the message of this salvation' (Acts 13:26).

includes sanctification (the subject of Rom. 6 – 8) and is consummated in final glory (5:2; 8:30). In this comprehensive sense 'salvation' may well be regarded as the key 'to unlock the wards of Paul's theology'.[1]

II. SIN AND RETRIBUTION:
THE UNIVERSAL NEED DIAGNOSED (1:18 – 3:20)

A. THE PAGAN WORLD (1:18–32)

Before Paul elaborates further the manner in which God's way of righteousness is set forth in the gospel, he shows why it is so urgently necessary that the way to get right with God should be known. As things are, human beings are 'in the wrong' with God, and his wrath is revealed against them. There is a moral law in life that men and women are left to the consequences of their own freely chosen course of action, and unless this tendency is reversed by divine grace, their situation will go from bad to worse. Three times over the words of doom recur: 'God gave them up' (verses 24, 26, 28).

Paul's aim is to show that the whole of humanity is morally bankrupt, unable to claim a favourable verdict at the judgment bar of God, desperately in need of his mercy and pardon.

He begins with an area of human life whose moral bankruptcy was a matter of general agreement among moralists of the day – the great mass of contemporary paganism. The picture which he draws of it is ugly enough in all conscience, but no uglier than the picture of it which we have from contemporary pagan literature. What is the cause, he asks, of this appalling condition which has developed in the world? Whence come these shameful perversions, this internecine enmity within the human family? It all arises, he says, from wrong ideas about God. And these wrong ideas about God did not arise innocently; the knowledge of the true God was accessible, but men and women closed their minds to it. Instead of appreciating the

---

[1] A. M. Hunter, *Interpreting Paul's Gospel* (1954), p. 9; see p. 39, above.

glory of the Creator by contemplating the universe which he created, they gave to created things that glory which belongs to God alone. Idolatry is the source of immorality. So the author of the book of Wisdom had already said:

'For the idea of making idols was the beginning of fornication, and the invention of them was the corruption of life' (Wisdom 14:12).

With Paul's language about the visible creation as a source of knowledge concerning the nature of its invisible Creator (verses 19–20) we may compare the speech at Lystra in Acts 14:15–17 and especially that at Athens in Acts 17:22–31. There is a difference of emphasis between the speech at Athens and Paul's argument here, but no contradiction: there Paul was trying to gain a hearing from pagans, whereas here he is addressing established Christians. In the Athenian speech God's creation of the world and his providential arrangement of the seasons of the year and the habitable zones of the earth for men and women's well-being are intended to lead them to 'feel after him and find him' (Acts 17:27). If, nevertheless, they acknowledge that he is an 'unknown God' to them, their self-confessed ignorance is not condoned as venial, although God in his mercy overlooked 'the times of ignorance' before the coming of Christ.

The culpable character of men and women's ignorance of God is emphasized still more here: it is a deliberate ignorance. They had the knowledge of God available to them but 'did not see fit to acknowledge God' (verse 28). The truth was accessible to them, but they suppressed it unrighteously and embraced the 'lie' in preference to it. Therefore 'God gave them up' to the consequences of their choice. And precisely here he has manifested his 'wrath' – that principle of retribution which must operate in a moral universe.

To a man so convinced as Paul was that the world was created and controlled by a personal God of righteousness and mercy, this retribution could not be an impersonal principle; it was God's own wrath. If it is felt that the word 'wrath' is scarcely suitable to be used in relation to God, it is probably because wrath as we know it in human life so constantly involves sinful,

self-regarding passion. Not so with God: his 'wrath' is the
response of his holiness to wickedness and rebellion. Paul
would certainly have agreed with Isaiah in describing the
execution of God's wrath as his 'strange deed' (Is. 28:21), to
which he girds himself slowly and reluctantly; indeed, he sets
forth the revelation of God's wrath here as the background to
his 'proper work' of mercy, which is so congenial to his
character that he speeds with joyful haste to lavish it on
undeserving penitents.

But even if the picture of divine retribution, operating as a
stern principle in human life, does provide a background to the
everlasting mercy, it is a real and terrible background, and one
that must be seriously reckoned with.

18. *The wrath of God is revealed.* Not in the gospel (in which
the saving 'righteousness of God' is revealed) but in the facts
of human experience: 'the history of the world is the judgment
of the world' (J. C. F. Schiller). The revelation of 'the wrath to
come' at the end-time (1 Thes. 1:10) is anticipated by the revelation of the same principle in the on-going life of the world. 'The
idea that God is angry is no more anthropopathic than the
thought that God is love. The reason why the idea of the divine
anger is always exposed to misunderstanding is because among
men anger is ethically wrong. And yet, even among men do
we not speak of a "righteous anger"?'[1] The exposure of pagan
idolatry and immorality in these verses follows lines laid down
in such works of Jewish apologetic as the book of Wisdom
quoted above (see especially Wisdom 12 – 14), and the *Epistle
of Aristeas*; it reappears in the Christian apologists of the second
century AD (*e.g.* the author of the *Epistle to Diognetus*, Aristides,
Tatian, Athenagoras, and the *Preaching of Peter* mentioned by
Clement of Alexandria, *Stromateis* 6.5, 39.1 – 43.3).

Who by their wickedness suppress the truth. 'In their wickedness
they are stifling the truth' (NEB). 'The truth' is more precisely
defined in verse 25 as 'the truth about God'.

20. *His invisible nature.* Lit. 'his invisible things', particularized

---

[1] E. Brunner, *The Mediator* (1934), p. 478.

as *his eternal power and deity*. The adjective *aïdios* (otherwise found in the New Testament only in Jude 6) might be rendered 'everlasting', to distinguish it from the commoner *aiōnios*, 'eternal' (*cf*. Rom. 2:7, *etc*.). This is the only New Testament instance of *theiotēs*, 'divinity', 'divine nature' (NIV). If God's divinity is shown in creation, his full deity or divine essence (*theotēs*) is embodied in Christ (Col. 2:9).

Have been clearly perceived. Lit. 'being understood are perceived' (*nooumena kathoratai*), where the former verb refers strictly to the intelligence and the latter to physical sight. 'Both the verbs . . . describe how, on contemplating God's works, man can grasp enough of His nature to prevent him from the error of identifying any of the created things with the Creator, enabling him to keep his conception of the Deity free from idolatry.'[1]

22. *They became fools*. As in the wisdom literature of the Old Testament, folly (*cf*. 'their senseless minds' in verse 21) implies moral obtuseness rather than mere deficiency in intelligence.

23. *And exchanged the glory of the immortal God for images. Cf*. Psalm 106:20, 'They exchanged the glory of God for the image of an ox that eats grass' (a reference to the worship of the golden calf). Here the language is generalized. The threefold classification of non-human living creatures, *birds or animals* (lit. 'quadrupeds') *or reptiles* (*cf*. Gn. 1:20–25), and the terms 'glory', 'image' and 'resembling' (*cf*. Gn. 1:26) suggest that 'Paul's account of man's wickedness had been deliberately stated in terms of the Biblical narrative of Adam's fall'.[2]

24, 26, 28. *God gave them up. Cf*. Acts 7:42 where, because of the idolatrous tendencies of the Israelites, 'God . . . gave them over to worship the host of heaven'. An impressive modern statement of this principle of divine retribution is provided by C. S. Lewis in *The Problem of Pain* (1940), pp. 115 f.: the lost, he says, 'enjoy forever the horrible freedom they have demanded, and are therefore self-enslaved'.

[1] B. Gärtner, *The Areopagus Speech and Natural Revelation* (1955), p. 137.
[2] M. D. Hooker, 'Adam in Romans 1', *NTS* 6 (1959–60), p. 301.

25. *A lie.* Lit. 'the lie' – the basic lie which contradicts God's truth; *cf.* 2 Thessalonians 2:10–12.

27. *The due penalty for their error.* NEB, better, 'the fitting wage of such perversion'. In modern English 'error' is too weak a word to render *planē* in a context like this; *cf.* Jude 11, where 'Balaam's error' (*planē*) is the idolatry and fornication of Baal-peor into which the Israelites were seduced by his counsel (Nu. 25:1–9; 31:16).

28. *A base mind.* NEB 'their own depraved (*adokimos*, "counterfeit") reason'.
Improper conduct. The phrase translated 'improper' (*ta mē kathēkonta*) is a technical term of Stoic philosophy, *kathēkonta* denoting actions that were 'fitting'. A similar expression is used in Ephesians 5:4, of things 'which are not fitting' (*ha ouk anēken*).

29. *Filled with all manner of wickedness.* The list of vices in verses 29–31 belongs to a category well attested in Greek literature of this period. *Cf.* 1 Corinthians 6:9–10; Galatians 5:19–21; Colossians 3:5.

30. *Insolent.* Greek *hybristēs*, one who behaves with humiliating and unconscionable arrogance to those who are not powerful enough to retaliate.

B. THE MORALIST (2:1–16)

Paul's style is that appropriate to the type of composition which the ancients called *diatribē*, in which questions or objections are put into the mouth of an imagined critic in order to be answered or demolished.[1]

One can almost envisage him as he dictates his letter, suddenly picking out the complacent individual who has been enjoying the exposure of those sins he 'has no mind to', and

---

[1] See S. K. Stowers, *The Diatribe and Paul's Letter to the Romans* (1981); *cf.* p. 91, n. 1, below.

telling him that he is no better than anyone else. He imagines an interruption by some objector, and turns to refute his objection, first squashing it with 'By no means!' ('Perish the thought!') and then giving a reasoned reply to it. He starts a new phase of his argument with such a rhetorical question as 'What shall we say?' or 'What then?'[1] And all the time his thought races ahead of his words, so that his words have to leap over a gap to catch up with his thought. We can only try to imagine how Tertius's pen kept up with the apostle's words. No wonder that, especially in impassioned moments, his Greek is full of breaks in construction and unfinished sentences.

We know that there was another side to the pagan world of the first century than that which Paul has portrayed in the preceding paragraphs. What about a man like Paul's illustrious contemporary Seneca, the Stoic moralist, the tutor of Nero?[2] Seneca might have listened to Paul's indictment and said, 'Yes, that is perfectly true of great masses of mankind, and I concur in the judgment which you pass on them – but there are others, of course, like myself, who deplore these tendencies as much as you do.'

Paul imagines someone intervening in terms like these, and he addresses the supposed objector: 'My good sir, in judging others you are passing judgment on yourself, whoever you may be, for in principle you do the same things as you condemn in them.' And how apt this reply would have been to a man like Seneca! For he could write so effectively on the good life that Christian writers of later days were prone to call him 'our own Seneca'.[3] Not only did he exalt the great moral virtues; he exposed hypocrisy, he preached the equality of all human beings, he acknowledged the pervasive character of evil ('all vices exist in all men, though all vices do not stand out prominently in each man'), he practised and inculcated daily self-examination, he ridiculed vulgar idolatry, he assumed the role of a moral guide. But too often he tolerated in himself vices not

---

[1] *Cf.* 3:5; 4:1; 6:1; 7:7; 8:31; 9:14, 30, and the similar 'You will say to me then' in 9:19; 11:19.

[2] See J. N. Sevenster, *Paul and Seneca* (1962).

[3] '*Seneca saepe noster*', says Tertullian; 'Seneca, so often one of ourselves' (*On the Soul* 20).

so different from those which he condemned in others – the most flagrant instance being his connivance at Nero's murder of his mother Agrippina.

Even in this section of chapter 2, however, as more explicitly from verse 17 onwards, Paul is thinking chiefly of a Jewish critic. Such denunciation of pagan idolatry as we find in chapter 1 was common form in Jewish propaganda. Religious Jews found ample scope for passing adverse moral judgment on their Gentile neighbours.

That Paul has a Jewish critic more particularly in mind is evident from his repetition of the words 'the Jew first and also the Greek' (see 2:9 and 10), in which he emphasizes that the Jews are the first to experience the judgment of God as well as the first to receive the good news of his saving grace (1:16). This twofold primacy of the people of Israel, in salvation and judgment alike, was taught by the prophets in earlier days; eight centuries before this Epistle was written, for example, we hear the word of God to his people through Amos: 'You only have I known of all the families of the earth; therefore I will punish you for all your iniquities' (Am. 3:2).

We have seen how the portrayal of pagan idolatry in chapter 1 echoes the book of Wisdom. Similarly now, in turning to convict the Jews of *their* moral bankruptcy, Paul takes up themes from the same book. According to the author of Wisdom, God afflicted the Gentiles (such as the Egyptian oppressors of Israel in the days of Moses) by way of retribution for their wickedness, whereas the same afflictions were remedial in intention when they fell on the Israelites:[1]

'For thou didst test them as a father does in warning,
but thou didst examine the ungodly as a stern king does in condemnation . . .
So while chastening us thou scourgest our enemies ten thousand times more,
so that we may meditate upon thy goodness when we judge,
and when we are judged we may expect mercy'
(Wisdom 11:10; 12:22).

[1] Compare Paul's argument in 1 Cor. 11:32.

'Agreed', says Paul; 'you do well to acknowledge God's goodness to you in spite of all your disobedience, but do you not realize that his goodness is intended to give you an opportunity to repent? Beware of despising his goodness and presuming on his mercy. If, instead of repenting, you maintain a hard and impenitent heart, then be sure that you are simply storing up for yourself an accumulation of divine wrath which will be discharged on you at the judgment day.'

When divine judgment comes, it will be absolutely impartial. God 'will render to every man according to his works' (2:6). While, for Paul, forgiveness and eternal life are utterly of God's grace, divine judgment (as uniformly in the Bible) is always passed in accordance with what men and women have done. Every material factor is taken into consideration. People are held accountable for such knowledge of the truth as was accessible to them, not for what was not accessible. Jews, says Paul, will be judged on the basis of the written law, for *they* had access to that source of divine knowledge. Gentiles will be judged by another criterion, for among them too God did not leave himself without witness. If the knowledge of God's character was available to them through the starry heavens above (*cf.* 1:20), it was available to them also through the moral law within. They did not have the law of Moses, as the Jews had, but they had the law of conscience, the distinction between right and wrong, engraved on their hearts. When they violate that law, says Paul, they know that they are doing wrong, and by that knowledge they will be judged on the day when the inmost secrets of hearts are brought to light. Whether the will of God is known by the law of Moses or by the voice of conscience, knowledge of his will is not enough; it is the doing of his will that counts.

4. *God's kindness is meant to lead you to repentance.* Cf. Wisdom 11:23, 'But thou art merciful to all, for thou canst do all things, and thou dost overlook men's sins, that they may repent.' See also Romans 11:22.

6. *For he will render to every man* (better, 'every one') *according to his works.* Cf. Job 34:11; Psalm 62:12; Proverbs 24:12; Jeremiah 17:10; 32:19 for Old Testament statements of this principle; it recurs in the New Testament in Matthew 16:27; 1 Corinthians 3:8; 2 Corinthians 5:10; Revelation 2:23; 20:12; 22:12. See also Romans 14:12.

7. *To those who by patience in well-doing seek for glory and honour and immortality, he will give eternal life.* Paul is not teaching salvation by works here, but emphasizing God's impartiality as between Jew and Gentile. *Cf.* Peter's surprised confession in Acts 10:34–35: 'Truly I perceive that God shows no partiality, but in every nation any one who fears him and does what is right is acceptable to him.' God showed his acceptance of the Gentile Cornelius, to whom these words were spoken, by sending Peter to him with a message by which he and his household would be saved (Acts 11:14).

8. *For those who are factious.* The NEB rendering, 'for those who are governed by selfish ambition', does more justice to the basic sense of *eritheia*, which is derived from *erithos* ('hireling'). Even in antiquity, however, its meaning tended to be assimilated to that of *eris*, 'strife' ('faction', 'contention').

11. *God shows no partiality. Cf.* Deuteronomy 10:17; 2 Chronicles 19:7; Job 34:19; Acts 10:34; Galatians 2:6; Ephesians 6:9; Colossians 3:25; 1 Peter 1:17. Our Lord stated the same truth graphically when he described how the Father in heaven 'makes his sun rise on the evil and on the good, and sends rain on the just and on the unjust' (Mt. 5:45).

12. *All who have sinned without the law will also perish without the law.* Sin unchecked leads to perdition one way or another, but Gentiles will not be condemned for failure to conform to a law-code which was not accessible to them. The principle is laid down that men and women are judged by the light that is available to them, not by light that is not available.

13. *It is . . . the doers of the law who will be justified.* Paul may have in mind Leviticus 18:5, 'You shall therefore keep my statutes and my ordinances, by doing which a man shall live' – a scripture which he quotes later in 10:5. The course of his argument goes on to indicate that, while one who was a 'doer' of the law would be justified, yet, since no-one does it perfectly, there is no justification that way. The antithesis between merely hearing the law and actually doing it is elaborated in James 1:22-25. The expression 'the doers of the law' is found in Qumran literature (*cf.* p. 76, above).

14. *When Gentiles who have not the law do by nature what the law requires.* The word order strongly suggests that 'by nature' (*physei*) is to be construed with 'do' (as in RSV); since, however, it comes between the two clauses in the Greek text it could just be taken with what precedes. Gentiles, that is to say, are born with no knowledge of the law, but when they come to faith in Christ they do, not 'by nature' but by the Spirit (*cf.* 8:4), *what the law requires* (see Cranfield, *ad loc.*). But this construction is less probable. Despite the dark picture drawn above (1:18-32), Paul and his readers knew pagans who led upright lives in accordance with the dictates of conscience (although this was not their ground of justification before God).

15. *They show that what the law requires is written on their hearts.* An echo of the prophecy of the new covenant in Jeremiah 31:33 (see p. 153). K. Barth holds that Gentile Christians are in view here[1] (similarly Cranfield, *ad loc.*), but this scarcely suits the context.

Their conscience also bears witness. The word 'conscience' (*syneidēsis*) is not current in classical Greek. It belonged to the vernacular tongue and attained literary status only a short time before the beginning of the Christian era. It meant 'consciousness of right or wrong doing', but Paul uses it (and perhaps he was the first to do so) in the sense of an independent witness within, which examines and passes judgment on one's conduct. In Christians this examination and judgment should be specially accurate because their conscience is enlightened by the Holy Spirit (*cf.* 9:1).

---

[1] *Church Dogmatics* I/2 (1956), p. 304; II/2 (1957), pp. 242, 604; IV/1 (1956), pp. 33, 369, 395.

C. THE JEW (2:17 – 3:8)

1. Privilege brings responsibility (2:17–29)
In 2:17 Paul addresses the moralizer explicitly as a Jew. 'You
bear the honoured name of Jew,' he says, 'your possession of
the law gives you confidence, you glory in the fact that it is the
true God whom you worship and whose will you know.' Here
perhaps there is a further echo of Wisdom:

'For even if we sin we are thine, knowing thy power;
but we will not sin, because we know that we are accounted
   thine.
For to know thee is complete righteousness,
and to know thy power is the root of immortality'
(Wisdom 15:2–3).

'You approve the more excellent way,' Paul continues, 'for you
have learnt it from the law. You regard yourself as better taught
than those lesser breeds without the law; you consider yourself
a guide to the blind and an instructor of the foolish.

'But why not take an honest look at yourself? Have *you* no
defects? You know the law, but do you keep it? You say, "You
shall not steal"; but do you never steal? You say, "You shall
not commit adultery"; but do you always keep that commandment? You detest idols, but do you never rob temples? You
glory in the law, but in fact your disobedience to the law brings
you and the God whom you worship into disrepute among the
pagans.

'To be a Jew will do one good in the sight of God only if he
keeps the law of God. A Jew who breaks the law is no better
than a Gentile. Conversely, a Gentile who keeps the law's
requirements is as good in the sight of God as any law-abiding
Jew. Indeed, a Gentile who keeps the law of God will condemn
a Jew who breaks it, no matter how well-versed that Jew may
be in the sacred scriptures, no matter how canonically circumcised he is. You see, it is not a matter of natural descent and
an external mark like circumcision. The word "Jew" means
"praise", and the true Jew is the man whose life is praiseworthy
by God's standards, whose heart is pure in God's sight, whose

87

circumcision is the inward circumcision of the heart. He is the true Jew, I say – the truly praiseworthy man – and his praise is not a matter of human applause, but of divine approval.'

18. *Know his will.* Lit. 'know the will'; God's will is 'the will' *par excellence. Cf.* 1 Maccabees 3:60, RV: 'as may be the will in heaven, so shall he do.'

Approve what is excellent. The word *diapheronta* means primarily 'things that differ' and then also 'things that differ from others by surpassing them', *i.e.* 'things that excel'. While RSV accepts this latter sense here, NEB prefers the former sense ('you are aware of moral distinctions'). The same phrase appears in Philippians 1:10 ('so that you may approve what is excellent'; NEB 'may thus bring you the gift of true discrimination').

22. *Do you rob temples?* What Paul has in mind is difficult to say: perhaps he refers to some scandalous incident like that of AD 19 recorded by Josephus (*Antiquities* 18.81–84), when four Jews of Rome, led by one who professed to teach the Jewish faith to interested Gentiles, persuaded a noble Roman lady, a convert to Judaism, to make a munificent contribution to the temple at Jerusalem, but appropriated it for their own uses. When the matter came to light, the Emperor Tiberius expelled all resident Jews from Rome (see p. 16). An incident like this brought the honoured name of 'Jew' into disrepute among the Gentiles. There, however, it was the temple of the God of Israel that was robbed; here the conjunction with idolatry suggests the robbing of pagan temples. Either way, temple robbery (*hierosylia*) was reckoned a most heinous crime; in Acts 19:37 Paul and his associates are declared to be guiltless of it in relation to the temple of Artemis at Ephesus.

24. *For, as it is written, 'The name of God is blasphemed among the Gentiles because of you.'* The reference is to Isaiah 52:5, 'continually all the day my name is despised.' The sad plight of the Jews in exile caused the Gentiles to speak lightly of their God, as though he were powerless to help his people. Now it is not his people's misfortune, but their misconduct, that causes the Gentiles to conclude that the God of such people cannot be of much account. Members of the Qumran community were warned to be careful in their dealings with Gentiles, 'lest they blaspheme'.[1]

25. *Circumcision indeed is of value if you obey the law.* Cf. Galatians 5:3, 'every man who receives circumcision . . . is bound to keep the whole law.' Circumcision, undergone as a legal requirement, carries with it the obligation to keep all the rest of the law, whether it be accepted in later life, as by proselytes (which is what Paul has in view in Galatians), or administered to Jewish infants (which is what he has in mind here). But as neither category of circumcised persons can keep the whole law but must inevitably default on their obligation, Paul adds: *but if you break the law, your circumcision becomes uncircumcision.*

This lesson had already been taught in part by Jeremiah: 'Behold, the days are coming, says the LORD, when I will punish all those who are circumcised but yet uncircumcised – Egypt, Judah, Edom, the sons of Ammon, Moab . . . for all these nations are uncircumcised, and all the house of Israel is uncircumcised in heart' (Je. 9:25–26). Israel's neighbours for the most part practised circumcision (the Philistines were a notorious exception); but the circumcision of Israel's neighbours was not a sign of God's covenant, as Israelite circumcision was intended to be. Yet, if Israel and Judah departed in heart from God, their physical circumcision would be in God's sight no better than that of their neighbours: so far as any religious value was concerned, it was no circumcision at all. What God desired was a purified and obedient heart. Cf. Deuteronomy 10:16, 'Circumcise therefore the foreskin of your heart, and be no longer stubborn' (also Je. 4:4).

27. *Those who are physically uncircumcised but keep the law will condemn you.* That is, the shortcomings of an unworthy Jew will be shown up by the example of a Gentile who, with none of the distinctive Jewish privileges, nevertheless pleases God.

29. *His praise is not from men but from God.* The Jews derived

[1] G. Vermes, *The Dead Sea Scrolls in English*, p. 114.

their name from their ancestor Judah (Heb. *Yᵉhûḏâ*), whose name is associated in the Old Testament with the verb *yāḏâ*, 'praise'; *cf.* his mother's words at his birth, 'This time I will praise the LORD' (Gn. 29:35), and his father's deathbed blessing, 'Judah, your brothers shall praise you' (Gn. 49:8).

2. Objections answered (3:1–8)

Here Paul imagines someone breaking into his argument and saying, 'Well then, if it is being a Jew inwardly that counts, if it is the "circumcision" of the heart that matters, is there any advantage in belonging to the Jewish nation, or in being physically circumcised?' We might have expected Paul to answer this supposed question quite categorically: 'None at all!' But, rather to our surprise, he replies, 'Much in every way.' Of course it is an advantage to belong to the circumcised nation. Think of all the privileges[1] granted by God to that nation – privileges in which other nations had no part. It would be asking too much of Paul to expect him to deny his true ancestral heritage, especially as now he had found, in the gospel to which his life was devoted, the fulfilment of the age-old hope of his people.

Among the ancestral privileges of Israel, Paul reckons as of first importance the fact that they were the custodians of 'the oracles of God'. To have the revelation of God's will and purpose committed to them was a high honour indeed. But if it was a high honour, it carried with it a great responsibility. If they proved unfaithful to their trust, their case was worse than that of the nations to which God had not revealed himself.

Now in fact Israel had not proved faithful to this trust. And this might have been put as an objection to Paul when he argued that it was a great advantage to belong to the nation which had received the divine oracles. But his reply is that men's faithlessness never alters God's faithfulness or frustrates his purpose. Their unfaithfulness simply sets his truth in relief: his righteousness is always vindicated over against their unrighteousness.

Then a further objection is dealt with. Someone may say: 'If my faithlessness sets God's faithfulness in bolder relief, if my

---

[1] A further list is given in Rom. 9:4–5.

unrighteousness establishes his righteousness, why should he find fault with me? He is really the gainer by my sin; why should he exact retribution for it?' This objection seems so foolish to Paul that he apologizes for mentioning it. The answer is plain: God is the moral governor of the universe, the judge of all the earth; how could he exercise that function which is inseparable from his Godhead if he did not exact retribution for sin?

The supposed objector, however, is persistent, and repeats his argument in different words: 'If my falsehood makes God's truth shine more brightly by contrast, it redounds to his glory; why then does he insist on condemning me as a sinner? The end – God's glory – is good; why is the means – my sin – counted wrong? Surely the end justifies the means?'

'As a matter of fact', says Paul, 'that is precisely what some people say my gospel amounts to; but their charge is not only slanderous, it stands self-condemned because it is such a contradiction in terms.' The gospel of justification by faith, apart from 'works of righteousness', has always called forth this criticism, but the criticism is amply refuted by the fact that the same gospel insists unequivocally on the 'fruits of righteousness' which must follow justification.[1]

4. *Let God be true though every man be false.* The second clause may echo the psalmist's dismayed outcry: 'Men are all a vain hope' (Ps. 116:11). 'Let every human being be convicted of falsehood', says Paul, 'rather than God's veracity be impugned.'

'That thou mayest be justified in thy words, and prevail when thou art judged.' Better: 'That thou mayest be vindicated when thou speakest, and win the case when thou enterest into judgment' (*krinesthai* should be taken as middle voice here, not passive). The quotation is from Psalm 51:4, where MT means simply '. . . when thou judgest' (RSV 'in thy judgment'; NEB 'in passing sentence').

8. *Why not do evil that good may come?* It is easy to see how Paul's gospel could be misrepresented as though it taught this. Those, whether Jews or Christians, who regarded religion as

---

[1] The diatribe pattern (see p. 81) is commonly thought to be followed in verses 1–8, but see D. R. Hall, 'Romans 3.1–8 reconsidered', *NTS* 29 (1983), pp. 183–197.

essentially a matter of law (however liberally 'law' might be interpreted), could not but conclude that a doctrine of justification apart from 'works of law' undermined the place of law in mankind's approach to God, and therefore undermined religion and morality.

Their condemnation is just. This may mean either 'To condemn such men as these is surely no injustice' (NEB) or 'such an argument is quite properly condemned' (J. B. Phillips). The pronoun translated 'their' may refer back either to the people who say such things (as RSV, NEB, NIV assume) or to the things they say (as Phillips and some others suppose). In the latter case 'refutation' would be a better rendering than 'condemnation'. For a reasoned answer to the accusation see 6:2–23.

D. ALL MANKIND FOUND GUILTY (3:9–20)

'Well then,' the interlocutor proceeds, 'you have said that it is an advantage to belong to the Jewish nation. Does it not follow that we Jews are superior to those Gentiles who lack the privileges we enjoy?' 'No indeed,' says Paul; 'we may have received greater advantages, but we are in fact in no better case than they are. They have sinned, it is true; but then, so have we. All, Jews and Gentiles alike, are bound to plead guilty before the bar of God. The situation is well summed up in the words of Scripture.'

Here Paul adduces a catena of Old Testament quotations in which the general sinfulness of humanity is summed up. The catena comes in here to clinch a case already established by various arguments. If the quotations were examined one by one, it would be necessary to relate them to their historical contexts; some at least of them had a particular rather than a universal reference. But the general picture which they here present rounds off the case which Paul has been building up. And if he supposes an objection to his use of these quotations, the objection is not that he has detached them from their historical contexts, but that they refer to the wicked Gentiles only, not to Israel. 'No,' he replies, 'these quotations are taken from the Jewish Scriptures, and therefore the people whom they have primarily in view are Jews.' What is written in the law (here meaning the Hebrew Bible as a whole) applies naturally to the people of the law. The law brings out men and women's sinfulness but does nothing to cure it. Jews as well as Gentiles, then, have to confess themselves morally bankrupt. If there is any hope for either group, it can be found only in the mercy of God and not in any claim that individuals or nations may try to establish on him. Because of the universal fact of sin, the way of acceptance with God by reason of our works of righteousness is closed – the notice is clearly worded: 'No Road This Way.'

9. *No, not at all.* There is a *prima facie* clash between this answer to 'Are we Jews any better off?' and the answer in verse 2 to 'Then what advantage has the Jew?' – 'Much in every way.' But that earlier answer had reference to the privileges inherited by Jews as members of the elect nation; 'No, not at all' relates to their standing before God. Privileges or no privileges, Jews and Gentiles stand equally in need of his grace. N. A. Dahl omits 'No, not at all' (following the uncial P) and takes the preceding question to mean 'What do we hold before us as a defence?' (answer: 'Nothing; we are all alike held fast by sin').[1]

10–12. *'None is righteous . . . no one does good, not even one.'* Quoted from Psalm 14:1c, 2b–3 (repeated in Ps. 53:1c, 2b–3).

13. *'Their throat is an open grave, they use their tongues to deceive.'* Quoted from Psalm 5:9.

14. *'Their mouth is full of curses and bitterness.'* Quoted from Psalm 10:7.

15–17. *'Their feet are swift to shed blood . . . the way of peace they do not know.'* Quoted from Isaiah 59:7–8.

18. *'There is no fear of God before their eyes.'* Quoted from Psalm 36:1.

---

[1] N. A. Dahl, 'Romans 3.9: Text and meaning' in *Paul and Paulinism*, ed. M. D. Hooker and S. G. Wilson (1982), pp. 184–204. The question can be rendered at least three ways; the answer at least two ways.

19. *Whatever the law says.* The reference is to the preceding quotations; but since none of them is taken from the Law in the stricter sense (the Pentateuch) – they are all drawn from the Psalter, with one exception, which comes from Isaiah – 'law' here must mean the Hebrew Scriptures in general. See pp. 51f.

20. *No human being will be justified in his sight by works of the law.* A free quotation and amplification of Psalm 143:2, '(Enter not into judgment with thy servant [*cf.* Ps. 51:4, quoted in verse 4 above]; for) no man living is righteous before thee.' *Cf.* Galatians 2:16 ('a man is not justified by works of the law'); 3:11 ('no man is justified before God by the law'). Paul adds the reason why no-one can be justified in God's sight 'by works of the law'; it is that *through the law comes knowledge of sin*. This affirmation is repeated and expanded in 5:20; 7:7–11.

III. THE WAY OF RIGHTEOUSNESS:
THE UNIVERSAL NEED MET (3:21 – 5:21)

A. GOD'S PROVISION (3:21–31)

But now a new way to acceptance with God has been opened up, a completely different way from that of legal obedience. Yet this is no new-fangled way, thought up by ourselves; it has ample witness borne to it in advance in the Old Testament writings – in the Law and the Prophets. It is the way of faith in Jesus Christ, and it lies open to all who believe in him, Jews and Gentiles alike. We have already seen that there is no distinction between these two divisions of humanity, since both Jews and Gentiles have sinned and fall short of God's glory, the true end for which God created them. But by this new way both Jews and Gentiles can be brought into a right relationship with God, can have the assurance of acceptance by him and receive his free pardon. They receive it freely, by his sheer grace, because of the redemptive work accomplished by Christ. It is Christ whom God has set forth before our eyes as the one whose sacrificial death has atoned for our guilt and removed the imminent retribution which our rebellion against God had incurred. What Christ has thus procured for us we can make effectively our own by faith.

This, then, is the way in which God has demonstrated his righteousness – he has vindicated his own character and at the same time he bestows a righteous status on sinners. This is why God, in his patient dealing with men and women, could pass over the sins which they committed before the coming of Christ, instead of exacting the full penalty; he was showing them mercy in prospect of the demonstration of his righteousness in this present era. And this demonstration shows us how God remains perfectly righteous himself while he pardons those who believe in Jesus and puts them in the right before his judgment bar.

If this is so, who has any right to boast? All ground of boasting in one's personal righteousness is removed, not by the works prescribed by the law but by the principle of faith. Where Jew and Gentile alike are justified by God's grace, through no merit of their own, none can say, 'I achieved this by my own effort.' The conclusion of Paul's argument is that human beings are set right in God's sight by faith, quite apart from the law's requirements. If acceptance by God could be attained only by keeping the Jewish law, then God would be in a special sense the God of the Jews. But he is as much the Gentiles' God as the God of the Jews, for in the gospel one and the same way of righteousness is opened up for both. He will accept Jews by virtue of their faith, and he will accept Gentiles on exactly the same basis.

For Paul, the division between Jews and Gentiles was the basic division in the human race. He himself was a Jew by birth and upbringing and had been taught to look on non-Jews as benighted sinners, lacking the knowledge of God's law by which alone it was possible to gain acceptance in his sight. And indeed the cleavage between Jew and Gentile was one of the most unbridgeable in the ancient world. There are other cleavages which may appear larger in our eyes today – cleavages of race, nationality, class and colour – whose recalcitrance presents us with far more acute problems than does the division between Jew and Gentile. But Paul's argument is as valid in the light of our contemporary cleavages as it was in the face of those of his own day: there is no distinction between east and west, black and white, for all are equally in need of the free mercy of God and all may receive his mercy on the same terms.

The Roman poet Horace, laying down some guide-lines for writers of tragedies in his day, criticizes those who resort too readily to the device of a *deus ex machina* to solve the knotty problems which have developed in the course of the plot. 'Do not bring a god on to the stage', he says, 'unless the problem is one that deserves a god to solve it' (*nec deus intersit, nisi dignus uindice nodus / inciderit*).[1]

Luther took up these words and applied them to the forgiveness of sins: here, he said, is a problem which needs God to solve it (*nodus Deo uindice dignus*).[2] True, for sinful man cannot solve it, though he desperately needs a solution to it: it is his problem; it is he who needs to be forgiven. And what Paul tells us here is that the problem has been worthily solved by the grace of God, who has presented Christ as the solution, the means of forgiveness, the guarantor of our acceptance. All that is required of sinful men and women is that they should embrace by faith what God's grace has provided.

It might be asked, however, if God's law is not nullified by this principle of faith. Far from it, says Paul. By the principle of faith the law is upheld, sin is condemned, righteousness is vindicated and the Old Testament scriptures are fulfilled. This he now proceeds to show.

21. *The righteousness of God.* 'God's way of righteousness', as in 1:17.

22. *Through faith in Jesus Christ.* Lit. 'through faith of Jesus Christ', where the genitive is objective: Jesus Christ is the one in whom faith is placed (this is confirmed by the unambiguous wording of verse 26: 'who has faith in Jesus').

There is no distinction. As here there is no distinction between Jews and Gentiles (or between any other opposed categories of

---

[1] Horace, *Ars Poetica* 131 f.

[2] I owe the quotation from Luther to T. R. Glover, *Jesus in the Experience of Men* (1921), p. 72.

mankind) in respect of sin, so in 10:12 'there is no distinction' between them in respect of the mercy of God.

23. *All have sinned.* These identical words (*pantes . . . hēmarton*) appear at the end of 5:12 where, however, the reference may be to the participation of all in 'man's first disobedience'; here the meaning is that all human beings, as individuals, have sinned.

Fall short of the glory of God. The image of God in which man was created was believed to involve a share in the divine glory, which was forfeited through sin. The words of Isaiah 43:7, 'whom I created for my glory' (spoken, in the context, of 'every one who is called by my name'), came to be applied to humanity in general. *Cf.* also 1 Corinthians 11:7. The 'hope of sharing the glory of God' awaits believers in the coming age (5:2).

24. *They are justified by his grace as a gift.* Paul's hope, before he became a Christian, was that, by dint of perseverance in observing the law of God, he might at length be pronounced righteous by God when he stood before his judgment-seat. But in this way of righteousness apart from the law, the procedure is reversed: God pronounces believers righteous at the beginning of their course, not at the end of it. If he pronounces them righteous at the beginning of their course, it cannot be on the basis of works which they have not yet done. Such justification is, on the contrary, 'an act of God's free grace, wherein he pardoneth all our sins, and accepteth us as righteous in his sight'.[1]

And when it comes to the question of our *acceptance* by God, how much more satisfying it is to know oneself justified freely by his grace than to hope to be justified 'by works of law'! In the latter case, I can never be really satisfied that I have made the grade, that my behaviour has been sufficiently meritorious to win the divine approval. Even if I do the best I can (and the trouble is, I do not always do that), how can I be certain that my best comes within measurable distance of God's requirement? I may hope, but I can never be sure. But if God in sheer grace

---

[1] *Westminster Shorter Catechism*, from Answer to Question 33.

assures me of his acceptance in advance, and I gladly embrace his assurance, then I can go on to do his will without always worrying whether I am doing it adequately or not. In fact, to the end of the chapter I shall be an 'unprofitable servant', but I know whom I have believed:

> 'He owns me for his child;
> I can no longer fear.'

In Isaiah 40 – 55 Israel's deliverance from exile in Babylonia is Israel's 'justification' – and God's. 'Only in the LORD . . . are righteousness and strength' (Is. 45:24), and his righteousness and strength are shown in his people's deliverance: 'In the LORD all the offspring of Israel shall triumph (lit. "shall be justified") and glory' (Is. 45:25); 'This is the heritage of the servants of the LORD and their vindication (lit. "righteousness") from me, says the LORD' (Is. 54:17). Why is their deliverance their justification? Had they not deserved their punishment of exile? Yes; Jerusalem had 'received from the LORD's hand double for all her sins' (Is. 40:2); but God's free grace restored them, and their restoration was both his victorious vindication of his name among the nations (Is. 42:13; 48:9–11) and his people's salvation.

Through the redemption which is in Christ Jesus. The redemption (*apolytrōsis*) or ransom is the buying of a slave out of bondage in order to set him free.[1] Here too God's merciful dealings with Israel provide an Old Testament background to Paul's language, whether we think of Israel's redemption from Egyptian bondage (Ex. 15:13; Pss. 77:15; 78:35) or of their later deliverance from the Babylonian exile (Is. 41:14; 43:1). The grace of God which 'justifies' those who believe has been actively manifested in the redemptive work of Christ.

'As I was walking up and down in the house, as a man in a most woful state, that word of God took hold of my heart, Ye are "justified freely by his grace, through the redemption

---

[1] See L. Morris, *The Apostolic Preaching of the Cross* ([3]1965), pp. 1–52; also his *The Atonement* (1983), pp. 107–110. In LXX this word and its cognates are frequently used of redemption by one who is under a special obligation because of kinship or some comparable relation to the person redeemed – by a *gōʾēl*, to use the Hebrew word (*e.g.* Lv. 25:47–49).

that is in Christ Jesus" (Rom. 3:24). But oh, what a turn it made upon me! Now was I as one awakened out of some troublesome sleep and dream, and listening to this heavenly sentence, I was as if I had heard it thus expounded to me: Sinner, thou thinkest that because of thy sins and infirmities I cannot save thy soul, but behold my Son is by me, and upon him I look, and not on thee, and will deal with thee according as I am pleased with him.'[1]

25. *Whom God put forward as an expiation by his blood, to be received by faith.* The two phrases 'by his blood' and 'to be received by faith' (lit. 'through faith') are independently epexegetic of 'expiation'. The key-word is 'expiation', as RSV renders *hilastērion*. This Greek form may be taken as masculine, the accusative singular of *hilastērios* ('propitiatory', 'agent of propitiation'), in agreement with 'whom' (*hon*), or as neuter ('means of propitiation', 'place of propitiation'). The commonest LXX usage of the word (in the neuter) is as the equivalent of Hebrew *kappōreth* (the place where sins are atoned for, or blotted out), the golden slab or 'mercy seat' which covered the ark in the holy of holies (so more than twenty times in the Pentateuch). In Ezekiel 43:14, 17, 20 (five times) it is used to render Hebrew *'azārâ*, the 'ledge' round the altar of burnt-offering in Ezekiel's temple.

The form *hilastērion* is related to the verb *hilaskomai*, which in pagan Greek means 'placate' or 'make gracious', but in LXX takes on the meaning of Hebrew *kipper* ('make atonement') and cognate words, among which is included *kappōreth* ('mercy-seat'). Exception has been taken to the use of the verb 'propitiate' and the noun 'propitiation', used to render these words in the older English versions of the New Testament, on the ground that the English terms smack of placating or appeasing.[2] We may compare the avoidance of these terms here in RSV, NEB ('God designed him to be the means of expiating sin by his sacrificial death, effective through faith') and GNB

---

[1] John Bunyan, *Grace Abounding*, §§ 257 f.
[2] *Cf.* C. H. Dodd, *ad loc.*; also in *The Bible and the Greeks* (1935), pp. 82–95; for a defence of the rendering 'propitiation' and a full discussion of the subject see L. Morris, *The Apostolic Preaching of the Cross*[3], pp. 143–213; also his *The Atonement*, pp. 151–176.

('God offered him, so that by his death he should become the means by which people's sins are forgiven through their faith in him'). But if *hilaskomai, hilastērion* and their cognates acquired a new meaning from their biblical setting, it might be expected that by dint of long usage the English terms 'propitiate' and 'propitiation' should have acquired a biblical meaning in the same way. In any case, misunderstanding is excluded by Paul's insistence that it is God, and not the sinner, who has provided this *hilastērion*. The Old Testament similarly ascribes the initiative in this matter to God's grace: 'The life of the flesh is in the blood; and I have given it for you upon the altar to make atonement for your souls; for it is the blood that makes atonement, by reason of the life' (Lv. 17:11). It is an Old Testament text like this, moreover, that explains Paul's use of the expression 'by his blood' in the present context and justifies the NEB interpretation of it as 'by his sacrificial death'.

The death of Christ, then, is the means by which God does away with his people's sin – not symbolically, as in the ritual of Leviticus 16 in which the material mercy-seat figured, but *really*. And *really* in a twofold sense: the sin has been removed not only from the believer's conscience, on which it lay as an intolerable burden, but also from the presence of God. The writer to the Hebrews similarly associates the sacrifice of Christ with the realization of God's promise in Jeremiah's prophecy of the new covenant: 'I will remember their sins no more' (Heb. 8:12, quoting Je. 31:34).

Once justice is done to the initiative of divine grace in the efficacy of Christ's self-offering, there is no reason for excluding from the meaning of *hilastērion* the averting of divine wrath, if the context so warrants. And the context does warrant the inclusion of the averting of divine wrath in the meaning of *hilastērion* in Romans 3:25. Paul has already said in 1:18 that 'the wrath of God (NEB 'divine retribution') is revealed from heaven against all ungodliness and wickedness'; how then is this 'wrath' to be removed? The *hilastērion* which God has provided in Christ not only removes the ungodliness and wickedness, but at the same time averts the retribution which is the inevitable sequel to such attitudes and actions in a moral universe.

If it were not that it is awkward to have Jesus spoken of as an object or place – the mercy-seat – a strong case could be made out for giving *hilastērion* that meaning here. Before the disappearance of the ark of the covenant at the time of the Babylonian exile, the mercy-seat which covered it was the place where national atonement was effected in the annual ceremony of the Day of Atonement (Lv. 16:15–16). Paul 'informs us that in Christ there was exhibited in reality that which was given figuratively to the Jews' (Calvin, *ad loc.*).[1]

According to T. W. Manson, the contrast between the old *hilastērion* and the new is pointed by the words 'whom God put forward'. The old *hilastērion* was concealed behind the curtain which separated the holy of holies from the outer sanctuary, and was seen by none except the high priest, when he went through the curtain on the Day of Atonement. But in Christ 'the mercy-seat is no longer kept in the sacred seclusion of the most holy place: it is brought out into the midst of the rough and tumble of the world and set up before the eyes of the hostile, contemptuous, or indifferent crowds.'[2] This is an impressive statement in support of the rendering 'mercy-seat'. But 'mercy-seat' would in any case be used by metonymy for 'atoning sacrifice' and perhaps it is best to translate *hilastērion* as 'atoning sacrifice'. Christ, that is to say, is the atoning sacrifice whom God has 'put forward' or (as NEB has it, preferring the alternative sense of the middle *proetheto*) 'designed'.

The phrase *by his blood* refers to the sacrificial death of Christ as the means by which the one effective atonement for sin has been made (*cf.* 5:8–9, 'while we were yet sinners Christ died for us. Since, therefore, we are now justified by his blood, much more shall we be saved by him from the wrath of God').

Paul has thus pressed into service the language of the law-court ('justified'), the slave-market ('redemption') and the altar ('expiation', 'atoning sacrifice') in the attempt to do justice to the fullness of God's gracious act in Christ. Pardon, liberation,

---

[1] *Cf.* J. N. Darby's *New Translation*: 'whom God has set forth a mercy-seat'. See also E. K. Simpson, *Words Worth Weighing in the Greek New Testament* (1944), pp. 10–12; W. D. Davies, *Paul and Rabbinic Judaism* (1948), pp. 237–242. Against this interpretation see G. A. Deissmann, 'Mercy Seat', *Encyclopaedia Biblica* III (1902), cols. 3033–3035; L. Morris, 'The Meaning of *hilastērion* in Romans iii.25', *NTS* 2 (1955–56), pp. 33–43; *The Apostolic Preaching of the Cross*[3], pp. 184–202; C. E. B. Cranfield, *ad loc.*

[2] T. W. Manson, 'Hilastērion', *JTS* 46 (1945), pp. 1–10 (p. 5).

atonement – all are made available to men and women by his free initiative and may be appropriated by faith. And faith in this sense is not a kind of work that is specially meritorious in God's sight; it is that simple and open-hearted attitude to God which takes him at his word and gratefully accepts his grace.

This was to show God's righteousness, because in his divine forbearance he had passed over former sins. That is, 'to demonstrate that God was not unrighteous when he passed over sins committed in earlier days, in the period of his forbearance'. The redemption accomplished by Christ has retrospective as well as prospective efficacy. His atonement avails for the whole human family; 'he is the expiation for our sins', as a later New Testament writer puts it (using the word *hilasmos*, from the same stock as *hilastērion*), 'and not for ours only but also for . . . the whole world' (1 Jn. 2:2). With the description of the ages before Christ as the period of God's forbearance may be compared Paul's announcement to the Athenians: 'The times of ignorance God overlooked, but now . . .' (Acts 17:30). Although the problem in theodicy may not be as obvious to the modern mind as it was to Paul's, yet to pass over wrong is as much an act of injustice on the part of a judge as to condemn the innocent (see comment on 4:5, p. 106).

26. *It was to prove.* Lit. 'for the demonstration of his righteousness' (*pros tēn endeixin tēs dikaiosynēs autou*), practically a repetition of 'This was to show God's righteousness' (*eis endeixin tēs dikaiosynēs autou*) in verse 25. The repetition has been explained, notably by R. Bultmann[1] and E. Käsemann[2], by the suggestion that in verses 24 and 25 Paul reproduced (with minor amplifications) a primitive formula, the gist of which he then repeated (verse 26) in his own words. The repetition, with the general amplitude of style, is more probably due to Paul's carefulness to omit no element in the situation.

At the present time. Catching up 'But now' (verse 21); *cf.* 'but now' in Acts 17:30.

That he himself is righteous and that he justifies him who has faith

---

[1] R. Bultmann, *Theology of the New Testament*, I (1952), p. 46.
[2] E. Käsemann, *ad loc.*; 'Zum Verständnis von Röm. 3, 24–26', *ZNW* 43 (1950–51), pp. 150–154.

in Jesus. In the self-offering of Christ, God's righteousness is vindicated and the believing sinner justified. For Christ occupies a unique position as God's representative with man and man's representative with God. As the representative man he absorbs the judgment incurred by human sin; as the representative of God he bestows God's pardoning grace on men and women. The words recall Isaiah 45:21 ('a righteous God and a Saviour') and Zechariah 9:9, LXX ('righteous and saving').[1]

28. *Apart from works of law.* Paul does not mean that such works need not be performed, but that, even when they are performed tolerably well, one is not thereby justified in God's sight. He is cutting the ground from under the feet of those who say, 'I always do the best I can . . . I try to live a decent life . . . I pay my lawful dues, and what more can God expect of me?'

Luther (like Origen and others before him) emphasizes 'apart from works of law' by adding 'alone' to *justified by faith*: 'man becomes righteous without works of the law, through faith alone.'[2] He pours scorn on the criticisms which he incurred for this 'addition' to the Word of God. In fact, he expressed Paul's meaning accurately: it is by faith alone, and not by legal works, or by any other fancied means of justification, that men and women receive the righteous status which God by his grace bestows. When this is grasped, it can be seen that they have no ground for self-congratulation as they contemplate the way of salvation: it is *sola gratia, sola fide, soli Deo gloria* ('by grace alone, through faith alone; to God alone be the glory').

Yet, while justification in this sense is received by faith alone, 'the faith which justifies is not alone'; it is, as Paul says in Galatians 5:6, 'faith working through love' – and just how it so

[1] R. St. John Parry, *ad loc.*, translates Paul's phrase 'just even when He justifies him that hath faith in Jesus'. R. V. G. Tasker approves this rendering because it brings out the tension between the justice and mercy of God involved in the mystery of atonement ('The Doctrine of Justification by Faith in the Epistle to the Romans', *EQ* 24 (1952), pp. 43 f.).

[2] 'So halten wir nun dafür, dass der Mensch gerecht werde ohne des Gesetzes Werke, allein durch den Glauben' (Luther's Bible). *Cf.* Romans 11:20, RSV ('you stand fast *only* through faith'); Galatians 2:16, NEB ('but *only* through faith in Christ Jesus'). A parallel to this use of 'faith' in the sense of 'faith alone' is adduced from Diogenes Laertius in W. Bauer, *Griechisch-Deutsches Wörterbuch zu den Schriften des Neuen Testaments* (⁵1958), *s.v. pistis.*

works is set out in practical detail in Romans 12:1 – 15:13. But this belongs to a later stage of the argument; what is important at this stage is to insist that it is by faith, not by what they *do*, that human beings receive the justifying grace of God.

31. *We uphold the law.* If Paul had expressed himself in Hebrew, he would have used the verb *qiyyēm*. This is the verb used in the rabbinical assertion that Abraham 'fulfilled the law'. Paul may have some such assertion in mind when he goes on to argue that Abraham did indeed fulfil or 'uphold' the law, but that, according to the testimony of Scripture, he upheld it through receiving God's gift of righteousness by faith.[1]

B. TWO OLD TESTAMENT PRECEDENTS (4:1–8)

Paul has already said that this 'righteousness of God . . . apart from law' is attested by the Law and the Prophets – *i.e.* by the Old Testament. This must now be shown more fully, and Paul undertakes to show it principally from the story of Abraham, with a side-glance at the experience of David.

Of all the righteous people in the Old Testament record, none could surpass Abraham – 'Abraham, my friend', as God calls him in Isaiah 41:8. God's own testimony to Abraham is recorded in Genesis 26:5, 'Abraham obeyed my voice and kept my charge, my commandments, my statutes, and my laws.' What about Abraham, then? If it is by works that a person is justified in God's sight, Abraham would have a better title than most, and he would be entitled to take some credit for it. But that is not God's way. God's way is clearly indicated in the record of Genesis 15:6: when the divine promise came to Abraham, in spite of the extreme improbability of its fulfilment by all natural considerations, 'he believed the Lord; and he reckoned it to him as righteousness.' Paul had already made this statement the basis of an *ad hominem* argument to the churches of Galatia, when some of their members were disposed to abandon the principle of faith for that of legal works. Now he makes it

---

[1] *Cf.* further C. T. Rhyne, *Faith Establishes the Law* (1981).

the text for a more systematic exposition of the principle of faith.

Abraham's acceptance with God was clearly not based on his works, good as they were. Paul's argument is not merely textual and verbal, dependent on a selection of Genesis 15:6 in preference to other texts from the patriarchal narrative which might have pointed in another direction. For Abraham's good works, his obedience to the divine commandments, were the fruit of his unquestioning faith in God; had he not first believed the promises of God he would never have set out for the promised land or conducted his life there in the light of what he knew of God's will. No; when God gave Abraham a promise (in the fulfilment of which, incidentally, the whole gospel was bound up), he simply took God at his word, and acted accordingly.

Now mark the difference, Paul goes on. When a man works for some reward, that reward is his due; when he simply puts his trust in God, it is by pure grace that his faith is reckoned to him for righteousness.

Nor is Abraham an isolated instance of the principle of justification by faith: another Old Testament example lies ready to hand in the case of David. Paul now quotes the opening words of Psalm 32 in which the psalmist, in joyful relief at the assurance of divine pardon, celebrates the blessedness of one 'whose transgression is forgiven, whose sin is covered, . . . to whom the Lord imputes no iniquity'. Here, plainly, is someone else, of whose guilt there could be no question, who nevertheless has received God's free pardon and been pronounced 'Not guilty' before the tribunal of heaven. And if we examine the remainder of the psalm to discover the ground on which he was acquitted, it appears that he simply acknowledged his guilt and cast himself in faith on the mercy of God.

Thus, in addition to the text from the Prophets (Hab. 2:4b) quoted already in 1:17, Paul now appeals to texts from the Law (Gn. 15:6) and from the Writings (Ps. 32:1–2), showing that God's way of righteousness through faith is attested in all three divisions of the Hebrew Bible.

1. *What then shall we say about Abraham . . .?* Several other versions adopt the fuller (and preferable) reading, 'What then shall we say that Abraham has found?' To the question in this form the answer would be: justification by faith, through God's grace.

Our forefather according to the flesh. In view of the qualifying phrase 'according to the flesh' (*cf.* 1:3; 9:3, 5), 'our' means 'of us Jews'; in another sense (*cf.* verses 11-12, 16-17 below), Abraham is the father of all believers, whether they be Jews or Gentiles by birth.

3. *'Abraham believed God, and it was reckoned to him as righteousness.'* See Galatians 3:6 for Paul's earlier quotation and application of Genesis 15:6.

5. *To one who . . . trusts him who justifies the ungodly, his faith is reckoned as righteousness.* The God whose grace Paul proclaims is the God who alone does great wonders. He created the universe from nothing (1:19-20), he calls the dead to life (4:17), he *justifies the ungodly.* That is the greatest of all his wonders: creation and resurrection are manifestations of the power of the living and life-giving God, but the justifying of the ungodly is *prima facie* a contradiction of his character as the righteous judge of all.

Abraham was not ungodly; he was a man of outstanding piety and righteousness. But the principle on which Abraham was justified, being one that excludes the idea of accumulating merit by works of piety and righteousness, is one that is equally available to the ungodly, who have no such works to rely on. So the tax-collector in the parable went home 'justified' rather than the Pharisee, not because his merit was greater (it was much less) but because, realizing the futility of self-reliance, he cast himself entirely on God's grace (Lk. 18:9-14). But the description of God as the one 'who justifies the ungodly' is so paradoxical as to be startling – not to say shocking. In the Old Testament the acquittal of the guilty and the condemnation of the innocent are alike repeatedly denounced as the acts of unjust judges. Indeed, for the better guidance of judges in the administration of justice the God of Israel offers himself as their example: 'I will not acquit the wicked', he says (Ex. 23:7) – or, as it might well be rendered, 'I will not justify the ungodly.' In the LXX version of those words the same Greek terms are used to convey what God forbids in the law as Paul here uses to declare what God in fact does in the gospel. No wonder that Paul thought it necessary above to maintain that God, in justifying sinners, nevertheless preserves his personal integrity. Once they are justified, indeed, the ungodly should cease to be ungodly, but it is not on the basis of any foreseen amendment of their ways that they are justified. If we fail to appreciate the moral problem involved in God's forgiving grace, it may be because we have 'not yet considered how serious a thing is sin'.[1] The paradox of the justifying of the ungodly is resolved in 5:6, 'Christ died for the ungodly'.

6. *So also David* . . . Psalm 32 is ascribed to David in the titles of both MT and LXX. There is a formal link between Psalm 32:1–2, quoted in verses 7–8, and Genesis 15:6, quoted in verse 3, in that the verb 'reckon' is common to both passages. In rabbinical exegesis such a link was held to encourage the interpretation of the one passage by the other, by the principle called *gᵉzērâ šāwâ* ('equal category').[2] Paul uses this principle here, but the link is not a merely formal one: the non-imputation of sin, in which the psalmist rejoices, amounts to the positive imputation of righteousness or pronouncement of acquittal, for there is no verdict of 'Not proven' in God's law-court.

C. THE FAITH OF ABRAHAM (4:9–25)

To return now to Abraham: a further crucial question arises. What relation, if any, lies between Abraham's being justified by faith and the rite of circumcision? For a Jew, this was a matter of great importance: circumcision was the outward and visible sign of God's covenant with Abraham. No uncircumcised man could claim any share in that covenant; circumcision

---

[1] *Cf.* Anselm's words to Boso in *Cur Deus Homo* 1.21: '*nondum considerasti quanti ponderis sit peccatum.*'

[2] This principle might have moved some rabbis to adduce a third text – Psalm 106:30–31, where Phinehas's drastic intervention in the Baal-peor apostasy 'has been reckoned to him as righteousness from generation to generation for ever'. But this would not have been appropriate to Paul's argument.

entitled Jews or Gentile proselytes[1] to all the covenant privileges, apart from those who by wilful repudiation of the divine
commandments cut themselves off from the covenant people.
One might, therefore, think of a Jew as replying to Paul's argument here: 'Granted that Abraham's faith in God was credited
to him for righteousness, this principle is applicable only to
Abraham and his circumcised offspring.' But Paul has a ready
answer to this. What was Abraham's condition when he was
justified by faith? Was he circumcised, or uncircumcised? To
this there could be only one answer. He was uncircumcised.
The covenant of circumcision was not introduced until a later
stage in Abraham's life (Gn. 17:10–14) – at least fourteen years
later, according to the Genesis chronology.[2] When at last
Abraham was circumcised, his circumcision was but the external
seal of that righteous status which God had granted him long
before, by virtue of his faith. Quite plainly it was faith, not
circumcision, that God required of him. Here then is hope for
Gentiles: the example of Abraham shows that circumcision or
uncircumcision is irrelevant to a man's status before God.

Abraham, accordingly, is the true father of all who, like him,
believe in God and take him at his word. He is the father of
uncircumcised believers, for he was himself uncircumcised
when his faith was reckoned to him for righteousness; he is the
father of circumcised believers too, not so much on the ground
of their circumcision as on the ground of their faith.

If circumcision had nothing to do with Abraham's justification
by God, with all the promised blessings that accompanied it,
the law had even less to do with it. For, as Paul had pointed
out to the Galatians, the law was given 430 years later than
God's promise to Abraham and could not invalidate it or restrict
its scope (Gal. 3:17). If, long after the promise was given, it had

---

[1] Even proselytes, who might have been regarded as Abraham's children by adoption,
were not permitted to call him 'our father'; in the synagogue liturgy they called the
patriarchs *'your* fathers' when those who were Jews by birth referred to them as *'our*
fathers'.

[2] Thirteen years after Ishmael's birth (Gn. 17:25; *cf.* 17:1, 24, with 16:16). And the narrative
sequence of Genesis implies that Ishmael's conception (Gn. 16:3–4) came after the promise
of Genesis 15:4–5, that Abraham would yet have a son of his own to be his heir and that
his descendants would be as numerous as the stars. It was through believing acceptance
of this promise that Abraham was justified (Gn. 15:6).

been made conditional on obedience to a law which was not mentioned in the original terms of the promise, the whole basis of the promise would have been nullified. The promise was a promise of blessing, and is fulfilled in the gospel. The Mosaic law does indeed pronounce a blessing on those who keep it, but at the same time it invokes a curse on those who break it. And in view of the universal failure to keep the law, the curse is more prominent and relevant than the blessing: *the law brings wrath* (verse 15). A sinful tendency may indeed be present in the absence of any law; but it takes a legal enactment to crystallize that tendency into a positive transgression or breach of law. And for each such transgression the law fixes an appropriate penalty; this is inherent in the principle of retribution which is inseparable from the idea of law. The law does not fix rewards for those who keep it, but it does necessarily lay down penalties for those who break it. A gracious promise such as God made to Abraham belongs to a totally different realm from law.

No; Abraham's justification and attendant blessings were based on his faith in God; they were not earned by merit or effort on his part (as would have been the case had they been conditional on law-keeping) but conferred on him by God's grace. And the principle on which God thus dealt with Abraham extends to his descendants – not to his natural descendants as such, for they have become subject to the obligations of the law, but to his spiritual descendants, those who follow the precedent of Abraham's faith. This, says Paul, is what God meant when he gave him the name Abraham (in place of Abram, as he was formerly called), and said, 'I have made you the father of a multitude of nations' (Gn. 17:5). These comprise all who believe in God, Jews and Gentiles alike: Abraham is the father of all believers.

Consider, too, the quality of Abraham's faith. It was faith in the God who brings the dead to life, who calls non-existent things as though they really existed – and gives them real existence by doing so. When God told him that he would have a vast multitude of descendants, Abraham was still childless. Not only so, but he was beyond the age at which a man might reasonably hope to become a father, and Sarah his wife was even more certainly beyond the age of motherhood. Abraham did not shut his eyes to these unfavourable circumstances; he took them all into careful consideration. But, when he set over against them the promise of God, he found that the certainty of God's ability and will to fulfil his promise outweighed them all. Having nothing to rest upon but the bare word of God, he relied on that, in face of all the opposing indications which pressed on him from every side. In fact, his faith was strengthened by the very force of the obstacles which lay in its path. And his faith won him the favour of God.

Now, adds Paul, the statement that Abraham's faith was counted to him for righteousness does not apply to Abraham alone. The principle which it enshrines holds good for all believers in God, and especially for believers in God as he is revealed in the gospel – the God who raised Jesus from the dead. Jesus had been delivered up to death because of his people's sins; but God raised him up to secure their justification.

11. *He received circumcision as a sign or seal.* In Genesis 17:11 God tells Abraham that circumcision is to be 'a sign of the covenant between me and you'. Paul's exegesis identifies this covenant with that of Genesis 15:18, in which (fourteen years at least before Abraham was circumcised) God showed Abraham effectively how he counted his faith to him as righteousness. Circumcision is thus treated as a subsequent and external seal of that righteous status which Abraham already possessed as God's free gift; it neither created nor enhanced that righteous status.

13. *That they should inherit the world.* 'They' is literally 'it' (*auto*, neuter), referring to 'offspring' (*sperma*, neuter, here translated 'descendants'); there is a much better attested variant reading 'he' (*auton*, masculine), referring to Abraham. This is not a formal quotation of any recorded promise to Abraham, but an interpretation of those promises which speak of 'all the families of the earth' (Gn. 12:3) or 'all the nations of the earth' (Gn. 18:18; 22:18) as 'blessing themselves' (MT) or 'being blessed' (LXX) by Abraham and his offspring. When Abraham's heritage is delimited in geographical terms it lies between Egypt and the

Euphrates (Gn. 15:18; *cf.* 13:14–15), but in the spiritual and permanent sense in which the promises are interpreted in the New Testament it cannot be confined within such earthly frontiers: it is as world-wide as the gospel (*cf.* Rom. 10:18). (In Heb. 11:16 the promised land is no earthly Canaan but 'a better country, that is, a heavenly one'.)

Did not come through the law. Referring to the promise of blessing through Abraham's offspring, Paul had argued in Galatians that the word 'offspring', being a collective singular, can and does point primarily to Christ (3:16) and consequently also to the people of Christ (3:29). Here his point is that the validity of the promise has nothing to do with the law (which came centuries later, as is noted in Gal. 3:17) or with legal righteousness, but comes *through the righteousness of faith.*

14. *If it is the adherents of the law who are to be the heirs, faith is null.* Because the inheritance promised to Abraham would now depend on a new principle – that of works, not faith.

And the promise is void. Because if its fulfilment depends on law-keeping, men and women's inability to keep the law will ensure that the promise will in fact never be fulfilled.

15. *For the law brings wrath.* That is, law inevitably imposes penalties for failure to keep it.

But where there is no law there is no transgression. Here, as in 5:13 ('sin is not counted where there is no law'), Paul appears to be enunciating a current legal maxim (like the Roman maxim *nulla poena sine lege*).

16. *That is why it depends on faith, in order that the promise may rest on grace.* A summary of the principle that what God provides by his free grace can be appropriated by human beings only through faith. What, on the contrary, is earned by works (not faith) is bestowed as a matter of merit (not grace).

17. *'I have made you the father of many nations.'* From Genesis 17:5, 'I have made you the father of a multitude (Heb. *'aḫ-hᵃmōn*) of nations', where *'aḫ-hᵃmōn* is given as the explanation of his new name Abraham.

In the presence of the God in whom he believed. These words follow on (after a parenthesis) from the clause *in order that the promise may . . . be guaranteed to all his descendants* (verse 16) – *i.e.* that the promise might be valid in God's sight for all Abraham's spiritual posterity (whether Jews or Gentiles by natural birth).

Who gives life to the dead. This general designation of God in Jewish liturgy is used here with special reference to Abraham's 'own body, which was as good as dead' and 'the barrenness (lit. 'deadness', *nekrōsis*) of Sarah's womb' (verse 19).

And calls into existence the things that do not exist. The reference here is to the 'many nations' which were to spring from Abraham; not only had they no existence as yet, but (since Abraham and Sarah had now entered a childless old age) nothing seemed less likely than that they should ever exist.

18. *That he should become the father of many nations.* In Genesis these are his descendants through Isaac (the Israelites and Edomites), together with the twelve tribes of the Ishmaelites (Gn. 25:12–18) and his descendants by Keturah (Gn. 25:2–4). For Paul they are the multiplicity of Jewish and Gentile believers.

'So shall your descendants be.' From Genesis 15:5, where God tells Abraham (while he is still childless) that his offspring will be as countless as the stars.

19. *He considered his own body, which was as good as dead.* He made allowance for every relevant factor, including his great age and the high improbability, by all natural reckoning, that he would ever have a child (*cf.* Heb. 11:12, where the same participle is similarly rendered 'as good as dead', with regard to this very situation). Yet, having taken account of all these factors, he concluded that the certainty of the divine promise outweighed every natural improbability.

25. *Who was put to death for our trespasses.* This may be a quotation from some primitive confession of faith; the language appears to be based on Isaiah 53. The verb *put to death* is literally 'delivered up' (*paradidōmi*), which occurs twice in the LXX version of that chapter: in Isaiah 53:6, 'the Lord has delivered him [the suffering Servant] up for our sins' and Isaiah 53:12, 'because of their sins he was delivered up'. (This last clause deviates considerably from MT, 'he . . . made intercession for the transgressors'; see note on Rom. 8:34, p. 170.) There is a verbal resemblance also to Isaiah 53:5 in the Targum of Jonathan, where the Aramaic clause *'ithmᵉsar ba'ᵃwāyāthānā*, if it stood by itself, might mean 'he was delivered up for our iniquities' (in the Targum, however, it is the temple that is the subject: the Servant-Messiah 'will build the sanctuary which was profaned by our trespasses and delivered up for our iniquities'). When the same Greek verb is used in 1 Corinthians 11:23, one may wonder if the sense there is not so much 'on the night when he was betrayed' (by Judas) but rather '. . . when he was delivered up' (by God).

And raised for our justification. Elsewhere it is by the sacrificial death of Christ that his people are justified (*cf.* 3:24–25; 5:9), but his sacrificial death would not have been efficacious apart from the resurrection. The preposition 'for' in both clauses of this verse represents *dia* ('because of'); Christ was 'delivered up' to atone for his people's sins and raised to guarantee their justification. (We must not interpret the two clauses so woodenly as to suggest that his resurrection had nothing to do with the atonement for their sins and his death nothing to do with their justification.)

D. THE BLESSINGS WHICH ACCOMPANY JUSTIFICATION: PEACE, JOY, HOPE, LOVE (5:1–11)

Having set out God's way of justifying sinners, and established it on a scriptural basis, Paul now lists the blessings which accrue to those whose faith has been counted to them for righteousness. The first of these is peace with God. Men and women who were formerly in a state of rebellion against him have now been reconciled to him by the death of Christ. It was the purpose of God, as Paul says in another place, to 'reconcile to himself all things' through Christ, but pre-eminently to reconcile those who once were 'estranged and hostile' to him at heart (Col. 1:20–22). And the fact that the death of Christ has accomplished this reconciliation has been a matter of plain experience in the lives of successive generations of believers. The reconciliation is something that God has already effected through Christ, and men and women are called upon to accept it, to enter into the good of it, to be at peace with God.

This peace carries with it free access to God; the former rebels are not merely forgiven by having their due punishment remitted; they are brought into a place of high favour with God – 'this grace in which we stand'. It is through Christ that they have entered into this state of grace, and through him, too, that they rejoice in their hope of glory. Peace and joy are twin blessings of the gospel: as an old preacher put it, 'peace is joy resting; joy is peace dancing.'

Three objects of joy are mentioned here: the first is the hope of glory. More about this glory will come into view in the eighth chapter. But the glory of God is the end for which he created mankind (see note on 3:23), and it is through the redemptive work of Christ that this end will be achieved. So long as his people exist in mortal body, it remains a *hope*, but it is a sure hope, one that is certain of fulfilment, because those who cherish it have already received the guarantee of its realization in the gift of the Holy Spirit, who fills their hearts with the love of God.

The second object of joy is unexpected: 'we rejoice in our sufferings' (verse 3). If this seems strange to us, let us remind ourselves that in the New Testament suffering is viewed as the normal experience of a Christian. New converts were warned that the kingdom of God could be entered only 'through many tribulations' (Acts 14:22); and when tribulation came their way, as it regularly did, they could not complain that they had not been prepared for it. But suffering was not only regarded as an inevitable feature of the Christian lot; it was looked upon as a token of true Christianity, as a sign that God counted those who endured it worthy of his kingdom (*cf.* 2 Thes. 1:5). Besides, it had a salutary moral effect on those who experienced it, for it helped them to cultivate endurance and steadfastness of character, and when these were linked to Christian faith, Christian hope was the more stimulated.

Above all, believers learnt to rejoice in God himself (verse

11). The coming glory was not merely recompense for the suffering of the present; it was the *product* of that suffering (*cf.* 8:17b; 2 Cor. 4:17). Every one who discerned the hope of glory in the suffering could rejoice in the one and the other, but chiefly in God – 'God my exceeding joy', as the psalmist said (Ps. 43:4).

And why not rejoice in God? His people have been reconciled to him by the death of Christ and experience daily deliverance from evil through Christ's resurrection life, while the end to which they confidently look forward is no longer the outpouring of divine wrath but the unveiling of divine glory. And from first to last they ascribe their blessings to God's love. It was because of that love that Christ laid down his life for them when they were weak, sinful and totally unattractive. Human love will go to death itself for those who are its natural objects, but hardly for the unlovely and unloving. Yet this is where the love of God shines most brightly: God confirms *his* love to us in the fact that Christ died for us while we were in a state of rebellion against him. So entirely at one are the Father and the Son that the self-sacrifice of the latter can be presented as a token of the love of the former. The death of Christ is indeed the supreme manifestation of God's love. What a perversion of the divine character it is to imagine that Christ died for human beings in order to make God love them! That a change in their relation to God is brought about by the death of Christ is clearly taught here and elsewhere; but no change is involved in the reality of God's love.

Love, joy, peace and hope, then, the true fruit of the Spirit, mark the lives of those who have been justified by faith in God. The guilty past has been cancelled, the glory of the future is assured, and here and now the presence and power of the Spirit of God secure to believers all the grace they need to endure trial, to resist evil, and to live as befits those whom God has declared righteous.

1. *We have peace with God.* Should we read 'we have peace' (*echomen*, indicative) or, with the margin, 'let us have peace' (*echōmen*, subjunctive)? The attestation for the latter is rather stronger (it is exhibited by the first hand in the Alexandrian codices *Aleph* and B and by the western codex D and the Latin versions) than for the former (to which the text in *Aleph* and B was corrected by a later hand and which is exhibited by the western codex G and by the majority of later witnesses). But the context supports 'we have peace' (*cf*. verse 11, 'we have now received our reconciliation'). NEB 'let us continue at peace with God' tries to do justice to both readings.[1]

2. *Through him we have obtained access to this grace in which we stand*. Many witnesses (including *Aleph*, A and the majority of later manuscripts) add 'by faith' after 'we have obtained access' (*cf*. RSV mg.). Even if not originally expressed, it is implied (*cf*. 11:20, 'you stand fast only through faith'). *Cf*. Ephesians 2:18, 'through him we . . . have access in one Spirit to the Father.' 'Access' denotes the privilege of approaching or being introduced into the presence of someone in high station, especially a royal or divine personage. Here Christ is viewed as ushering believers into their new state of grace and acceptance before God (*cf*. also Eph. 3:12).

And we rejoice in our hope of sharing the glory of God, for which we were created and from which through sin we fall short (3:23). RSV adds *sharing* to complete the sense; it is not expressed in the Greek text. The verb 'rejoice' (as also in verse 3) might, so far as the form (*kauchōmetha*) goes, be either indicative ('we rejoice') or subjunctive ('let us rejoice'); the indicative suits the context better. 'We rejoice' (like 'we have obtained access') is probably linked with 'through him'; *cf*. Colossians 1:27, 'Christ in you, the hope of glory.'

5. *Hope does not disappoint us*. Lit. 'does not put to shame'; *cf*. Isaiah 28:16, LXX (quoted in 9:33; 10:11). A hope which fails of realization does put one to shame, but the hope which is based on the promise of God is assured of fulfilment (*cf*. 8:24–25).

---

[1] Suitability to the context is the determinant factor. In 14:19 the strongly attested indicative *diōkomen* ('we pursue') must be rejected in favour of the less well attested *diōkōmen* ('let us pursue') because only the latter makes sense in the context. Such variations are common because, with the strong stress accent on the antepenultimate syllable (as in Byzantine and Modern Greek), the distinction between the long and the short vowel in the penultimate syllable disappears in pronunciation. When copying was done by dictation the reader might intend one form and the scribe write down the other.

God's love has been poured into our hearts through the Holy Spirit which has been given to us. This reference to the Spirit's work in the believer anticipates the fuller account given below in chapter 8. His indwelling presence is the pledge of that glory for which the believer hopes. The love which is his primary 'fruit' (Gal. 5:22) has its origin in God and is reproduced in the children of God.

6. *At the right time.* That is, at the time of greatest need, when nothing but his death would help.

Christ died for the ungodly. And therefore the paradox of 4:5, that God 'justifies the ungodly', is seen to be righteously based.

7–8. *Perhaps for a good man one will dare even to die.* 'A good man' is literally 'the good man' (RV), where the definite article indicates a particular type of man. There is little distinction between 'righteous' and 'good' in this verse; 'good' represents *agathos*, not *chrēstos* ('kindly'). Some would take 'good' as neuter here, as though it denoted a good cause rather than a good man, but this is unlikely. 'Even for one who is righteous or good', Paul argues, 'you will scarcely find any one willing to sacrifice his life – well, perhaps a few people might go so far as to do so – *but God shows his love for us* in Christ's sacrificing *his* life for those who were neither righteous nor good, but ungodly sinners' (*cf.* 1 Jn. 4:10).

9. *Since, therefore, we are now justified by his blood.* His 'blood', as in 3:25, denotes his sacrificial death; 'by his blood' here is parallel to 'by the death of his Son' in verse 10.

Much more shall we be saved by him from the wrath of God. Lit. 'from the wrath'; the RSV addition 'of God' is epexegetic (*cf.* 12:19). In 1 Thessalonians 1:10 Jesus is called our deliverer 'from the wrath to come'; here, as there, the outpouring of judgment at the end-time is in view. See also 1 Thessalonians 5:9, 'God has not destined us for wrath, but to obtain salvation through our Lord Jesus Christ.' Those who have been pronounced righteous by God can rejoice already in their deliverance from the end-time 'wrath'.

10. *While we were enemies we were reconciled to God by the death of his Son.* Cf. Colossians 1:21–22, 'And you, who once were estranged and hostile in mind, doing evil deeds, he has now reconciled in his body of flesh by his death.' The hostility and estrangement which require to be removed lie in human beings, not in God; it is he who takes the initiative in good will by providing 'the redemption which is in Christ Jesus'.

Much more, now that we are reconciled, shall we be saved by his life. That is, by his present resurrection life. This statement is expanded below in 6:8–11.

11. *Through whom we have now received our reconciliation.* Where reconciliation is mentioned in the New Testament, God or Christ is always the reconciler, and human beings are the object (or among the objects) of his reconciling act. God 'through Christ reconciled us to himself'; men and women are accordingly summoned in Christ's name to 'be reconciled to God' (2 Cor. 5:18, 20). The situation may be compared to that of a king proclaiming an amnesty for rebellious subjects, who are urged to accept his gracious pardon while it is extended to them. God's abhorrence of sin does not make him the enemy of sinners or seek their ill; his desire is for all 'to be saved and to come to the knowledge of the truth' (1 Tim. 2:4).[1]

E. THE OLD AND THE NEW SOLIDARITY (5:12–21)

The portrayal of Christ as the 'last Adam', the counterpart of the 'first Adam', is a prominent feature of Paul's Christology. It is not peculiar to him among the New Testament writers, and we cannot even be sure that it was original with him, but he develops it more fully than any other, especially in Romans 5:12–21 and in his discussion of resurrection in 1 Corinthians 15:22, 45–49.

The idea of God's man as the fulfiller of God's purpose is a recurring one in the Old Testament: he is 'the man of thy right

---

[1] For another angle on the subject of reconciliation see the full treatment by L. Morris, *The Apostolic Preaching of the Cross* (³1965), pp. 219–250; also his later book, *The Atonement* (1983), pp. 132–150.

hand, the son of man whom thou hast made strong for thyself'
for whose prosperity and victory prayer is offered in Psalm
80:17. When one man fails in the accomplishment of God's
purpose (as, in measure, all did), God raises up another to take
his place – Joshua to replace Moses, David to replace Saul,
Elisha to replace Elijah.

But who could take the place of *Adam*? Only one who was
competent to undo the effects of Adam's fall and become the
inaugurator of a new humanity. The Bible – and, indeed, the
history of the world – knows of one man only who has
the necessary qualifications. Christ stands forth (in Carlyle's
rendering of Luther's *Ein' feste Burg*) as

'the proper Man
Whom God Himself hath bidden'.

And for those whom he has set right with God the old solidarity
of sin and death, which was theirs in association with the first
Adam, has given way to a new solidarity of righteousness and
life in association with 'the last Adam'.

Paul rounds off the argument of the letter thus far by drawing
a parallel and antithesis between Adam and Christ. Adam is
for Paul a counterpart or 'type' of Christ. As death entered the
world through Adam's disobedience, so new life comes in
through Christ's obedience. As Adam's sin involves his
posterity in guilt, so Christ's righteousness is credited to his
people.

To Paul, Adam was more than a historical individual, the first
man; he was also what his name means in Hebrew – 'humanity'.
The whole of humanity is viewed as having existed at first
in Adam. Because of his sin, however, Adam is humanity in
alienation from God: the whole human race is viewed as having
originally sinned in Adam. In the fall narrative of Genesis 3 'all
subsequent human history lies encapsuled';[1] its incidents are
re-enacted in the life of the race and of each member of the
race.[2]

Paul was apparently conversant with what is widely called

---

[1] Quoted by E. K. Simpson, *The Pastoral Epistles* (1954), p. 47.
[2] See comments on 1:23 (p. 80); 7:7-13 (p. 141).

the Hebrew concept of corporate personality,[1] and his thought could readily oscillate on the one hand between the first Adam and sinful humanity, and on the other hand between Christ, 'the second man', and the community of the redeemed. And very properly so: our solidarity with our fellows is a reality which we tend to overlook in the assertion of our individual independence. 'No man is an island, entire of itself; every man is a piece of the continent, a part of the main; if a clod be washed away by the sea, Europe is the less, as well as if a promontory were, as well as if a manor of thy friends or of thine own were; any man's death diminishes *me*, because I am involved in mankind; and therefore never send to know for whom the bell tolls; it tolls for thee.' John Donne's oft-quoted words express a permanent truth. Because we live in separate bodies we tend to think that all other aspects of our personality are equally separate and self-contained, but they are not.

Here, however, two different kinds of solidarity are distinguished. A new creation has come to birth: the old 'Adam-solidarity' of sin and death has been broken up, to be replaced by the new 'Christ-solidarity' of grace and life. Yet the break is not as sharp and clear-cut as might be thought: at present there is an overlap between the two. 'As in Adam all die' applies in the physical realm to believers as much as 'so also in Christ shall all be made alive' does, so long as this mortal existence endures. But here and now they have the assurance that, because they are 'in Christ', they will indeed be 'made alive', because here and now through faith in him they have received from God that justification which brings life in its train. 'In God's sight', said Thomas Goodwin, seventeenth-century President of Magdalen College, Oxford, 'there are two men – Adam and Jesus Christ – and these two men have all other men hanging at their girdle strings.'

The obedience of Christ to which his people are here said to owe their justification and hope of eternal life is not confined to his death. His death was the crown and culmination of that 'active obedience' which characterized his life throughout its

---

[1] *Cf.* H. W. Robinson, *Corporate Personality in Ancient Israel*, revised edition (1981); also J. W. Rogerson, 'The Hebrew Conception of Corporate Personality: A Re-examination', *JTS*, new series 21 (1970), pp. 1–16.

course. It was a perfectly righteous life that he offered up in death on his people's behalf. The righteous life in itself would not have met their need had he not carried his obedience to the point of death, 'even death on a cross'; but neither would his death have met their need had the life which he thus offered up not been a perfect life. Paul's language here echoes the words of the fourth Servant Song: 'by his knowledge shall the righteous one, my servant, make many to be accounted righteous; and he shall bear their iniquities' (Is. 53:11).

So, if the fall of Adam brought all his posterity under the dominion of death, the obedience of Christ has brought a new race triumphantly into the realm of resurrection life.

'But', says someone, 'in all this discussion of Adam and Christ, have you not forgotten Moses? Where does he come in? Surely the introduction of the law (roughly midway between Adam and Christ, according to the chronology of MT) means that there are three ages, inaugurated respectively by Adam, Moses and Christ, and not just two, inaugurated respectively by Adam and Christ?'

No, says Paul. The law has no permanent significance in the history of redemption. It was introduced as a temporary measure for a practical purpose. Sin was present in the world ever since Adam's fall, but the law served the purpose of bringing sin right out into the light of day, so that it might be more clearly recognized for what it really is. It is not merely that in the presence of specific laws sin takes the form of specific transgressions of these laws; the presence of law can positively stimulate sin. An express prohibition may tempt people to do what is prohibited, whereas they might never have thought of doing it if the prohibition had not brought it to their attention. Paul shows sound insight into human nature. There is substance in the old story of the parishioner who objected to the recitation of the Ten Commandments in church 'because they put so many ideas into people's heads'.

But the law introduced no new principle into the situation; it simply revealed more plainly the principle of sin which was already present. The gospel, on the other hand, has introduced a completely new principle – the principle of God's grace. However fast the operation of law stimulates sin and causes it to increase, faster still does the grace of God increase and remove the accumulation of sin.[1]

12. *As sin came into the world through one man and death through sin.* The 'one man' is Adam; the reference is to the story of 'man's first disobedience' in Genesis 3. *Cf.* Wisdom 2:23-24,

'God created man for incorruption,
  and made him in the image of his own eternity,
but through the devil's envy death entered the world,
  and those who belong to his party experience it.'

The same point is made in the outcry of 2 Esdras 7:118: 'O Adam, what have you done? For though it was you who sinned, the fall was not yours alone, but ours also who are your descendants.' Ben Sira characteristically draws a misogynistic moral from the narrative: 'From a woman sin had its beginning, and because of her we all die' (Ecclus. 25:24; see p. 142). But none of these writers sees anything of the deeper significance in the fall of man which is now unfolded by Paul.

Death spread to all men because all men sinned. Does this mean that all have sinned in their personal lives (which is apparently the meaning of the words in 3:23) or that all sinned in Adam's primal sin? In support of the latter it might be argued that human beings are mortal before they commit any sin, so that the mortality of the race is the result of the original racial sin. This seems to be implied by verse 14, where those who lived between Adam and Moses are said to have died even if they did not sin in the manner of 'the transgression of Adam'. The construction, with the underlying thought, is paralleled in 2 Corinthians 5:14: 'one has died for all; therefore all have died'

---

[1] Two monographs on Romans 5:12–21 are K. Barth, *Christ and Adam* (E.T., 1956), and J. Murray, *The Imputation of Adam's Sin* (1959). Murray also devotes Appendix D of his commentary on *Romans* (I, pp. 384–390) to a critique of 'Karl Barth on Romans 5'. Another critique of Barth's monograph, from a standpoint far removed from Murray's, is R. Bultmann, 'Adam and Christ according to Romans 5', in *Current Issues in New Testament Interpretation*, ed. W. Klassen and G. F. Snyder (1962), pp. 143–165. See also C. K. Barrett, *From First Adam to Last: A Study in Pauline Theology* (1962); R. Scroggs, *The Last Adam: A Study in Pauline Anthropology* (1966); S.-H. Quek, 'Adam and Christ according to Paul', in *Pauline Studies*, ed. D. A. Hagner and M. J. Harris (1980), pp. 67–79.

– where, however, it is the racial implication of Christ's death, not of Adam's fall, that Paul has in view. It is not simply because Adam is the ancestor of mankind that all are said to have sinned in his sin (otherwise it might be argued that because Abraham believed God all his descendants were necessarily involved in his belief); it is because Adam *is* mankind.

For a defence of the other interpretation – that the reference is to all having sinned in their personal lives – see Cranfield, *ad loc.*: after a careful examination of various interpretations of the words 'because all sinned' he concludes that this interpretation is 'most probable'.[1]

Paul does not conclude his sentence with a 'so' clause to match the 'as' clause at the beginning of verse 12. His mention of death as spreading to all humanity because of sin leads him to introduce the long parenthesis of verses 13–17; after the parenthesis, instead of providing the principal clause for which the reader has been waiting, he repeats the 'as' clause of verse 12 in different words in verse 18 and follows up the new 'as' clause with a balancing 'so' clause. An apodosis in correlative terms to the protasis (the 'as' clause) of verse 12 would be worded more or less like this: 'so through one man God's way of righteousness was introduced, and life by righteousness.'

13. *Sin indeed was in the world before the law was given.* Once sin gained an entrance into the human family, death followed. The sentence on Adam, 'in the day that you eat of it you shall die' (Gn. 2:17), was executed on his descendants, even although, until the law was given, there was no positive commandment for them to break as there had been for Adam.

But sin is not counted where there is no law. (Cf. 4:15.) Yet sin was all-pervasive, and mortal in its effect, even in the absence of any positive commandment with penalty attached. Sin manifests itself in the form of specific transgressions when there are specific commandments to be transgressed. Later Jewish tradition regarded the seven commandments to Noah in Genesis 9:1–7 as binding on all the Gentiles. Paul makes no reference to them. But the oldest form of the tradition recog-

---

[1] See also C. E. B. Cranfield, 'On Some of the Problems in the Interpretation of Romans 5:12', *SJT* 22 (1969), pp. 324–341.

nized that six of them were already creation ordinances (the only new one being the ban on eating flesh with blood in it); and in Paul's eyes it was in disobedience to the creation ordinances that the death-deserving ungodliness of the pagan world consisted (1:18–32).

14. *Who was a type of the one who was to come.* That is, Adam, the first man, is a counterpart (*typos*) of Christ, whom Paul elsewhere calls 'the last Adam' and 'the second man' (1 Cor. 15:45, 47). It is noteworthy that Adam is the only Old Testament character who is *explicitly* called a 'type' of Christ in the New Testament. There is a fitness in this, even if the typological relation between them involves as much contrast as resemblance; in Paul's thought Christ replaces the first man as the archetype and representative of a new humanity:

> 'Adam, descended from above,
> Federal head of all mankind.'

15. *If many died through one man's trespass, much more have the grace of God and the free gift in the grace of that one man Jesus Christ abounded for many.* In both clauses 'many' is literally 'the many' (*cf.* verse 19), 'the many' being the great mass of mankind (like the twofold 'all' in 1 Cor. 15:22). See also Romans 11:32 (pp. 210–211). 'The many' can by no means denote a minority: on the contrary, it follows from these words, as Calvin put it, 'that the grace of Christ belongs to a greater number than the condemnation contracted by the first man'. Calvin knew, indeed, of some who envisaged the elect as a minority, and who accordingly argued that Paul was here 'merely debating a point'; his own reasoning, however, was 'that if Adam's fall had the effect of producing the ruin of many, the grace of God is much more efficacious in benefiting many, since admittedly Christ is much more powerful to save than Adam was to ruin.'[1]

16. *And the free gift is not like the effect of that one man's sin.* Through the one disobedient act of the primal sinner sentence

[1] J. Calvin, *Romans*, E.T. (1961), pp. 114 f.

of condemnation was passed; but the 'free gift' (*charisma*, as in 6:23; whereas *dōrea*, 'gift', is used in verses 15, 17, and the related *dōrēma* in verse 16a), bestowed after the commission of many sins, issues in God's reversal of that adverse judgment and his conferment of a righteous status on many sinners.

17. *The free gift of righteousness, i.e.* the gift (*dōrea*) of justification received from God by believers.

Will . . . reign in life through the one man Jesus Christ. When death reigns, human beings are its helpless victims; when Christ reigns, they share his risen life and royal glory (*cf.* 8:17).

18. *One man's trespass . . . one man's act of righteousness.* The RV rendering, 'through one trespass . . . through one act of righteousness', is grammatically as permissible as the RSV rendering, but RSV gives a better parallel to verse 19 ('by one man's disobedience . . . by one man's obedience'). One man's 'act of righteousness' (*dikaiōma*)[1] is the crowning act of Christ's life-long obedience (verse 19), when he yielded up his life; the second man's act, which brought salvation, is contrasted with the first man's 'trespass', which brought perdition.

To acquittal and life, lit. 'to justification of life'. 'Justification of life' is justification which issues in life (just as condemnation issues in death). 'Acquittal' renders *dikaiōsis*, translated 'justification' in 4:25 (Paul might have repeated *dikaiōma*, translated 'justification' at the end of verse 16, but the intervening use of this word earlier in verse 18 in the sense of 'righteous act' may have moved him to use *dikaiōsis* here instead).

19. *As by one man's disobedience many were made sinners, so by one man's obedience many will be made righteous.* As in verse 15, the twofold 'many' is literally 'the many'. The second clause here is probably a deliberate echo of Isaiah 53:11, where the obedient Servant causes *the many* (MT, LXX) 'to be accounted righteous'.[2] From the second clause, 'the many' is introduced into the first clause by way of balance (and the influence of

---

[1] This word (*dikaiōma*) is used in a variety of senses – 'justification' in verse 16, 'decree' in 1:32 (*cf.* 'precept' in 2:26); 'just requirement' in 8:4.

[2] See L. C. Allen, 'Isaiah liii.11 and its Echoes', *Vox Evangelica* 1 (1962), pp. 24–28.

Isaiah 53:11 may also be present in the twofold 'the many' of verse 15). 'O the sweet exchange, O the inscrutable creation, O the unlooked-for benefits, that the sin of many should be put out of sight in one righteous man, and the righteousness of one should justify many sinners!' (*Epistle to Diognetus* 9.5). The obedience of Christ accomplished more than Abraham's could ever have done; by his passion and triumph he has won the right and power to beat back the hostile cosmic forces – to 'retrieve the cosmic situation', as C. K. Barrett puts it[1] – and ensure for his people participation in his victory.

20. *Law came in, to increase the trespass*. The verb 'came in' is literally rendered 'came in beside' in RV (NEB 'intruded into this process'); it is used in Galatians 2:4 of the 'false brethren' who 'slipped in' or 'infiltrated' (*pareiserchomai*) as spies into the apostolic company. The sense of verse 20 reproduces that of Galatians 3:19: 'Why then the law? It was added because of transgressions (NEB 'to make wrongdoing a legal offence'), till the offspring should come to whom the promise had been made.' Law increased the trespass by providing opportunities for violating a multiplicity of specific commandments; there may be the further suggestion that it 'also *increases sin in the sense that it makes men sin more*'.[2] In any case, both epistles imply that the law of Moses is a parenthetic dispensation in the course of God's dealings with the human race.

IV. THE WAY OF HOLINESS (6:1 – 8:39)

A. FREEDOM FROM SIN (6:1–23)

1. A supposed objection (6:1–2)
'Well,' someone might say, 'if God's grace so abounded over sin, why should we not go on sinning so as to give his grace

---

[1] *From First Adam to Last*, p. 93.
[2] C. E. B. Cranfield, 'St. Paul and the Law', *SJT* 17 (1964), pp. 46 f. – especially, he considers, because it tempts sinners 'to try to use it as a means to the establishment of a claim upon God'.

the opportunity of abounding all the more?'

This is not a completely hypothetical objection. In fact, there have always been people to insist that this is the logical corollary of Paul's teaching about justification by faith; and unfortunately, in every generation, people claiming to be justified by faith have behaved in such a way as to lend colour to this charge. James Hogg's *Private Memoirs and Confessions of a Justified Sinner* (1824) provides an outstanding literary example of such deliberate antinomianism; a notable historical instance may be seen in the Russian monk Gregory Rasputin, the evil genius of the Romanov family in its last years of power. Rasputin taught and exemplified the doctrine of salvation through repeated experiences of sin and repentance. He held that, as those who sin most require most forgiveness, a sinner who continues to sin with abandon enjoys, each time he repents, more of God's forgiving grace than any ordinary sinner. The case-books of many soul-physicians[1] would reveal that this point of view has been commoner than is often realized, even when it is not expressed and practised so blatantly as it was by Rasputin.

Some of Paul's own converts gave him much cause for concern on this very score. It was bad enough to have his theological opponents misrepresenting his gospel as being tantamount to 'Why not do evil that good may come?' (3:8); it was worse when his converts played into their hands by behaving as though the gospel gave them licence to do whatever they liked. Paul's Corinthian correspondence shows how much trouble his converts gave him in this regard: it is plain that some of them imagined that sexual irregularities, for example, were matters of very small importance. From the terms in which he directs the church of Corinth to excommunicate a man who was living in an incestuous relation, it appears that some members of that church, far from expressing any disapproval of this scandalous state of affairs, thought that it was rather a fine assertion of Christian liberty (1 Cor. 5:1–13). No wonder that other Christians maintained that the only way to inculcate the principles of sound morality in such people was to require them to keep the law of Moses – indeed, to impose that law on

---

[1] *Cf.* Hannah Whitall Smith, *Religious Fanaticism* (1928).

them as a condition of salvation, over and above the requirement of faith in Christ. But Paul's own experience had taught
him that all the law-keeping in the world could not bring the
assurance of pardon and peace with God, whereas faith in
Christ did so at once. He could never consider legalism as the
remedy for libertinism; he knew a more excellent way. When
men and women yielded their lives to the risen Christ and the
power of his Spirit, their inward being was radically transformed: a new creation took place. They received a new nature
which delighted to produce spontaneously the fruit of the Spirit,
those graces which were manifested in perfection in the life of
Christ himself. To many people this appeared (as to many it
still does) impracticably optimistic. But Paul trusted the Spirit
of Christ in his converts, and in the long run his trust was
vindicated, though he had to endure many heart-breaking
disappointments in his spiritual children until at last he could
see Christ 'formed' in them (Gal. 4:19).

In the division of the Epistle to the Romans on which we
have now entered we see him expound this teaching at length,
in reply to the preposterous argument that one ought really to
go on sinning, so that God's grace might abound the more.

2. The meaning of baptism (6:3-14)
'Anyone who can argue like that', says Paul, 'shows that he
has not begun to understand the gospel. Life in sin cannot co-
exist with death to sin.' But what is meant by 'death to sin'?

'Listen,' he says. 'Do you not remember what happened
when you were baptized?' From this and other references to
baptism in Paul's writings, it is plain that he did not regard
baptism as an 'optional extra' in the Christian life. He took it
for granted that the Roman Christians, who were not his
converts, had been as certainly baptized as his own converts
were. His remarks on baptism in 1 Corinthians 1:14-17,
concluding with the statement that he was not sent 'to baptize
but to preach the gospel', do not mean that he regarded the
sacrament itself as unimportant; what was unimportant was the
identity of the baptizer. He assumes that all the members of
the Corinthian church have been baptized (1 Cor. 1:13; 6:11;
10:1-2; 12:13).

In apostolic times baptism appears to have followed immediately on confession of faith in Christ. The repeated accounts of baptism in Acts give ample proof of this; the incident of the twelve disciples at Ephesus (Acts 19:1–7) is the exception that proves the rule. What is expressly related in Acts is implied in the Epistles. Faith in Christ and baptism were, indeed, not so much two distinct experiences as parts of one whole. Faith in Christ was an essential element in baptism, for without it the application of water, even accompanied by the appropriate words, would not have been Christian baptism.

But when believers were baptized, what happened? This, says Paul. Their former existence came to an end; a new life began. They were, in fact, 'buried' with Christ when they were dipped in the baptismal water, in token that they had died so far as their old life of sin was concerned; they were raised with Christ when they emerged from the water, in token that they had received a new life, which was nothing less than participation in Christ's own resurrection life. 'Are we to continue in sin that grace may abound?' But how could they continue in sin, if the life which they now lived, even while yet in mortal body, was the life which was theirs by union with the risen Christ? The very idea was a moral contradiction in terms.

But how is this going to work out in practice? 'Yield yourselves to God,' says Paul; 'present your bodies to him as instruments for the doing of his will. Formerly you were enslaved to sin, but your old relation to sin has been broken – broken irrevocably, by death. What death? The death that you have died with Christ. Now that you are united to him by faith, his death has become yours; your "old self" has been "crucified" on his cross. Christ had to do with sin, as well as you; you have had to do with it as sinners, he had to do with it as sin-bearer. As the bearer of his people's sins, he died; but now he lives his resurrection life. He no longer bears his people's sins; when once he had died for their sins, he rose from the dead, and now death can touch him no more. If you consider yourselves to have died in his death, and risen to a new way of life in his resurrection, sin will dominate you no more. You now live under a regime of grace, and grace does not stimulate sin, as law does; grace liberates from sin and enables you to triumph over it.'

3. *Baptized into Christ Jesus. Cf.* Galatians 3:27, 'as many of you as were baptized into Christ have put on Christ' – *i.e.* you have been incorporated in him, have become members of his body (*cf.* 1 Cor. 12:13), and so have shared by faith-union with him those experiences which were his historically: his crucifixion and burial, his resurrection and exaltation. Further light on Paul's doctrine of baptism is provided in 1 Corinthians 10:2, where all the Israelites who left Egypt are said to have been 'baptized into Moses in the cloud and in the sea'. Baptism thus seals the believer's exodus, his deliverance from the bondage of sin and his entry into a new life of freedom.

4. *Buried . . . with him by baptism into death. Cf.* Colossians 2:12, 'buried with him in baptism.' Burial sets the seal on death; so the Christian's baptism is a token burial in which the old order of life in sin comes to an end, to be replaced by the new order of life in Christ.

Christ was raised from the dead by the glory of the Father. The 'glory' here is more especially God's glorious power – 'the working of his great might which he accomplished in Christ when he raised him from the dead' (Eph. 1:19-20; *cf.* Col. 2:12).

We too might walk in newness of life. This is the new mode or quality of life which results from the impartation of Christ's risen power to the believer. Paul and other New Testament writers frequently use the verb 'walk' in this ethical sense (*cf.* 8:4; 13:13; 14:15).

5. *United with him in a death like his.* Lit. 'planted together in the likeness of his death' (*cf.* the 'sowing' figure of 1 Cor. 15:36-44, although there it is the believer's personal death that is meant, not, as here, death with Christ).

United with him in a resurrection like his. A reference to the future resurrection-harvest of the people of Christ, patterned on the resurrection of 'Christ the first fruits' (1 Cor. 15:23).

6. *Our old self was crucified with him.* 'The man we once were has been crucified with Christ' (NEB). This 'crucifixion' is not a present experience but a past event, expressed by the aorist tense in Greek; those who are united by faith to Christ are reckoned as having been crucified with him when he was crucified. Cf. Galatians 2:20, 'I have been crucified [perfect tense] with Christ; it is no longer I who live, but Christ who lives in me; and the life I now live in the flesh I live by faith in the Son of God.' Similarly in Galatians 6:14 Paul boasts in the cross of Christ, 'by which the world has been crucified [perfect tense] to me, and I to the world'. In the latter passage there may be a side-glance at an alternative meaning of the verb 'crucify' (stauroō), namely 'fence off'. The person I now am ('in Christ') has been fenced off by the cross from the person I formerly was ('in Adam'), when I belonged to the current world-order. (In both these Galatians passages the perfect tense denotes a present state produced by the past event of Romans 6:6.) For the 'old self' or 'old man' (anthrōpos) cf. Colossians 3:9 and Ephesians 4:22 (quoted on p. 43).

So that the sinful body might be destroyed. 'For the destruction of the sinful self' (NEB), lit. 'the body of sin' – *i.e.* so that the 'flesh', the unregenerate nature with its downward tendency, in which sin found a ready accomplice, might be rendered inoperative. The 'sinful body' is more than an individual affair; it is 'the sin-dominated nature that was ours in Adam' (J. I. Packer[1]), the old solidarity of death which has been broken by the death of Christ, with a view to the creation of the new solidarity of life of which believers are made part 'in Christ'. It is not the human body in the ordinary sense that is to be destroyed or put out of action; baptism does not have this effect. (Cf. 7:24, 'this body of death'; 8:3, 'sinful flesh'.)

7. *He who has died is freed from sin* (lit. 'has been justified from sin'). The point of this is paraphrased by NEB: 'a dead man is no longer answerable for his sin.' Death pays all debts, so those who have died with Christ have the slate wiped clean, and are ready to begin their new life with Christ freed from the entail of the past.

[1] *NIDNTT* I, p. 73 (*s.v.* 'Abolish'); see also R. H. Gundry, *'Sōma' in Biblical Theology* (1976), pp. 39, 57 f.

8. *We shall also live with him* – in our present 'newness of life' (*cf.* verse 11) as well as in the resurrection age.

10. *He died to sin, once for all.* This adverb (*ephapax*) is used repeatedly in Hebrews to emphasize the finality of the sacrifice of Christ. In his death he dealt effectively and conclusively with sin, winning a victory 'that needs no second fight, and leaves no second foe'.

11. *You also must consider yourselves dead to sin and alive to God in Christ Jesus.* This is no game of 'let's pretend'; believers should consider themselves to be what God in fact has made them. It is no vain exercise but one which is morally fruitful: the Spirit has come to make effective in them what Christ has done for them, and to enable them to become in daily experience, as far as may be in the present conditions of mortality, what they already are 'in Christ Jesus' and what they will be fully in the resurrection life. (This is the subject of 8:1–27.)

12. *To make you obey their passions.* Cf. 13:14, 'to gratify its desires.'

14. *Sin will have no dominion over you, since you are not under law but under grace.* The law demanded obedience, but grace supplies the will and the power to obey; hence grace breaks the mastery of sin as law could not. See pp. 153f.

3. The slave-market analogy (6:15–23)
Paul repeats the objection of verse 1 in slightly different terms (suggested by the wording of verse 14) and uses the analogy of the slave-market to answer it.

Paul's language about believers' being no longer enslaved to sin because, having died with Christ, they are dead to sin might have led him to point out that, when a slave has died, the master's authority over him is at an end. Instead, he points out that the master's authority over a slave is at an end when the slave passes into the ownership of a new master. 'Once', says Paul, 'you were slaves of sin. Sin was your master, and you were forced to do all the evil things that sin ordered you to do; you had no power to say "No". But now you have passed from the service of sin into the service of God; your business now is to do what pleases God, not what sin dictates. There is a big difference indeed between the kind of thing you will do as servants of God and the kind of thing you used to do as servants of sin. Moreover, to serve God "under grace" is a liberating experience, as different as can well be from slavery to sin. And not only is there a great difference in character between the two forms of service; there is a great difference between the ends to which they lead. Sin pays wages to its servants, the wages being death. God does not pay his servants mere wages: he gives them something better and much more generous. In his grace he gives life eternal as a free gift – that life eternal which is theirs by union with Christ.'

What is to be said of this argument? Is it a legal fiction, or an exhortation to pull ourselves together and make a new start, a good resolution to do better in the future? 'Consider yourselves dead in relation to sin, but alive in a new relation to God by virtue of your incorporation into Christ,' Paul has said (verse 11). Is this just an exertion of the will, or an effort of the imagination? No, it is not. It is something that has proved its reality in the lives of many, and such people have no difficulty in understanding what Paul means. For the God of whom he speaks is the living God, and when men and women present themselves to him, to be used in his service, he accepts them as his servants and gives them the power to do his will. The Christ of whom Paul speaks is the Christ who truly died and rose again, and in the lives of those who put their trust in him 'He breaks the power of cancelled sin'.

15. *Are we to sin because we are not under law but under grace?* The antinomian argument of verse 1 is reworded in terms of verse 14. Paul's repeated *By no means!* implies that anyone who talks like this has not the remotest inkling what divine grace means. Those who are 'under grace' share the life of Christ. As the life of Christ was (and is) characterized by spontaneous and glad obedience to the Father's will, so the life of those who are 'in Christ' will be characterized by the same obedience. 'Love

133

and do as you please'[1] is a maxim which, in those who have God's love poured into their hearts by the Holy Spirit, can only result in their doing those things which please God. To treat being 'under grace' as an excuse for sinning is a sign that one is not really 'under grace' at all.

16. *Obedience, which leads to righteousness.* One might have expected '. . . which leads to life', to balance the preceding *sin, which leads to death,* but righteousness (justification) and life are two sides of the same coin (*cf.* 5:18, 21).

17. *You . . . have become obedient from the heart to the standard of teaching to which you were committed.* The 'standard' or 'pattern of teaching' (NEB) is probably the summary of Christian ethics, based on the teaching of Christ, which was regularly given to converts in the primitive church to show them the way of life which they were thenceforth to follow. It is the body of teaching which Paul elsewhere calls 'the tradition' or 'the traditions' (*cf.* 1 Cor. 11:2; 2 Thes. 2:15; 3:6) – the noun (*paradosis*) being from the same root as the verb 'commit' or 'deliver' (*paradidōmi*). It has been inferred from various summaries of this teaching in the Epistles that it was arranged in catechetical form at an early period. But the 'pattern of teaching' was embodied in Christ, to whom they now belonged (*cf.* 13:14).

18. *Having been set free from sin.* That is, having been liberated from the tyranny of sin, not 'justified' from sin as in verse 7.

19. *I am speaking in human terms, because of your natural limitations* (lit. 'because of the weakness of your flesh'). That is, I am using a human analogy (*cf.* 1 Cor. 15:32) in case you fail to grasp my meaning. See p. 42.

20. *You were free in regard to righteousness.* That is, sin and not righteousness was your master then.

21. *But then what return* (lit. 'fruit') *did you get. . . ?* Probably

---

[1] *'Ama, et fac quod uis'* (Augustine, *Homilies on 1 John*, 7.8).

a complete question, to which the answer is, *The things of which you are now ashamed.*

The end of those things is death. Cf. 'fruit for death' (7:5); also 1:32, 'God's decree that those who do such things deserve to die.'

22. *The return you get is sanctification.* Lit. 'you have your fruit for sanctification' (in contrast to the shameful and deadly 'fruit' of verse 21). Those who have been justified are now being sanctified; those who have no experience of present sanctification have no reason to suppose they have been justified.

23. *Death . . . eternal life.* Repeated from verses 21–22. Both the death and the life belong to the coming age, but by God's *free gift* (*charisma*) believers in Christ receive a share in his risen life here and now, and enjoy it in advance of its consummation at their own resurrection.

B. FREEDOM FROM LAW (7:1–25)

1. The marriage analogy (7:1–6)
The implication of Paul's words in 6:14 is revolutionary. If it is because 'you are not under law but under grace' that 'sin will have no dominion over you', then to be 'under law' is to be dominated by sin, and to be 'under grace' is to be liberated not only from the dominion of sin but also from the regime of law. For Paul, to be 'under grace' is to live according to the Spirit; to be 'under law' is to live 'according to the flesh' (8:5, 13).[1]

With the law of God Paul has no fault to find – naturally, because it is God's law. It forbids sin; it prescribes righteousness. Men and women of God in Israel had found the law to be a safeguard against sin. 'Great peace have those who love thy law,' said one psalmist; 'nothing can make them stumble' (Ps. 119:165); another could say, 'The law of the LORD is perfect, reviving the soul' (Ps. 19:7).

But Paul speaks differently, and he speaks out of his own

---

[1] Jesus, while born 'under the law' (Gal. 4:4), is the one exception to this rule.

experience. The law of God in itself is not only a declaration of God's will; it is a revelation of his character, 'holy and just and good' (7:12). What is at fault is the human material on which the law operates (8:3); this leads to the conception of religion as law-keeping, the idea that by painstaking conformity to a law-code, by 'working to rule', one can acquire merit in God's sight.

When Peter, at the Council of Jerusalem, describes the law as 'a yoke which neither our fathers nor we have been able to bear' (Acts 15:10), he speaks as a typical member of the Jewish rank and file, as an *'am hā'āreṣ*. And he is thinking, probably, not only of the written law, but of its oral amplification, the 'tradition of the elders' (as it is called in Mk. 7:5). This oral law, it was held, was received by Moses on Sinai together with the written law. Moses delivered it to Joshua and then it was transmitted in turn through the elders who outlived Joshua, the prophets and the 'men of the great synagogue' (set up, it was believed, under Ezra and Nehemiah). Simon the Just, one of the last survivors of the 'great synagogue', delivered it to Anti-gonus of Socoh, and after him it was delivered in turn to successive pairs of scholars, generation by generation, ending with Hillel and Shammai, founders of two leading schools of rabbinical study (*c.* 10 BC).[1]

Only those who dedicated themselves whole-heartedly to the keeping of the law, interpreted according to this tradition, had any hope of success; but for them it was a real hope. The rich man who told Jesus that he had kept all the commandments from his early days (Mk. 10:20) was not a liar or a hypocrite. When Paul, twenty years and more after his conversion, looks back on his earlier career as a Pharisee and says that, 'as to righteousness under the law', he was 'blameless' (Phil. 3:6), he is speaking in terms of sober fact. Yet he found in Christ a new life and a new power, a new joy and a new peace, such as he had never known before, together with a new 'righteousness' – 'not . . . a righteousness of my own, based on law, but that which is through faith in Christ, the righteousness from God that depends on faith' (Phil. 3:9).

In this section of Romans he tells us more clearly than

---

[1] *Pirqē Abōth* 1.1–15.

anywhere else how he found the law so inadequate as a way to secure a righteous standing before God. He has hinted at it before: 'through the law comes knowledge of sin' (3:20) – not only the objective recognition of sin as any breach of the law, but perhaps also the awareness of sin within. More than that: Paul could never forget that the sin of sins in his own life – his persecution of the church – was directly stimulated by his devotion to the law (Gal. 1:13–14; Phil. 3:6a). In his experience freedom from sin and freedom from law went closely together. If in chapter 6 he has illustrated freedom from sin in terms of the relation between a slave and his master, now in 7:1–6 he illustrates freedom from law in terms of the relation between a wife and her husband.

Marriage, he says, is a lifelong relationship. A wife is bound to her husband so long as he lives; if, during his lifetime, she leaves him for another man, she is branded as an adulteress. But if he dies, she is free to become the wife of another without incurring any disrepute. Death breaks the marriage-bond; similarly, death breaks a person's relation to the law. When Paul applies the analogy, we are conscious of a reversal of the situation. The believer in Christ is compared to the wife, and the law to her husband, but whereas in the illustration it was the husband that died, in the application it is not the law that has died, but the believer; the believer has died with Christ – and yet it is still the believer who, no longer bound to the law, is free to be united with Christ. If, however, the matter is put in simpler terms, Paul's meaning can be expressed easily enough: as death breaks the bond between a husband and wife, so death – the believer's death-with-Christ – breaks the bond which formerly yoked him to the law, and now he is free to enter into union with Christ. His former association with the law did not help him to produce the fruits of righteousness, but these fruits are produced in abundance now that he is united with Christ. Sin and death were the result of his association with the law; righteousness and life are the product of his new association; for (as Paul puts it elsewhere) 'the written code kills, but the Spirit gives life' (2 Cor. 3:6).

1. *I am speaking to those who know the law.* 'I am speaking to those who have some knowledge of law' (NEB); it is immaterial at this stage of the argument whether they knew it in the form of Jewish law or Roman law, for in either case it was true that 'a person is subject to the law so long as he is alive, and no longer' (NEB).

2. *A married woman is bound by law to her husband as long as he lives.* Again, the statement is generally true whether one thinks of Jewish or Roman law.

The law concerning her husband. The law (Jewish or Roman) which binds her to her husband and makes him her master.

3. *She will be called an adulteress.* Cf. Mark 10:12. The Greek verb used here is the intransitive *chrēmatizō*, 'be publicly known as' (used in Acts 11:26 of the disciples of Jesus coming to be known as Christians). 'She incurs the stigma of adultery' (J. B. Phillips).

4. *So that you may belong to another, to him who has been raised from the dead.* Having been raised from the dead, he will die no more (6:9); therefore this new marriage relationship will not be broken by death, as the old one was.

In order that we may bear fruit for God. It is somewhat far-fetched to think that the marriage metaphor is being continued, so that the 'fruit' here spoken of is viewed as the offspring of the new marriage. The fruit, like the 'fruit unto holiness' of 6:22 (AV), is a new life, characterized by those 'good works, which God prepared beforehand, that we should walk in them' (Eph. 2:10).

5. *While we were living in the flesh.* That is, when we were unregenerate.

Our sinful passions, aroused by the law, were at work in our members to bear fruit for death. How the law can arouse sinful passions appears in verses 7–13. The 'fruit for death' consists of those evil works whose 'end' is death, according to 6:21.

6. *But now we are discharged from the law, dead to that which held us captive.* It is by virtue of this death (death-with-Christ and death-to-sin) that believers have been 'discharged' from their former liability under the law.

Not under the old written code. Lit. 'not in the oldness of the letter' (for 'letter' in the sense of 'written code' *cf.* 2 Cor. 3:6). Paul views his pre-Christian life as an observant Jew as a life of submission to an external code. But now the Spirit supplies from within that regulative principle which once the law, and that imperfectly, supplied from without.

In the new life of the Spirit. Lit. 'in newness of spirit', that is, the life which believers now live 'in the Spirit' (*cf.* 8:9). This antithesis between 'letter' (*gramma*) and 'spirit' (*pneuma*) points to the gospel age as that in which the new covenant foretold in Jeremiah 31:31–34 is realized (*cf.* 8:4, below). See further, p. 46 with n. 1.

2. The dawn of conscience (7:7–13)
How does the law serve as a stimulus to sin? The answer is given in the first person singular in the remainder of the chapter; the past tense is used in verses 7–13, the present tense in verses 14–25. In verses 7–13 Paul shows how entry into life under the law coincides with the dawn of conscience and the first awareness of inward sin.

In considering how far the 'I' of these verses (and of verses 14–25) is strictly autobiographical or how far Paul is relating his personal experience, we must bear in mind that there is no evidence that Paul, before his conversion, suffered from an uneasy conscience. Up to the moment when the risen Lord appeared to him on the Damascus road, he was confident that his persecution of the church was an acceptable service to God. In so far as the 'I' is autobiographical, 'here Paul's auto-biography is the biography of Everyman.'[1]

Once upon a time, Paul tells us, he had no consciousness of sin. In his earliest days, before he made the acquaintance of the law, he led a carefree life. But 'shades of the prison-house begin to close upon the growing boy'; the day came when Paul had to take on himself the obligation to keep the law.[2] The obligation

---

[1] T. W. Manson, 'Romans', *Peake's Commentary on the Bible* ([2]1962), p. 945.

[2] 'At thirteen the age is reached for the fulfilment of the commandments' (Rabbi Judah ben Tema, *Pirqē 'Abōth* 5.24).

to keep the law involved first of all the obligation to know and obey the Ten Commandments. Prohibitions, as a matter of common knowledge, tend to awaken a desire to do the thing that is forbidden: the smoker may forget how much he wants to smoke until he sees a sign which says 'No Smoking'.

Here, then, were the Ten Commandments, all but one of them charged with prohibitions: 'You shall not. . . .' Paul was not greatly tempted to worship a graven image or to commit murder, adultery or theft. The commandment which caused the trouble was the tenth, which dealt with an inner attitude rather than with an overt action or word. 'You shall not covet' proved a stumbling-block. The commandment in its Old Testament formulation goes on to specify a number of objects which a man must not covet – his neighbour's house, wife, servants, animals or property in general. Paul was not necessarily stimulated to covet any of these: the trouble went deeper. Covetousness is itself a sin; it is indeed a basic element in many forms of sin. As Paul puts it elsewhere, covetousness is idolatry (Col. 3:5). It may be illicit desire; it may be desire for something lawful in itself, but desire of such a self-regarding intensity that it usurps the place which God alone ought to occupy in the human soul.

'So,' says Paul, 'I should never have come to know what covetousness was but for the commandment which says "You shall not covet". But that commandment provided sin with a bridgehead from which it launched an attack on me, and as a result it brought all kinds of covetousness to birth within me. Without a law to stir it into life sin lay dormant; but when I was confronted with the law, sin sprang to life and laid me low. Here is a paradox indeed! The law was given so that people might keep it and live; but it was death, not life, that this law brought to me.'

This autobiographical interpretation does not command the general acceptance today that once it did: one writer speaks of it as 'now relegated to the museum of exegetical absurdities'.[1] But the arguments against it are not conclusive. Paul did not think of his own experience as unique; the account he gives here is true in a greater or lesser degree of the human race. A

[1] P. Démann, 'Moïse et la loi dans la pensée de saint Paul', in *Moïse, l'homme de l'alliance* = *Cahiers Sioniens* 2–4 (1954), p. 229.

parallel can be traced between 7:13 – 8:2 and the outline of human history in 5:12–21; in both passages one can distinguish three phases: (*a*) before the law; (*b*) under the law; (*c*) set free from the law in Christ. It may be, too, that here as in 5:12–19 Paul has the fall narrative partly in mind. Covetousness, which in one form or another is common to mankind, played a part in Adam's downfall. Moreover, when Paul speaks of sin as 'deceiving' or 'beguiling' him (verse 11), there is an echo of Eve's complaint: 'The serpent beguiled me, and I ate' (Gn. 3:13). But Paul would not have re-told the fall story in the first person singular had he not recognized it as an authentic record of his own experience, as well as of the experience of humanity. In this respect, at least, he knew himself to be 'the Adam of his own soul' (2 Baruch 54:19).

7. *If it had not been for the law, I should not have known sin.* Cf. 3:20. The function of the law is propaedeutic: by revealing to men and women their sinfulness and inability, it reveals to them also their need of that deliverance which only the grace of God can effect.

You shall not covet (Ex. 20:17; Dt. 5:21). It is natural for human beings to want things; when it is brought to their attention that certain things which they want are forbidden them by law, there is a tendency to want them all the more, to set their hearts on them.

8. *Sin, finding opportunity in the commandment.* In this and the following verses sin is personified as a powerful enemy, who has established a base of operations (*aphormē*) within the citadel of Mansoul.

Wrought in me all kinds of covetousness. 'Produced in me all kinds of wrong desires' (NEB). C. K. Barrett points out that covetousness, the breach of the law, is the perversion of love, which is 'the fulfilling of the law' (13:10).[1]

9. *I was once alive apart from the law.* So Adam was not conscious of any sinful inclination until his obedience was tested

---

[1] *From First Adam to Last* (1962), p. 100.

by the commandment 'you shall not eat'. But Paul understands the fall narrative all the better in the light of general human experience (including his own).

10. *The very commandment which promised life.* A reference to Leviticus 18:5, quoted below in 10:5 (*cf.* 2:13).

11. *Deceived me.* The verb (*exapataō*) is the same as in 2 Corinthians 11:3 ('the serpent deceived Eve') and 1 Timothy 2:14 ('the woman was deceived and became a transgressor'); *cf.* the simple verb *apataō* in Genesis 3:13, LXX. But the parallel with the fall story must not be pressed too far, for Paul's doctrine is that mankind fell 'in Adam' and not in Eve, and in Genesis 3, as is pointed out in 1 Timothy 2:14, 'it was not Adam who was deceived' (NEB).

12. *The law . . . the commandment . . . The law* is the law in its entirety; *the commandment* is each of the precepts which it comprises (613, according to the traditional reckoning). *The law is holy*, because God, whose character it reflects and whose will it declares, is himself holy (*cf.* Lv. 11:45; 19:2).

13. *Did that which is good, then, bring death to me?* Cf. 2 Esdras 9:36-37, 'For we who have received the law and sinned will perish, as well as our heart which received it; the law, however, does not perish but remains in its glory.'
It was sin, working death in me through what is good, in order that sin might be shown to be sin. Although to be 'under law' involves in practice being 'under sin', Paul has indignantly repudiated any attempt to equate the law with sin (verse 7). The law is good and, in its own nature, life-giving; it could not bring one into a state of death. The villain of the piece is sin: sin seized the opportunity afforded it when the law showed me what was right and what was wrong, without supplying the power to do the former and avoid the latter. Sin forced me against my better judgment to do what the law showed me to be wrong, and thus made me incur condemnation and death. In consequence I appreciated, as I should not otherwise have done, just how sinful, how contrary to God and goodness, sin actually is.

3. The conflict within (7:14-25)

In this section the first person singular is carried on from verses
7-13, but the past tense is replaced by the present. Not only
so, but there is an inward tension here which was absent from
the preceding section. There, sin assaulted the speaker by
stealth and struck him down; here, he puts up an agonizing
resistance, even if he cannot beat back the enemy. There, he
described what happened to him when he lived in 'this present
age'; here, the 'age to come' has already arrived, although the
old age has not yet passed away, and he is caught up in the
tension between the two.[1] He is like a person living simul-
taneously on two planes, eagerly longing to lead a life in
keeping with the higher plane, but sadly aware of the strength
of indwelling sin that keeps on pulling him down to the lower
plane.

Here is a picture of life under the law, without the aid of the
Spirit, portrayed from the perspective of one who has now
experienced the liberating power of life in the Spirit. When Paul
himself lived under the law, before the Damascus-road event,
he does not seem to have been aware of any such inward
tension as is here described. But he may well have known
believers in Christ who were nevertheless living in legal
bondage because they had not appreciated or appropriated the
fullness of gospel freedom. And he knew that Christians in
general live in two worlds, with the tension that this involves.
Temporally they live in this world; as men and women of flesh
and blood they are subject to the conditions of mortal life. Like
all their fellows, they are children of Adam and subject to the
law that 'in Adam all die'. Spiritually, however, they have
passed from death to life, from the realm of darkness to the
kingdom of light. As sharers in Christ's death, burial and resurrection, they have been raised to 'walk in newness of life',
citizens of the new world, members of the new creation, no
longer 'in Adam' but 'in Christ'.

One day this present order will pass. The new age will be
established in glory, and the tension between the two ages will
be resolved. But, so long as Christians live 'between the times',

---

[1] This tension is not identical with that between the good and evil inclination (yēṣer ha-
ṭōb and yēṣer hā-rā') in Jewish thought, with which it has been compared.

their lives provide the battleground for the conflict summarized in Galatians 5:17, 'the desires of the flesh are against the Spirit, and the desires of the Spirit are against the flesh; for these are opposed to each other, to prevent you from doing what you would.'[1]

The conflict of Galatians 5:17, however, is not identical with that depicted here. Here there is no mention of the Spirit; if there were, the picture would be different and the outlook brighter. Here is the portrait of one who is conscious of the presence and power of indwelling sin in his life; indwelling sin is a tyrant whose dictates he hates and loathes, but against whose power he struggles in vain by his own strength. When he is compelled by *force majeure* to obey the tyrant's dictates, he does not recognize the ensuing acts as his own; they are the very opposite of what he desires to do. What he desires to do is the law of God, he delights in it, he acknowledges that it is 'holy and just and good'. But, for all his desire to obey God's law, he is compelled by the malignant power within to disobey it. 'I do not do the good I want, but the evil I do not want is what I do' (verse 19).

This unequal struggle against 'the law of sin which dwells in my members' (as Paul calls it) has been the real experience of too many Christians for the confident assumption to be made that Paul cannot be speaking autobiographically here, that his 'I' is purely dramatic. Paul can entreat his friends 'by the meekness and gentleness of Christ' (2 Cor. 10:1); but did this meekness and gentleness come to him naturally? A man of his imperious zeal must have found it no easy matter to 'crucify the flesh' – to win the victory over a hasty tongue, a premature judgment, a resentment at any encroachment on the sphere of his apostolic service. M. Goguel may be right in assigning Paul's personal experience of this inner conflict to the period immediately following his conversion.[2] But, whatever may be said about this, the man who, even at the height of his apostolic career, made it his daily business to discipline himself so as not

---

[1] For the counterpart in Romans to Gal. 5:16 see p. 148. On the interpretation, and relation to the argument of Romans, of Gal. 5:16 f. see F. F. Bruce, *The Epistle of Paul to the Galatians* (1982), pp. 242–245.

[2] M. Goguel, *The Birth of Christianity*, E.T. (1953), pp. 213 f.

to be disqualified in the spiritual contest, the man who pressed on to the goal of God's upward calling in Christ Jesus, knew that the 'immortal garland' was to be run for 'not without dust and heat'. He was too constantly given to portraying the way of holiness as a race to be run, a battle to be fought, for us to imagine that victory came to him 'sudden, in a minute'.

True, but victory did come. The present passage leads up to a paean of triumph, although it begins with a sad confession of inability. The inability persists only so long as I fight the battle in my own strength, for then I serve the law of God with my mind, but my body willy-nilly goes on rendering obedience to the law of sin. Must I always know defeat? Must I always carry this incubus? Will deliverance never come? Thank God it will, through Jesus Christ our Lord!

14. *I am carnal, sold under sin.* The nature which I have inherited 'in Adam' finds the law uncongenial. The law is 'spiritual' because it is God's law; but this nature of mine is unspiritual (*sarkinos*, 'fleshly'), enslaved to a power which my will repudiates. There is something in humanity, even in regenerate humanity, which objects to God and seeks to be independent of him. This 'something' is what Paul here calls his 'flesh' (*cf.* verse 18), which lays him wide open to the tyranny of indwelling sin. The phrase 'sold under sin' has a parallel in Wisdom 1:4, where wisdom refuses to 'make her home in a body that is mortgaged to sin' (NEB).

15. *I do not understand my own actions.* 'I do not even acknowledge my own actions as mine' (NEB).[1]

For I do not do what I want, but I do the very thing I hate. It is customary to quote as classical parallels Horace's *quae nocuere sequar, fugiam quae profore credo*, 'I pursue the things that have done me harm; I shun the things I believe will do me good' (*Epistles* 1.8.11), or Ovid's *uideo meliora proboque; deteriora sequor*, 'I see and approve the better course, but I follow the worse one'

---

[1] Plato uses the same verb (*gignōskō*) in *Protagoras* 355C, where he rejects the idea that 'one may acknowledge evil things to be evil, and nevertheless do them'. But experience is against him.

(put into the mouth of Medea in *Metamorphoses* 7.20 f.).[1] C. K. Barrett (*ad loc.*) points out an even closer verbal parallel in Epictetus, according to whom (*Dissertations* 2.26.4) the thief does not do what he wishes; but he also points out, and very pertinently, that neither Ovid nor Epictetus (not, it may be added, Horace) is saying exactly what Paul says. Paul has within him an independent witness, the voice of conscience (see note on 2:15, p. 86), which, by condemning his failure to keep the law, bears testimony to the perfection of the law.

17, 20. *It is no longer I that do it, but sin which dwells within me.* But as soon as my will consents to it, then it is I who do it, even if it was not so before.

22. *I delight in the law of God, in my inmost self.* And therefore I can sing 'O how I love thy law!' and everything else in Psalm 119, but the problem is to express that love by obedience. The 'inmost self' is the 'new nature' in Christ that is daily being renewed in the Creator's image (Col. 3:10; *cf.* 2 Cor. 4:16). In the light of 8:7–8 it is difficult to view the speaker here as other than a believer.

23. *The law of sin.* The evil principle, or the tyranny of indwelling sin. With *nomos tēs hamartias* here A. A. T. Ehrhardt compares the paradoxical Latin term *lex iniuriae* ('law of injustice'), used paradoxically by Cicero in *Verrines* ii.3.211.[2]

24. *Wretched man that I am!* The impassioned outcry shows that the preceding words express 'no abstract argument but the echo of the personal experience of an anguished soul'.[3] Alexander Whyte speaks with scorn of those commentators who treat this section as a 'studied artifice of Pauline rhetoric', setting forth 'the spiritual experiences of a man of straw'.[4]

---

[1] Ovid's Medea echoes her counterpart in Euripides' *Medea* 1078–1080: 'I understand that such things as I am about to do are evil, but anger, cause of the greatest ills among mortals, is stronger than my (rational) resolves.'

[2] 'A Penitentiary Psalm from the Dead Sea Scrolls and its Allies', *Texte und Untersuchungen* 73 = *Studia Evangelica* 1 (1959), p. 589.

[3] M. Goguel, *The Birth of Christianity* (1953), pp. 213 f.

[4] *Bible Characters: New Testament* (1952), p. 260.

'Believers are perfect as to their justification, but their sanctification is only begun. It is a progressive work. When they believed in Christ, they knew but very little of the fountain of corruption that dwells in them. When Christ made Himself known to them as their Saviour, and the Beloved of their souls, the carnal mind seemed to be dead, but they found out afterwards that it was not dead. So some have experienced more soul trials after their conversion than when they were awakened to a sense of their lost condition. "O wretched man that I am! . . ." is their cry till they are made perfect in holiness. But He that hath begun a good work in them will perform it until the day of Jesus Christ.'[1]

Who will deliver me from this body of death? One can find no lack of verbal parallels to this exclamation in classical literature and elsewhere. Cicero, Philo, Epictetus and Marcus Aurelius all describe the soul throughout earthly life as burdened by, or shackled to, a dead body.[2] Some commentators have adduced Virgil's account of the Etruscan king Mezentius, who tormented his living captives by tying them to decomposing corpses.[3]

But Paul is no Platonist or Stoic. He has just spoken of himself as held 'captive to the law of sin which is in my members' (verse 23), and *this body of death* is similarly his body, or human nature under hostile occupation. The body as such, however, is not denigrated: it is destined to share in the redemption accomplished by Christ (8:23) and meanwhile, when the longed-for deliverance has been obtained through 'the law of the Spirit of life in Christ Jesus' (8:2), it serves as a vehicle for the glorifying of God (1 Cor. 6:20).

25. *Thanks be to God through Jesus Christ our Lord!* It is astonishing to find this outbreak of triumph immediately after the anguished cry, 'Who will deliver me?' But here is the answer: 'God alone, through Jesus Christ our Lord! Thanks be to God!'

---

[1] D. MacFarlane, in *The Free Presbyterian Pulpit* (1961), p. 20.

[2] *Cf.* Cicero, *Hortensius* (in Augustine, *Against Julian the Pelagian* 5.78); Philo, *On Husbandry* 25; Epictetus, *Dissertations*, fragment 23; Marcus Aurelius, *Meditations* 2.12; 4.41. Plato (*Phaedrus* 250C) speaks of the soul as imprisoned in the body like an oyster in its shell.

[3] *Aeneid* 8.485–488.

147

(NEB). Just how this deliverance from the power of indwelling sin may be appropriated is described more fully in the next chapter; for the moment, after this brief indication that the situation is not so hopeless as the 'wretched man' feared, Paul goes back to summarize the moral predicament of verses 14–24.

So then, I of myself serve the law of God with my mind, but with my flesh I serve the law of sin. It is unnecessary to treat this sentence as misplaced. Moffatt makes it stand as a parenthesis after verse 23, which, he says, 'seems its original and logical position before the climax of ver. 24' – a transposition which C. H. Dodd says is 'surely right' (*ad loc.*). G. Zuntz thinks that it 'may be an addition by Paul himself or a summing up by some early reader; in any case, its present position is unsuitable and suggests that a marginal gloss has been inserted into the text'.[1] It appears in its present position, however, in our earliest authorities; and it is precarious to rearrange the words of Paul in the interests of a smoother logical sequence.

The *mind* with which the law of God is served is the mind responsive to the voice of conscience (but scarcely the Spirit-renewed mind of 12:1); the *flesh* which does the bidding of the law of sin is the fallen nature which death alone will annihilate. It is *I of myself* (*autos egō*) that experience defeat and frustration; but 'I', as a believer, am not left to 'myself'; the power of the indwelling Spirit makes an almighty difference (*cf.* 8:9–11).

C. FREEDOM FROM DEATH (8:1–39)

1. Life in the Spirit (8:1–17)
'Walk by the Spirit,' Paul had said to the Galatians, 'and you will by no means fulfil the desire of the flesh' (Gal. 5:16).[2] Here he expands those words. The Holy Spirit has not been mentioned in chapter 7, but he pervades chapter 8, which describes the life of victory and hope lived by those who 'are

---

[1] *The Text of the Epistles* (1954), p. 16.
[2] RSV wrongly renders the second clause not as a promise but as a command ('do not gratify the desires of the flesh'). The sense is: 'if you walk by the Spirit you will not fulfil the desire of the flesh.'

in Christ Jesus' (verse 1) and 'walk not according to the flesh but according to the Spirit' (verse 4).

So long as they endeavour to rely on their own resources, they fight a losing battle; when they avail themselves of the resources of life and power that are theirs 'in Christ Jesus', they are more than conquerors. There is therefore no reason why they should go on in a life of penal servitude, bound to carry out the dictates of the tyrannical law of sin and death. Christ dwells in them by his Spirit, and his Spirit infuses into them a new principle – the law of life – which is stronger than indwelling sin and sets them free from its tyranny.

Under the old order, before the coming of the Spirit, it was impossible to do the will of God, and if people's lives are still dominated by that old order, to do his will remains an impossibility. But those who belong to the new order of the Spirit do the will of God from the heart. Their own spirit, formerly dead and insensitive, is now instinct with the life which the Spirit of God imparts. Their body may still for the time being be subject to the law of death which results from the entry of sin into the world; but the last word remains with the Spirit of life.

For not only does the Spirit maintain life and power in the spirit of believers here and now; his indwelling presence is a token that their body, still subject to mortality, will rise to new life as Christ's own body rose. The body is not excluded from the benefits of 'the redemption which is in Christ Jesus'. Paul has already used this fact in an appeal to members of the Corinthian church to regard their bodies and bodily actions in a spirit of Christian responsibility: 'you were bought with a price. So glorify God in your body' (1 Cor. 6:20). Here he suggests that intimations of a coming immortality are conveyed by the Spirit even in this period of mortality: this is one of the many ways in which the presence of the Spirit in this phase of existence is the first-fruits of a heritage of glory yet to be realized. If those who go on in conformity with the old order have the sentence of death within themselves, those who reckon the old order as belonging to the dead past and follow the guidance of the Spirit of God have the assurance that life immortal has already begun within them. Indeed, the fact that they respond to the leading of the Spirit of God is a clear proof that they are children of God.

For Paul, the leading of the Spirit is not a matter of sporadic impulse, but the believer's normal experience; it is the very principle of the freedom of the Christian life. 'If you are led by the Spirit you are not under the law' (Gal. 5:18). The old legal bondage has been thrown off; the Spirit introduces believers into a new relationship as God's free-born sons and daughters. It is the prompting of the Spirit that causes them to address God spontaneously as their Father, using the expression which Jesus himself used when speaking to God as his Father – an expression proper to the intimate atmosphere of family affection. No wonder that, as Paul says elsewhere, the Spirit sent by God into his children's hearts, crying 'Abba! Father!', is 'the Spirit of his Son' (Gal. 4:6). They have, in other words, received that Spirit who descended in power on Jesus at his baptism (Mk. 1:10), led him in the wilderness (Lk. 4:1–2), supplied the energy for his mighty works (Mt. 12:28) and animated his whole life and ministry (Lk. 4:14, 18).

Thus the Spirit of God bears consentient witness with the personal spirit of Christians that they are children of God. God's children, moreover, are his heirs – heirs to that glory which is Christ's by unique right, and which by grace he shares with his people, who are thus joint-heirs with him. Those who in this present life experience the fellowship of his sufferings can look forward to the fellowship of his glory. 'Suffering now, glory hereafter' is a recurring New Testament theme, and one that corresponded to the realities of early Christian life. The warning given by Paul and Barnabas to their converts in South Galatia, that 'through many tribulations we must enter the kingdom of God' (Acts 14:22), was repeated as each new community was formed, and was speedily confirmed by experience. 'If we endure, we shall also reign with him' (2 Tim. 2:12) means the reproduction in the lives of Christians of the pattern perfectly exemplified in their Master, who by divine necessity passed through suffering, and so entered into his glory (*cf.* Lk. 24:26; 1 Pet. 1:11; 5:1).

1. *There is therefore now no condemnation for those who are in*

Christ Jesus. If 'condemnation' were simply the converse of 'justification', Paul would be saying that those who are in Christ Jesus are justified; but that stage in the argument was reached in 3:21 – 4:25. The word *katakrima* here means 'probably not "condemnation", but the punishment following sentence' (BAGD, p. 413) – in other words, penal servitude. There is no reason for those who are 'in Christ Jesus' to go on doing penal servitude as though they had never been pardoned, never been released from the prison-house of sin.

'In Christ Jesus' (or 'in Christ') is Paul's description of the new order into which men and women are introduced when they put their trust in Christ. Christian baptism is baptism 'into Christ Jesus' (6:3); by faith-union with him his people are reckoned to have died with him, been buried with him and been raised with him. The common life in the body of Christ is Christ's own resurrection life shared with his people; if from one point of view he lives in them, from another they live in him (*cf.* Gal. 2:20). 'To be "in Christ" is to be a member of the church; not, of course, to have your name on the books, but to be in a real sense a limb or organ of Christ's body, dependent upon Him, dedicated to His ends' (*cf.* 12:4–5).[1]

2. *The law of the Spirit of life in Christ Jesus has set me free . . .* Compare 2 Corinthians 3:17, 'where the Spirit of the Lord is, there is freedom'; also Galatians 5:13, 'you were called to freedom.' 'Law' here probably means 'principle' (see p. 51). It is the 'law of the Spirit' by contrast with 'the law of sin which dwells in my members' (7:23); it is the 'law of life' by contrast with the commandment which 'promised life' but 'proved to be death' (7:10).[2] Even if *the law of sin and death* is not to be identified outright with the law of Moses, the law of Moses nevertheless stimulates sin and condemns to death. But the Spirit 'by His determining influences produces regulated action without any code'.[3]

[1] C. H. Dodd, *Gospel and Law* (1951), pp. 36 f.; *cf.* C. F. D. Moule, *The Origin of Christology* (1977), pp. 47–96. See also what is said above on corporate personality in the exposition of 5:12–21 (p. 120 with n. 1).
[2] The two genitives 'of the Spirit' and 'of life' may be treated as alike dependent on 'law'. Even so, it is implicit in Paul's argument that the Spirit is the 'Spirit of life'.
[3] N. Q. Hamilton, *The Holy Spirit and Eschatology in Paul* (1957), p. 30.

The mention of the Spirit here introduces a fuller exposition of his ministry, anticipated in 5:5, where his coming is said to flood the hearts of believers with the love of God, and 7:6, where 'the new life of the Spirit' is contrasted with 'the old written code' (*cf.* also the brief reference in 1:4 to the 'Spirit of holiness' in connection with Christ's being raised from the dead). Paul now shows what is involved in the 'new life' which the Spirit imparts and sustains. With the entry of the Spirit there is no further talk of defeat. The conflict goes on, but where the Spirit is in control the power of indwelling sin is mastered.

For 'me' in 'has set me free' some weighty authorities (including the eastern witnesses *Aleph* and B and the western witness G), followed by the Nestle-Aland text, read 'thee' (*cf.* NEB: 'has set you free').

3. *In the likeness of sinful flesh.* Lit. 'in likeness of flesh of sin'. 'In likeness of flesh' by itself would be docetic; it is of the essence of the gospel that the Son of God came 'in flesh' and not merely 'in likeness of flesh'. Paul might have said simply 'in flesh', but he wished to emphasize that human flesh was the realm in which sin gained a foothold and usurped dominion until the grace of God drew near. Hence he says not simply 'flesh' but 'flesh of sin' or 'sinful flesh'. But to say that the Son of God came 'in sinful flesh' might imply that there was sin in him, whereas (as Paul puts it elsewhere) he 'knew no sin' (2 Cor. 5:21). Hence he is described as being sent 'in the likeness of sinful flesh'.

For sin. Greek *peri hamartias*, which is the regular LXX rendering of Hebrew *ḥaṭṭā't*, 'sin-offering'.[1] This is probably its force here (*cf.* RSV mg. 'as a sin offering'; NEB 'as a sacrifice for sin').

Condemned sin in the flesh. Sentence was passed and executed on sin in Christ's 'flesh', in his human nature, and thereby in human nature as such. 'Paul wants to emphasize that the power of sin is a cosmic unity, but that it is broken into at one absolutely specific point' (O. Michel, *ad loc.*). For those who are

---

[1] In Is. 53:10 it is the LXX rendering of Heb. *'āšām*, 'guilt-offering' (the Servant of the Lord makes himself an *'ăšām*).

united to Christ, therefore, the power of sin has been broken (*cf.* 6:6–7).

4. *In order that the just requirement of the law might be fulfilled in us.* The law's 'just requirement' is summed up in 13:9 in the single commandment, 'You shall love your neighbour as your-self.' The Greek word is *dikaiōma*, used here as in 2:26 (for other meanings see p. 125, n. 1). Here is the fulfilment of Jeremiah's prophecy of the new covenant (quoted in part in 11:27), under which, said God, 'I will put my law within them, and I will write it upon their hearts' (Je. 31:33), and of the parallel promise of Ezekiel 11:19–20; 36:26–27, where God undertakes to give his people a 'new heart' and a 'new spirit' – in fact, his own Spirit, sent to dwell within them so that they will henceforth do his will spontaneously. The New Testament writers recognize in the gospel the fulfilment of these and similar prophecies.

Who walk not according to the flesh but according to the Spirit. To live 'according to the flesh' means for Paul to live 'under law' (*i.e.* in the old aeon of bondage); to live 'according to the Spirit' means to live 'under grace' (*i.e.* in the new aeon of freedom); *cf.* 6:14.

Christian holiness is not a matter of painstaking conformity to the specific precepts of an external law-code; it is rather a question of the Holy Spirit's producing his fruit in one's life, reproducing those graces which were seen in perfection in the life of Christ. The law prescribed a life of holiness, but it was powerless to produce such a life, because of the inadequacy of the human material on which it had to work. But what the law was powerless to do has been done by God. Now that God's own Son, sent to earth 'in the likeness of sinful flesh', has given up his life for the sin of the world, the death-sentence has been pronounced on sin. Sin found no foothold in the life of Jesus; it was effectively overcome in his death, and the fruits of that victory are now made good to all who are 'in him'. All that the law required by way of conformity to the will of God is now realized in the lives of those who are controlled by the Holy Spirit and are released from their servi-tude to the old order. God's commands have now become God's enablings.

> To run and work the law commands,
> Yet gives me neither feet nor hands;
> But better news the gospel brings:
> It bids me fly, and gives me wings.

'Grace was given', as Augustine said, 'that the law might be fulfilled.'[1]

'Not until, by the death and resurrection of Christ, the new creation had come into being, did it become possible for God to send the Spirit of his Son into the hearts of lost and helpless men; and with the Spirit came life, freedom and power. Those who live by the Spirit, as Paul says, produce the fruits of the Spirit. A vine does not produce grapes by Act of Parliament; they are the fruit of the vine's own life; so the conduct which conforms to the standard of the Kingdom is not produced by any demand, not even God's, but it is the fruit of that divine nature which God gives as the result of what he has done in and by Christ.'[2]

5. *Those who live according to the flesh set their minds on the things of the flesh, but those who live according to the Spirit set their minds on the things of the Spirit.* Cf. Galatians 5:16–17 (quoted on pp. 144, 148); also Galatians 5:25, 'If we live by the Spirit, let us also walk by the Spirit.'

6. *To set the mind on the flesh . . . to set the mind on the Spirit* . . . Lit. 'the mind of the flesh . . . the mind of the Spirit'. The two spheres of existence are so opposed that the one is described as *death*, the other as *life*. Compare the antithesis in Galatians 5:19-23 between 'the works of the flesh' and 'the fruit of the Spirit'.

9. *Any one who does not have the Spirit of Christ does not belong to him.* 'If a man does not possess the Spirit of Christ, he is no Christian' (NEB). Since it is the Spirit alone who brings people

---

[1] '*Gratia data est, ut lex impleretur*' (*On Spirit and Letter*, 34) – 'but not in order that by their fulfilment of the law the faithful might justify themselves' (C. E. B. Cranfield, *ad loc.*).
[2] S. H. Hooke, *The Siege Perilous* (1956), p. 264.

into living relation with Christ, there can be no such relation with Christ apart from the Spirit.

10. *If Christ is in you, although your bodies are dead because of sin, your spirits are alive because of righteousness.* Lit. 'the body is dead . . . the spirit is life'. 'The body is dead' in the sense that it remains subject to death as the wages of sin: 'dead' is used as being more emphatic than 'mortal'. The question further arises whether 'the spirit' is the believer's human spirit or the indwelling Spirit of God. Thus far in chapter 8 *pneuma* has denoted the Spirit of God, and this raises a presumption that the word has the same meaning here. However, in verse 16 below it is used of the believer's spirit (*cf.* 1:9, above). For Paul, the human spirit is not alive until it is quickened by the Spirit of God; hence if 'the (human) spirit is alive', it is because 'the (divine) Spirit is life'. The 'righteousness' mentioned at the end of the verse is the righteousness of God received by faith (1:17; 3:22) – justification. Paul's statement may be paraphrased: 'If you are believers, the risen Christ dwells within you. It is true, on the one hand, that your body is still subject to that temporal death which is the consequence of sin; but, on the other hand, the Spirit who has taken up his abode in you, the living and life-giving Spirit of Christ, imparts to you that eternal life which is the consequence of justification' (*cf.* 5:18, lit. 'justification of life').

Practically, be it noted, 'if Christ is in you' is equivalent to 'if the Spirit of God really dwells in you' (verse 9; *cf.* verse 11), even if the two may be distinguished theoretically. It is by the Spirit that the indwelling presence of the risen Christ is conveyed and maintained. Similarly, no practical distinction can be drawn between being 'in Christ Jesus' (verse 1) and 'in the Spirit' (verse 9).

11. *He who raised Christ Jesus from the dead will give life to your mortal bodies also through his Spirit which dwells in you.* Even if for the present 'the body is dead' (verse 10), it too has the promise of life. *Cf.* 1 Corinthians 6:14; 2 Corinthians 4:14; 1 Thessalonians 4:14, where the resurrection of believers is similarly made dependent on the resurrection of Christ (*cf.* note on 1:4, pp. 69f.).

But here the role of the indwelling Spirit as the earnest of coming resurrection is emphasized as it is not in those earlier passages; *cf.*, however, 2 Corinthians 5:5, 'he who has prepared us for this very thing [the putting on of the heavenly body] is God, who has given us the Spirit as a guarantee.'

13. *If by the Spirit you put to death the deeds of the body.* 'Put to death' is equivalent to 'consider . . . dead' (6:11); whereas in 6:11 believers are exhorted to consider themselves dead in relation to sin, here they are told to treat their former sinful practices as dead in relation to themselves (so also in Col. 3:5). We may compare Galatians 5:24, 'those who belong to Christ Jesus have crucified the flesh with its passions and desires', and our Lord's more vivid language about plucking out the eye or cutting off the hand or foot that leads one into sin (Mk. 9:43–47).

14. *All who are led by the Spirit of God are sons of God.* Cf. Galatians 5:18, 'if you are led by the Spirit you are not under the law.' In Galatians 3:23 – 4:7 Paul contrasts the former bondage of slaves ('under the law') with the new freedom of sons ('under grace'), into whose hearts 'God has sent the Spirit of his Son . . . crying, "Abba! Father!" '

15. *You did not receive the spirit of slavery to fall back into fear, but you have received the spirit of sonship.* For the construction compare 1 Corinthians 2:12, 'we have received not the spirit of the world, but the Spirit which is from God'; 2 Timothy 1:7, 'God did not give us a spirit of timidity but a spirit of power and love and self-control.' 'Here is a beautiful chain of experimental verses, all cast in the same mould, all built upon the same pattern, with the negative first and the positive second; on one side bondage, worldliness, and fear; on the other sonship, spiritual gifts, power, love, and sanctified common-sense.'[1]

The spirit of sonship is so called because it is those who are led by the Spirit of God that are sons of God (verse 14). The word 'sonship' (*hyiothesia*) is rendered 'adoption as sons' in verse 23. 'In Christ Jesus' believers 'are all sons (and daughters) of God,

---

[1] J. Rendel Harris, *Aaron's Breastplate* (1908), p. 92.

through faith' (Gal. 3:26), but their full instatement or manifestation as such will coincide with the resurrection (verses 19–23
below). The Spirit empowers them to anticipate this future
consummation and to appreciate their present relationship as
children to their Father. In Galatians 4:6 it is because they are
his sons and daughters that God has given them 'the Spirit of
his Son'; when they address God by the same name as Jesus
used, it is evident that the Spirit that animated Jesus has taken
up residence in their lives.

The term 'adoption' (used here in older English versions) may
have a somewhat artificial sound in our ears; but in the Roman
world of the first century AD an adopted son was a son deliberately chosen by his adoptive father to perpetuate his name and
inherit his estate; he was no whit inferior in status to a son born
in the ordinary course of nature, and might well enjoy the
father's affection more fully and reproduce the father's character
more worthily.

'*Abba! Father!*' This phrase occurs in two other places in the
New Testament – in Mark 14:36 (in Jesus' prayer in Gethse-
mane) and Galatians 4:6 (quoted in note on verse 14 above).
Abba is an Aramaic word (in the 'emphatic state') which came
to be used among Jews (as it is to this day in Hebrew-speaking
families) as the familiar term by which children address their
father. In synagogue worship Jews did (and do) address God
as their Father, but not by this form of the word. The fact that
this form made its way into the worshipping vocabulary of the
Gentile churches is best explained by Jesus' characteristic use
of it. There is strong presumption, too, that when he taught
his disciples to begin their prayers with 'Father, hallowed be
thy name' (Lk. 11:2), the word they were encouraged to use for
'Father' was *Abba*. When this non-Greek word passed into the
usage of Greek-speaking churches it was amplified by the
addition of its Greek equivalent, *ho patēr* (the two forms being
rendered together 'Abba! Father!'). It is noteworthy that Paul
takes it for granted that this invocation was as familiar to the
Roman Christians, who were not his converts, as it was to the
Galatian Christians, who were.

'This is but a little word, and yet notwithstanding it compre-

157

hendeth all things. The mouth speaketh not, but the affection of the heart speaketh after this manner. Although I be oppressed with anguish and terror on every side, and seem to be forsaken and utterly cast away from thy presence, yet am I thy child, and thou art my Father for Christ's sake: I am beloved because of the Beloved. Wherefore this little word, Father, conceived effectually in the heart, passeth all the eloquence of Demosthenes, Cicero, and of the most eloquent rhetoricians that ever were in the world. This matter is not expressed with words, but with groanings, which groanings cannot be uttered with any words or eloquence, for no tongue can express them.'[1]

16. *It is the Spirit himself bearing witness with our spirit.* This is the New Testament basis of the doctrine of the 'inward witness of the Holy Spirit' (*testimonium Spiritus sancti internum*); cf. 1 John 5:7–8. For the relation of the Spirit of God to the spirit of the person whom he indwells, see note on verse 10 above.

That we are children of God. The word here is *tekna*, and not *hyioi*, 'sons', as in verse 14; but the course of the argument shows that Paul is using the two terms interchangeably. In Galatians 3:23 – 4:7 he does indeed make a distinction between the period of infancy, when his readers were under the guardianship of the law, and the attainment of their responsible status as sons (*hyioi*) of God, now that the gospel has been introduced. But their previous status is indicated by the term *nēpioi* ('infants'), not *tekna* ('children'). Nowhere in the New Testament can a valid distinction be made between being 'children (*tekna*) of God' and 'sons (*hyioi*) of God'. In the Johannine writings this relationship is expressed throughout by *tekna* (*cf.* Jn. 1:12; 1 Jn. 3:1–2), *hyios* being reserved for Christ as the Son of God.

To call God 'Father', then, is as sure a token of the indwelling Spirit as to call Jesus 'Lord' (1 Cor. 12:3).

17. *And if children, then heirs.* Cf. Galatians 4:7 'you are no longer a slave but a son, and if a son then an heir.' The equival-

[1] Martin Luther, *Commentary on Galatians* ('Middleton' edition, 1575/1953), on 'Abba! Father!' (Gal. 4:6).

ence of *teknon* and *hyios* is again confirmed by the use of the former here in Romans, and of the latter in the Galatians parallel. Looking back in later years on what is commonly called his conversion, John Wesley described it as his exchanging 'the faith of a *servant*' for 'the faith of a *son*'.[1]

Heirs of God and fellow heirs with Christ. They are fellow heirs with Christ because the glory which they are to inherit by grace is the glory which is his by right (*cf.* Jn. 17:22–24).

Provided we suffer with him in order that we may also be glorified with him. The suffering is the indispensable prelude to the glory. Thus when Paul says (2 Cor. 4:16) that, 'though our outer nature is wasting away, our inner nature is being renewed every day', he means that the very afflictions and privations which wear down the 'outer nature' are the means used by the Spirit of God to renew the inner being more and more, until at last the outer nature disappears altogether and the inner being (the 'new man') is fully formed after the image of Christ (*cf.* 2 Cor. 3:18; Col. 3:10). So also, in 2 Corinthians 4:10, he speaks of himself and his fellow apostles as 'always carrying in the body the death [lit. 'dying'] of Jesus, so that the life of Jesus may also be manifested in our bodies'.

2. The glory to come (8:18–30)

But the glory to come far outweighs the affliction of the present. The affliction is light and temporary when compared with the all-surpassing and everlasting glory. So Paul, writing against a background of recent and (even for him) unparalleled tribulation, had assured his friends in Corinth a year or two before this that 'this slight momentary affliction is preparing for us an eternal weight of glory beyond all comparison' (2 Cor. 4:17). It is not merely that the glory is a compensation for the suffering; it actually grows out of the suffering. There is an organic relation between the two for the believer as surely as there was for the Lord.

When the day of glory dawns, the glory will be manifested on a universal scale in the people of God, the glorified community of Christ. Something of the glory is already visible:

---

[1] J. Wesley, *Journal*, i (1872 edition), pp. 76 f., footnotes.

Paul elsewhere sees a special splendour in the church as the fellowship of the reconciled, and thinks of it as being displayed even at this present time to celestial beings as God's masterpiece of reconciliation: 'that through the church the manifold wisdom of God might now be made known to the principalities and powers in the heavenly places' (Eph. 3:10). But what is now seen in a limited and distorted fashion will be seen in perfection when the people of God at last attain the goal which he has ever had in view for them – complete conformity to his glorified Son.

But it is not only the people of God that have this hope of glory. All creation, says Paul, is waiting with earnest longing for the day when the sons of God will be manifested in glory. At present, as the Preacher proclaimed, 'Vanity of vanities' is writ large over all things beneath the sun (Ec. 1:2; 12:8). But this vanity, this state of futility, frustration and bondage, is only temporary; just as humanity at present falls short of the glory of God, so creation as a whole cannot attend the full end for which it was brought into being. Like humanity, creation must be redeemed because, like humanity, creation has been subject to a fall.

The doctrine of a cosmic fall is implicit in the biblical record from Genesis 3 (where the ground is cursed for man's sake) to Revelation 22 (where the curse is finally removed); it is indeed demanded by a world-outlook which endeavours to do justice to the biblical doctrine of creation and to the facts of life as we know them. Man is part of 'nature', and the whole 'nature' of which he forms part was created good, has been involved in frustration and futility by sin, and will ultimately be redeemed. It is no accident that the redemption of 'nature' is here seen as coinciding with the redemption of man's body – that part of his being which links him with the material creation. Man was put in charge of the 'lower' creation and involved it with him when he fell; through the redemptive work of the 'second man' the entail of the fall is broken not only for man himself but for the creation which is dependent on him.

Even now man, who by selfish exploitation can turn the good earth into a dust bowl, can by responsible stewardship make the desert blossom like the rose; what then will be the effect of a completely redeemed humanity on the creation entrusted to its care? When Isaiah looked forward to the peaceful coexistence of wolf and lamb in the new age, he voiced his hope in the language of poetry, but his poetry enshrines no pathetic fallacy but something much more biblical and substantial:

> 'They shall not hurt or destroy
> in all my holy mountain;
> for the earth shall be full of the knowledge of the LORD
> as the waters cover the sea' (Is. 11:9).

The Christian will neither hold that at present 'all is for the best in the best of all possible worlds', nor will he write the world off as belonging to the devil. The world is God's world, and God will be glorified by all his works. And when the Creator is glorified, his creatures are blessed.

These words of Paul point not to the annihilation of the present material universe on the day of revelation, to be replaced by a universe entirely new, but to the transformation of the present universe so that it will fulfil the purpose for which God created it. Here again we hear the echo of an Old Testament hope – the creation of 'new heavens and a new earth in which righteousness dwells' (2 Pet. 3:13, quoting Is. 65:17; 66:22; cf. Rev. 21:1). But the transformation of the universe depends on the completion of man's transformation by the working of God's grace.

The grace of God has already begun to work in the lives of the justified; its continued working is sufficiently attested by the indwelling of the Spirit, and it is that same grace which, on 'the day of Jesus Christ', will bring to completion the work so well begun.

> 'Grace all the work shall crown
> To everlasting days;
> It lays in heaven the topmost stone,
> And well deserves the praise.'

But the indwelling of the Spirit is not only the evidence that God's grace is continually at work within believers now; it is the guarantee of their coming glory – and more than the guarantee, it is the first instalment of that glory. There is no discontinuity between here and hereafter, so far as God's working in and for his people is concerned.

If inanimate creation longs blindly for the day of its liberation, the community of the redeemed, who see the glory shining before them, strain forward intelligently for that consummation. For them it is the day when they will be publicly and universally acknowledged as the sons and daughters of God; for them, too, it is the day of resurrection, when the present body of humiliation will be transformed into the likeness of Christ's glorified body, when the whole human personality will finally experience the benefits of his redemptive work.

This is the hope of the people of God – 'Christ in you, the hope of glory', as Paul puts it in another letter (Col. 1:27). This hope is an essential element in their salvation; it enables them to accept the trials of the present, so that by patient endurance they may win their lives; it is, along with faith and love, one of the crowning graces of the Christian life.

In all the trials of the present, too, the indwelling Spirit aids by his intercession. The aspirations after holiness and glory which he creates in the lives of believers are too deep to be adequately articulated in words. At a certain stage of religious life the accurate form of words is regarded as essential to the efficacy of prayer; but when the human spirit is in closest harmony with the Spirit of God, words may not only prove inadequate; they may even hinder prayer. But God, before whom the thoughts of all are like an open book, recognizes in those unspoken 'sighs' deep in his people's hearts the voice of the Spirit interceding for them in tune with his own will, and answers them accordingly.

Indeed, God's overruling grace co-operates in all things for his people's good, even in those things which at the time are so distressing and perplexing and hard to bear. 'We know' that this is so, says Paul, speaking as one who had proved its truth in his own experience, finding, for example, that his hardships turned out for the furtherance of the gospel (Phil. 1:12) and that his sorest and most disagreeable trials were the means by which the power of Christ rested on him (2 Cor. 12:9–10).

And now he lets his mind run back and forth to survey the whole course of God's dealings with his people. Before the world's foundation God foreknew and foreordained them – foreordained them for the day of final redemption, when they would be fully conformed to the image of his Son. The Son of God is himself 'the image of the invisible God' (Col. 1:15; *cf.* 2 Cor. 4:4). God's creating mankind 'in his image' was an early step towards the accomplishment of his age-long purpose, to have creatures of his own sharing his glory as fully as it is possible for created beings to share their Creator's glory. When the image of God in the old creation was defaced by sin, so that man as he now is falls short of the glory for which he was made, the purpose of God was not frustrated. When the due time arrived, the divine image was displayed on earth in the new Man, into whose image those who are united with him by faith are progressively changed – from one degree of glory to another – until the day when, to quote another New Testament writer, they will be perfectly conformed to his likeness, because they will see him 'as he is' (1 Jn. 3:2).

18. *The sufferings of this present time are not worth comparing with the glory that is to be revealed to us.* Perhaps the idea of its being revealed 'in us' (*eis hēmās*) is also present. *Cf.* Luke 6:22–23, 'Blessed are you when men hate you . . . Rejoice in that day, and leap for joy, for behold, your reward is great in heaven.'

19. *The revealing of the sons of God.* That is, their 'adoption as sons' (verse 23), coinciding with the 'revelation' (*apokalypsis*) of the Son of God (*cf.* 1 Cor. 1:7).

20. *The creation was subjected to futility.* In addition to implying futility (frustration, vanity), *mataiotēs* can also mean the worship of false gods (*cf.* Acts 14:15); the creation has been enslaved to malignant powers (*cf.* 1 Cor. 12:2).

By the will of him who subjected it. Not Adam, or the devil, but God; only he could be said to have subjected creation to futility *in hope*. In the light of 16:20, the 'hope' may be understood as first expressed in the promise of Genesis 3:15.

21. *Because the creation itself will be set free from its bondage to decay.* RV, NEB margin, NIV take *hoti* to mean 'that' rather than 'because', making the clause the substance of the hope ('in hope that the creation itself . . .').

Obtain the glorious liberty of the children of God. They are thus the first-fruits of the redeemed creation; *cf.* James 1:18, 'Of his own will he brought us forth by the word of truth that we should be a kind of first fruits of his creatures.' Instead of 'glorious liberty' we might render, literally, 'liberty of the glory' – the glory of verse 18.

22. *The whole creation has been groaning in travail together until now.* This might be related to the current Jewish expectation of 'the birth-pangs of the Messiah' (the time of distress which would usher in the Messianic age; *cf.* Mk. 13:8, NEB 'the birth-pangs of the new age begin'). But the condition here described has apparently been going on since the fall; in any case, it carries with it the hope of new life for all creation.

23. *The first fruits of the Spirit.* The indwelling of the Spirit here and now is the 'first fruits' (*aparchē*), *i.e.* the 'first instalment' or 'initial down-payment' of the eternal heritage of glory that awaits believers. In 2 Corinthians 1:22; 5:5; Ephesians 1:14 the same teaching about the Spirit is conveyed by the use of Greek *arrhabōn*, 'earnest' or 'pledge'.

It has been suggested that some readers of the letter may have inferred from Paul's use of *aparchē* here that the possession of the Spirit is the believer's 'identification-card', since there is papyrus evidence for this sense of the word. Although that is not precisely what Paul means, they would not have been far astray if they did make this inference, as something of this sort is implied by the 'sealing' with the Spirit in 2 Corinthians 1:22; Ephesians 1:13; 4:30. For another use of the *aparchē* figure see Romans 11:16 (pp. 205f.).

Groan inwardly. Cf. 2 Corinthians 5:2, 'Here indeed we groan, and long to put on our heavenly dwelling.'

As we wait for adoption as sons, the redemption of our bodies. The 'adoption' here is the full manifestation of the status of believers when they are invested as sons and daughters of God (*cf.* verses

14–17) and enter on the inheritance which is theirs by virtue of that status. 'The redemption of our bodies' is the resurrection, a theme on which Paul had recently enlarged in 2 Corinthians 4:7 – 5:10. The same hoped-for occasion is called 'the day of redemption' in Ephesians 4:30, where believers are said to be sealed with the Spirit in view of it.

24. *In this hope we were saved.* The aorist tense (*esōthēmen*) implies that the salvation is already ours; the phrase 'in this hope' indicates that our full enjoyment of it lies in the future.

25. *If we hope for what we do not see.* Cf. 2 Corinthians 4:18, 'we look not to the things that are seen but to the things that are unseen; for the things that are seen are transient, but the things that are unseen are eternal.'

26. *The Spirit himself intercedes for us.* He is called the disciples' 'advocate' (*paraklētos*) in John 14:16, 26; 15:26; 16:7 (see also note on verse 34, below). Cf. Ephesians 6:18, 'Pray at all times in the Spirit, with all prayer and supplication.' When believers pray 'in the Spirit', the Spirit himself intercedes on their behalf. (See p. 48.)

With sighs too deep for words. 'Through our inarticulate groans' (NEB). The noun *stenagmos*, like the verb *stenazō* (used in verse 23), may denote either sighing or groaning. Speaking to God in the Spirit with 'tongues' (1 Cor. 14:2) may be included in this expression, but it covers those longings and aspirations which well up from the depths of the spirit and cannot be imprisoned within the confines of everyday words. In such prayer it is the indwelling Spirit who prays, and his mind is immediately read by the Father to whom the prayer is addressed (verse 27). Moreover, these 'inarticulate groans' cannot be dissociated from the groaning of verse 23, with which believers (together with all creation) express their longing for the coming resurrection-glory, which will consummate the answer to all their prayers. (See p. 49 with n. 1.)

27–28. *We know that in everything God works for good with those who love him.* 'We know' expresses the knowledge of faith.

Grammatically 'all things' may be either nominative (subject of 'works together'; *cf.* AV) or (as is more probable) accusative. If accusative, it is either direct object ('he works all things') or (as is again more probable) adverbial ('in everything'). RSV transfers the noun 'God' from its textual position as object after 'love' to an earlier point where it is made subject of 'works'. Some ancient witnesses (including P⁴⁶) read 'God' in both positions (*cf.* RV mg., 'to them that love God God worketh all things with them for good'); this makes the construction excessively heavy. NEB happily revives an ancient and attractive interpretation which has in general received little attention from translators and commentators, according to which the subject of 'works' is the subject of the previous clause – the Spirit. Its rendering, then (taking verses 27b and 28a closely together) is: '. . . he pleads for God's people in God's own way; and in everything, as we know, he co-operates for good with those who love God.'[1] (*Cf.* 1 Cor. 2:9 for the blessings prepared for those who love God.)

Who are called according to his purpose. They are 'called', not in the general sense in which 'many are called, but few are chosen', but in the sense of that 'effectual calling' which is 'the work of God's Spirit, whereby, convincing us of our sin and misery, enlightening our minds in the knowledge of Christ, and renewing our wills, he doth persuade and enable us to embrace Jesus Christ, freely offered to us in the gospel.'[2] *Cf.* 1:6 ('called to belong to Jesus Christ'); 1:7 ('called to be saints'); 9:11 ('because of his call').

29. *For those whom he foreknew he also predestined.* God's fore-knowledge here connotes that electing grace which is frequently implied by the verb 'to know' in the Old Testament. When God takes knowledge of people in this special way, he sets his choice on them. *Cf.* Amos 3:2 ('You only have I known of all the families of the earth'); Hosea 13:5 ('It was I who knew you in the wilderness'). We may compare Paul's language in 1 Corinthians 8:3 ('if one loves God, one is known by him'); Galatians

---

[1] *Cf.* M. Black, 'The Interpretation of Romans viii.28', *Neotestamentica et Patristica* (O. Cullmann *Freundesgabe*) = *Supplement to Novum Testamentum* 6 (1962), pp. 166–172.
[2] *Westminster Shorter Catechism*, Answer to Question 31.

4:9 ('you have come to know God, or rather to be known by God'). This aspect of the divine knowledge is emphasized also in the Qumran *Rule of the Community*: 'From the God of Knowledge comes all that is and shall be. Before ever they existed He established their whole design, and when, as ordained for them, they come into being, it is in accord with His glorious design that they fulfil their work.'[1]

To be conformed to the image of his Son, in order that he might be the first-born among many brethren. The new creation, the community of men and women conformed to the image of Christ, who is himself the image of God (2 Cor. 4:4; Col. 1:15), is seen to have been from the beginning the object of God's foreknowledge and foreordaining mercy. The fulfilment of this purpose is involved, for New Testament writers, in the creative words of Genesis 1:26, 'Let us make man in our image, after our likeness.' The old creation in itself is insufficient for the realization of this goal; it requires the redemptive work of Christ and his consequent status as head of the new creation. He who is 'the first-born of all creation' in the old order because 'all things were created through him and for him' is also by resurrection the head of a new order, 'the beginning, the first-born from the dead' (Col. 1:15–18). His 'many brethren' are, by the new birth, heirs of eternal life in him.

30. *Those whom he predestined he also called; and those whom he called he also justified.* The people of God respond to his call in faith, and by faith they are justified.

And those whom he justified he also glorified. The glorifying of God's people forms the climax of the 'sorites' – the literary construction employed in verses 29 and 30, in which the logical predicate of one clause becomes the logical subject of the next. More importantly, it forms the climax of the divine purpose; it involves their ultimate and complete conformity to the image of Christ. 'When Christ who is our life appears, then you also will appear with him in glory' (Col. 3:4; *cf.* 1 Jn. 3:2).

This, then, is the purpose of God's gracious predestination – the creation of a new race sharing and displaying the Creator's

---

[1] G. Vermes, *The Dead Sea Scrolls in English* (1962), p. 75.

glory (*cf.* 5:2). The successive stages in the accomplishment are set out clause by clause. The foreknowing and foreordaining belong to God's eternal counsel; the calling and the justifying have taken place in his people's experience; but the glory, so far as their experience is concerned, lies in the future. Why then does Paul use the same aorist tense for this as he uses for the other acts of God? Perhaps he is imitating the Hebrew use of the 'prophetic past', by which a predicted event is marked out as so certain of fulfilment that it is described as though it had already taken place.[1] As a matter of history, the people of God have not yet been glorified; so far as the divine decree is concerned, however, their glory has been determined from all eternity, hence – 'those whom he justified he also glorified.'

Why does Paul move directly here from justification to glory, without saying anything about the Christian's present experience of sanctification by the power of the Spirit? Partly, no doubt, because the coming glory has been in the forefront of his mind; but even more because the difference between sanctification and glory is one of degree only, not one of kind. Sanctification is progressive conformity to the mind or image of Christ here and now (*cf.* 2 Cor. 3:18; Col. 3:10); glory is perfect conformity to the image of Christ there and then. Sanctification is glory begun; glory is sanctification consummated. Paul looks forward to the consummation of the work of grace – a consummation guaranteed by its inception: 'he who began a good work in you will bring it to completion at the day of Jesus Christ' (Phil. 1:6).

3. The triumph of faith (8:31–39)

Could there be any stronger encouragement to faith than the contemplation of God's saving purpose for his people, moving forward to its predestined consummation? Since God is their strong salvation, what force can prevail against them? Since his love was supremely manifested in the sacrifice of his own Son on their behalf, what good thing will he withhold from them? Paul for a moment envisages the situation in terms of a court of justice, where the believer stands to be judged. But who will

---

[1] A similar use of the Greek aorist indicative to denote a future event is found in Jude 14 (quoting a Greek version of 1 Enoch 1:9): 'Behold, the Lord came with his holy myriads.'

dare to come forward as prosecutor? God himself, the Judge of all, has pronounced acquittal and justification; who can call his sentence in question? The prosecutor may not venture to appear, but counsel for the defence is present and active: the Christ who died and rose again is enthroned at God's right hand, making prevalent intercession for his people. Nothing can come between them and his love – not all the trials and afflictions which they have experienced or may yet experience. In the spiritual conflict mighty forces, supernatural as well as natural, are arrayed against them, but through him they overcome them all and remain irrevocably encircled and empowered by his unchanging love.

32. *He who did not spare his own Son.* An echo of Genesis 22:12, 15, where God says to Abraham, 'you have not withheld [LXX 'spared', Gk. *pheidomai*, as here] your son, your only son.' The 'binding of Isaac' (the title traditionally given by Jews to the narrative of Gn. 22:1–19) probably plays a greater part in Paul's thinking about the sacrifice of Christ than appears on the surface.[1] In Jewish interpretation it is treated as the classic example of the redemptive efficacy of martyrdom.

Will he not also give us all things with him? Cf. Matthew 6:33, 'all these things shall be yours as well.'

33–34. *It is God who justifies; who is to condemn?* In the forensic language of this passage we catch an unmistakable echo of the challenge of the Servant of the Lord in Isaiah 50:8–9, 'He who vindicates me is near. Who will contend with me? Let us stand up together. Who is my adversary? Let him come near to me. Behold, the Lord GOD helps me; who will declare me guilty?' When God enters into judgment, the outlook for the opposing party is bleak (Rom. 3:4); but if God takes the side of the defendant, no amount of evidence for the prosecution can procure an adverse verdict. A good Old Testament illustration is the silence of Satan, chief prosecutor in the heavenly court,

---

[1] *Cf.* H. J. Schoeps, *Paul*, E.T. (1961), pp. 141–149; L. Morris, *The Cross in the New Testament* (1965), p. 39, n. 62; p. 138, n. 67; N. A. Dahl, 'The Atonement – An Adequate Return for the Akedah? (Ro 8:32)', in *Neotestamentica et Semitica: Studies in Honour of Matthew Black*, ed. E. E. Ellis and M. Wilcox (1969), pp. 15–29.

when God declares his acceptance of Joshua the high priest (Zc. 3:1–5).

34. *Who is at the right hand of God.* An echo of Psalm 110: 1, 'The LORD says to my lord: "Sit at my right hand, till I make your enemies your footstool." ' These words, whose Messianic reference was apparently accepted by Jewish scribes of our Lord's time (*cf.* Mk. 12:35–37), were applied to Jesus from the earliest days of the church, and form the biblical foundation of the doctrine of his exaltation and session at the Father's right hand – that is, in the place of supremacy over the universe.

> 'But one day, as I was passing in the field, and that too with some dashes on my conscience, fearing lest yet all was not right, suddenly this sentence fell upon my soul, "Thy righteousness is in heaven"; and methought withal, I saw, with the eyes of my soul, Jesus Christ at God's right hand; there, I say, is my righteousness; so that wherever I was, or whatever I was a-doing, God could not say of me, "He wants my righteousness", for that was just before him. I also saw, moreover, that it was not my good frame of heart that made my righteousness better, nor yet my bad frame that made my righteousness worse; for my righteousness was Jesus Christ Himself, the same yesterday, and today, and for ever.'[1]

Who indeed intercedes for us. An echo of the fourth Servant Song (Is. 52:13 – 53:12): the Servant 'made intercession for the transgressors' (Is. 53:12; see note on Rom. 4:25, p. 113). The Targum of Jonathan speaks of the Servant-Messiah as making entreaty for trespasses not only in Isaiah 53:12 but also in verses 4 and 11. So believers have an intercessor or 'advocate' with the Father (*cf.* 1 Jn. 2:1) as well as an intercessor here (verse 27).

36. *As it is written, 'For thy sake we are being killed all the day long; we are regarded as sheep to be slaughtered.'* A quotation from Psalm 44:22, a plea to God for speedy aid in a time of sore distress for Israel.

---

[1] John Bunyan, *Grace Abounding*, § 229.

37. *In all these things.* Possibly a Hebraism, meaning 'despite all these things', 'for all that'.

We are more than conquerors. Greek *hypernikōmen,* 'we are super-conquerors.'

38. *Nor principalities, . . . nor powers.* The principalities and powers are the forces of evil in the universe, the 'spiritual hosts of wickedness in the heavenly places' of Ephesians 6:12. It may be that not all principalities and powers are hostile, but if any are well-disposed, they would not attempt to separate believers from the love of Christ.

Nor things present, nor things to come. Perhaps a reference to the two ages (this age and the coming one); but 'things to come' may well include hazards yet to be experienced in this mortal life.

39. *Nor height, nor depth.* 'Height' and 'depth' were technical terms in astrology, and later in Gnosticism. Paul need not have had their technical significance in mind; but if he had, they would be closely associated with the *principalities* and *powers* that were believed to control the movements of the heavenly bodies, especially the planets, and thus to control the destinies of mortals. But fate, whether real or imaginary, has no power over those whose 'life is hid with Christ in God' (Col. 3:3). Nothing in the course of time, nor in the expanses of space, nothing in the whole universe can sever the children of God from their Father's love, secured to them in Christ.

V. HUMAN UNBELIEF AND DIVINE GRACE (9:1 – 11:36)

A. THE PROBLEM OF ISRAEL'S UNBELIEF (9:1–5)

To many modern readers chapters 9 – 11 form a parenthesis in the course of Paul's argument. Had he proceeded straight from 8:39 to 12:1, we should have been conscious of no hiatus in his reasoning. He has just pointed forward to the culmination of God's purpose of grace, the glory that is to be revealed in the children of God. What more can he say than press home on his readers their responsibility to live in this world as befits heirs of the glory to come? If 'I appeal to you therefore' (12:1) came in at this point, we should be quite ready for it.

Not so Paul. The problem with which he proceeds to grapple was one of intense personal concern to him. He gloried in his ministry as apostle to the Gentiles, and rejoiced in their salvation. But his own kith and kin, the Jewish nation, had for the most part failed to accept the salvation proclaimed in the gospel, even though it was presented to them first. What then? Should they simply be written off as 'unworthy of eternal life' (Acts 13:46)? No indeed: they were his own people, and he neither would nor could dissociate himself from them. He too, like so many of them, had once opposed the gospel, but he had been arrested by the risen Jesus and set on the Christian way. How he longed that they too might have the scales removed from their eyes! Indeed, if their salvation could be purchased by his own damnation, right readily would he consent, if such a thing were possible, to be 'anathema from Christ' for their sakes. The ingathering of the Gentiles, no matter on how extensive a scale, could never compensate for the defection of his nation, which caused him such unceasing mental anguish.

He takes up the subject too, we may infer, because the situation in the Roman church required it. The original believers in Rome appear to have been Jews, but by this time they were becoming outnumbered by Gentiles. There was perhaps a tendency on the part of some of the Gentile Christians to think of their Jewish brethren as poor relations, mercifully rescued from an apostate nation but inhibited by a respect for outmoded customs. The tendency on the part of some at least of the Jewish Christians might be to resent Gentile aspersions on their fellow-Jews and to stress their continued solidarity with them, to a point where they were in danger of underestimating those distinctive features of Christian faith and life which forged a bond between them and their Gentile brethren in the Lord stronger than the bond which bound them to their Jewish brethren in the flesh. (It may well be that we meet a later stage of this tendency in the letter to the Hebrews.) Paul appreciated

the wisdom of showing both sides something of the part
played by both Jews and Gentiles in the saving purpose of
God.

But, above all else, a real problem in theodicy was involved.
The present situation called in question the whole exposition of
the gospel set out in the foregoing chapters. It was of the
essence of Paul's argument that the gospel which he (and his
fellow-apostles) preached was no innovation. It was attested in
the Hebrew Scriptures; it was the fulfilment of God's promise
to the patriarchs; it proclaimed that God's way of righteousness
through faith, by which Abraham had been blessed, was still
open to all who believed in God as Abraham did. How came
it, then, that it was pre-eminently Abraham's descendants who
declined to believe the gospel? Surely, had Paul's claims been
valid, the Jewish people would have been the first to acknowledge them? Such objections were no doubt voiced, and Paul
could appreciate their force, although he was well aware of the
fallacy which they involved. Yet it was a paradox, not to say a
scandal, that the very nation which had been specially prepared
by God for this time of fulfilment, the nation which could glory
in so many unique privileges of divine grace (including above
all the Messianic hope), the nation into which in due course
the Messiah had been born, should have failed to recognize
him when he came, while men and women of other nations
which had never enjoyed such privileges embraced the gospel
eagerly the first time they heard it. How could this be harmon-
ized with God's choice of Israel and his declared purpose of
blessing the world through Israel?

In the next three chapters (9 – 11), then, Paul wrestles with
this problem. This was not the first time that he had done so;
the contents of these chapters are the fruit of many years of
thought and prayer on his part, no doubt. It has indeed been
suggested that the three chapters existed already as a separate
treatise, but this is doubtful. It seems plain that, as Paul dictates
to Tertius, he wrestles with the problem afresh, pressing
towards a solution now along this road and now along that,
until at last he emerges into the full light of the wisdom of
God's overruling grace. He begins with one statement of God's
ways in election and ends with another, but at the end he sees

farther into the character and aim of the divine election than he did at the outset. He begins with the particular problem of Jewish resistance to the gospel, and ends with an unfolding of 'the divine purpose in history'[1] which in some ways goes beyond any comparable passage in the whole Bible.

The first two answers that he gives to the problem are:

i. This is how it has come about in the unchallengeable ordering of God's sovereign choice (9:6–29).

ii. Human responsibility also comes into the picture: Israel's resistance to the gospel follows the precedent repeatedly set throughout her history; 'disobedient and contrary' she had always been in face of God's overtures (9:30 – 10:21).

These are followed by two more, which are fraught with greater promise:

iii. The fact that a 'remnant' of Israel has already believed the gospel is the token that, in God's purpose, Israel as a whole will yet do so (11:1–16).

iv. If Israel's present rejection of the gospel has been the occasion of so much blessing for the Gentiles, Israel's future acceptance of the gospel will usher in the day of world-wide regeneration (11:17–32).

1. *My conscience bears me witness in the Holy Spirit.* A further example of the Spirit's consentient witness with the believer's spirit (*cf.* 8:15–16). For 'conscience' see note on 2:15 (p. 86).

3. *I could wish that I myself were accursed and cut off from Christ.* 'Accursed and cut off' renders the single Greek word *anathema.* Paul's wish recalls Moses' prayer after the incident of the golden calf: 'But now, if thou wilt forgive their sin – and if not, blot me, I pray thee, out of thy book which thou hast written' (Ex. 32:32). But whereas Moses refuses to survive if his people perish, Paul could almost welcome perdition for himself if it meant salvation for Israel. 'I could wish' (better, 'I could pray',

---

[1] The heading given to Romans 9 – 11 in C. H. Dodd's commentary and in NEB. William Manson entitles them 'The Righteousness of God in History' (*New Testament Essays in Memory of T. W. Manson*, ed. A. J. B. Higgins, 1959, p. 164) – which brings out even better their integrity with the main theme of the letter as a whole. See also H. L. Ellison, *The Mystery of Israel* (1966); J. Munck, *Christ and Israel*, E.T. (1967); W. D. Davies, 'Paul and the People of Israel', *Jewish and Pauline Studies* (1984), pp. 123–152.

imperfect of *euchomai*) implies the unexpressed protasis, 'if such a thing were possible.'

4. *To them belong the sonship.* The people of Israel are called collectively the 'son' of God (Ex. 4:22–23; Ho. 11:1) or individually his 'sons' (Ho. 1:10).

The glory. The Shekinah of God, the token of his dwelling among them, *e.g.* in the Mosaic tabernacle (Ex. 40:34) and in Solomon's temple (1 Ki. 8:10–11).

The covenants. There is weighty evidence (P 46, B, D, *etc.*) for the singular reading 'the covenant', in which case the covenant at Sinai (Ex. 24:8) would be meant. But the plural is probably to be preferred (*cf.* Eph. 2:12); 'the covenants' will then include those made by God with Abraham (Gn. 15:18; 17:4–21), with Israel in the days of Moses (Ex. 24:8; 34:10; Dt. 29:1 ff.) and Joshua (Dt. 27:2 ff.; Jos. 8:30 ff.; 24:25), and with David (2 Sa. 23:5; Ps. 89: 28); not to mention the new covenant, promised in the first instance to 'the house of Israel and the house of Judah' (Je. 31:31).

The giving of the law. The Mosaic legislation (Ex. 20:1 ff.).

The worship. The prescriptions for the cultus (*latreia*), especially those in the book of Leviticus, on which the temple ceremonial at Jerusalem was still based when Paul was dictating these words.

And the promises. Including the Messianic promises, God's 'steadfast, sure love for David' (Is. 55:3; *cf.* Acts 13:23, 32–34); but a special place must be given to the promise to Abraham and his offspring, which is basic to the receiving of God's righteousness through faith (4:13–21).

5. *To them belong the patriarchs.* Abraham, Isaac, Jacob and his twelve sons, the primary recipients of the promises just mentioned.

Of their race, according to the flesh, is the Christ. Compare the affirmation of Christ's Davidic descent in 1:3, and the later statement that 'Christ became a servant to the circumcised to show God's truthfulness, in order to confirm the promises given to the patriarchs' (15:8). In him all God's promises to Israel reach their consummation.

God who is over all be blessed for ever. The relation of these
words to those which precede is disputed. RSV takes them as
an independent ascription of praise to God, prompted by the
mention of God's crowning his many blessings on Israel by
sending them the Messiah (similarly NEB, GNB). They may be
taken, on the other hand, as in apposition to 'the Christ'; so
RSV margin: 'who is God over all, blessed for ever' (similarly
AV, RV, NIV).

The latter construction is more in keeping with the general
structure of the sentence (*cf*. 1:25, where the words 'who is
blessed for ever! Amen' are not an independent ascription of
praise but the integral peroration of the sentence, standing
in apposition to 'the Creator'). It is further supported by the
consideration that something is required to balance the phrase
'according to the flesh' (as in 1:3–4, where the same phrase is
balanced by 'according to the Spirit of holiness'). Here the
Messiah is said, with regard to his human descent, to have
come of a long line of Israelite ancestors; but as regards his
eternal being, he is 'God over all, blessed for ever'.

It is true that Paul is not in the habit of calling Christ 'God';
he reserves for him the title 'Lord': 'for us there is one God,
the Father, from whom are all things and for whom we exist,
and one Lord, Jesus Christ, through whom are all things and
through whom we exist' (1 Cor. 8:6). Yet for Paul Christ is the
one in whom, through whom and for whom all things were
created (Col. 1:16), in whom 'the whole fulness of deity dwells
bodily' (Col. 2:9). 'The judgment seat of God' (14:10) is called
in 2 Corinthians 5:10 'the judgment seat of Christ'. Moreover,
when Paul gives Jesus the title 'Lord', he does so because God
the Father has bestowed this title on him as 'the name which
is above every name' (Phil. 2:9). This title 'Lord' is given to
Jesus by Paul as the equivalent of Yahweh; his application of
Isaiah 45:23 (*cf*. Rom. 14:11) to Jesus in Philippians 2:10–11
indicates that to him the confession 'Jesus Christ is Lord' is
equivalent to 'Jesus Christ is Yahweh'.

It is, on the other hand, impermissible to charge those who
prefer to treat the words as an independent doxology with
Christological unorthodoxy. The words can indeed be so
treated, and the decision about their construction involves a

delicate assessment of the balance of probability this way and that.[1]

Amen. A proper conclusion to doxological language (*cf.* 1:25; 11:36; Gal. 1:5; Eph. 3:21; Phil. 4:20; 1 Tim. 1:17; 6:16; 2 Tim. 4:18). In addition, it forms a fitting conclusion here to the very positive catalogue of Israel's ancestral blessings (including, be it noted, 'the giving of the law') – a fuller answer to the question 'what advantage has the Jew?' (Rom. 3:1) than it received in its immediate context. Such a positive catalogue (which may also have been called for by the Jewish-Gentile situation in the Roman church) emphasizes the seriousness of the problem which Paul is about to propound.

B. GOD'S SOVEREIGN CHOICE (9:6–29)

Has God's plan gone awry? No indeed, says Paul. The present condition of Israel reproduces a pattern of divine action and human response which has been unfolded often enough in the past. Some have always opened their hearts to God's revelation, while others have hardened theirs; and by the variety of their response they have shown whether or not they were among those on whom God had set his sovereign choice.

Paul has already pointed out (2:28–29) that the true Jew is the one whose life brings forth praise to God, that natural descent and physical circumcision are not the things that matter most. Now he points out in similar vein that not all the descendants of Israel are Israelites in the inward sense, that not all the descendants of Abraham are 'children of Abraham' in the spiritual sense which has been explained in chapter 4. Throughout Old Testament history God's purpose was handed down through an inner group, an elect minority, a saving remnant. Abraham had a number of sons, but only through one of them, Isaac, the child of promise, was the line of God's promise to be traced. Isaac in his turn had two sons, but only through one of

---

[1] For the construction preferred here see O. Cullmann, *The Christology of the New Testament*, E.T. (1959), pp. 312 f.; J. Munck, *Christ and Israel*, E.T. (1967), pp. 32 f.; B. M. Metzger, *New Testament Studies* (1980), pp. 57–74. For the other see V. Taylor, *The Person of Christ in New Testament Teaching* (1958), pp. 55–57; E. Käsemann, *ad loc.*

them, Jacob, was the holy seed transmitted. And God's choice of Jacob and passing over of his brother Esau did not in the least depend on the behaviour or character of the twin brothers; he had declared it in advance before they were born.

So today, Paul implies, when some receive the light and others do not, the divine election may be discerned, operating antecedently to the will or activity of those who are its objects. If God does not reveal the principles on which he makes his choice, that is no reason why his justice should be called in question. He is merciful and compassionate because such is his will. 'The quality of mercy is not strained', and least of all when it is God who shows mercy; for if he were compelled to be merciful by some cause outside himself, not only would his mercy be so much the less mercy, but he himself would be so much the less God.

Nor is it only in his dealings with the 'chosen seed of Israel's race' that this principle operates. It can be seen in the Exodus story of his dealings with the king of Egypt, who stubbornly and repeatedly refused to let Israel go. Why did God endure Pharaoh's obstinacy so long? He supplies the answer himself: 'for this purpose have I let you live, to show you my power, so that my name may be declared throughout all the earth' (Ex. 9:16). All the recalcitrance and rebellion of a man like Pharaoh will never avail to thwart the purpose of God; God's glory will triumph, whether man obeys or not.

Well, the retort comes, if God foreordains people's ways by his own will, why does he blame them for their ways? They do not oppose his will; they act in accordance with it.

'My good sir,' is Paul's reply, 'who are you to answer back to God?' And he takes up the analogy of a potter and his pots, which came as readily to Hebrew prophets as it did to Omar Khayyam. Jeremiah learnt a lesson about God's dealings with his people the day he went down to the potter's house and saw how the potter moulded the clay as he saw fit, squeezing a vessel that had gone wrong into a shapeless lump so as to make a new vessel out of it again (Je. 18:1–10).

It may be granted that the analogy of a potter and his pots covers one aspect only of the Creator's relation to those whom he has created, especially to human beings, created in his own image. Pots are not made in the potter's image, and they do not in any case answer him back or find fault with his workmanship. But there are different ways of answering him back. There is the answering back of faith, as when a Job or a Jeremiah calls out for an account of God's mysterious ways with him. Even the Christ on the cross could cry, 'why hast thou forsaken me?' But when the man or woman of faith cries out like this, it is from a fundamental conviction that God is all-righteous as well as all-powerful. There is, on the other hand, the answering back of unbelief and disobedience, when an attempt is made to put God in the dock and sit in judgment on him. It is the person who adopts this attitude whom Paul, like Isaiah, rebukes so sternly and reminds of his creaturely status.

'Woe to him who strives with his Maker,
  an earthen vessel with the potter!
Does the clay say to him who fashions it, "What are you
  making?"
or "Your work has no handles"?' (Is. 45:9).

Paul has been misunderstood and unjustly criticized through failure to recognize that it is the God-defying rebel and not the bewildered seeker after God whose mouth he so peremptorily shuts. God, in his grace, does abide his people's question, but he will not be cross-examined at the judgment bar of a hard and impenitent heart.

Suppose that God wishes to display his righteous judgment and his power, says Paul, why should he not bear patiently with people like Pharaoh – pots (to carry on the metaphor) fashioned to be object-lessons of his wrath, fit only to be destroyed? And why should he not display the greatness of his glory by means of other 'pots' which are to be the object-lessons of his mercy, prepared in advance for this glorious purpose? Paul, more cautious than some of his systematizers, does not say outright that God does this, but asks, 'What if he does so? Who will bring him to book?'

While Paul will allow no questioning of God's right to do what he will with his own, he lets his emphasis fall, not on God's wrath towards the reprobate, but rather on the postponement of his wrath against those who have long since become ripe for destruction. As has been pointed out earlier (2:4), the mercy and forbearance of God are intended to afford people time for repentance; if, instead, they harden their hearts yet more, as Pharaoh did after repeated respites, they are simply storing up an increasing weight of retribution for themselves against the day of requital.

In some schools of theological thought, unfortunately, the doctrine of election has been formulated too much on the basis of this preliminary stage in Paul's present argument, without adequate account being taken of his further exposition of God's purpose in election at the conclusion of the argument (11:25–32). Yet this stage of his argument is undeniably in line with well-known facts of life which present a problem for any theodicy. Some people have better spiritual opportunities than others; and of those who have equal opportunities some profit by them and others do not. Some nations have received more gospel light than others, and are correspondingly accountable to God. Men and women who have experienced the forgiving grace of God will always wonder why their eyes should have been opened while the eyes of others remain closed.

The point on which Paul insists here is that all are guilty before God; no-one has a claim on his grace. If he chooses to extend his grace to some, the others have no ground for arguing that he is unjust because he does not extend it to them. If it is justice they demand, they can have it, but –

> 'Though justice be thy plea, consider this,
> That in the course of justice, none of us
> Should see salvation.'[1]

In point of fact, as appears with blessed clarity later in Paul's argument, God's grace is far wider than anyone could have dared to hope; but just because it is grace, no-one is entitled to it, and no-one can demand that God should give an account of the reasons for which he bestows his grace, or that he should bestow it otherwise than in fact he does. Grace in its sovereignty

---

[1] Shakespeare, *The Merchant of Venice*, Act 4, Scene 1.

may impose conditions, but it cannot be made subject to them.

But God delights to show mercy, and he has lavished it on men and women beyond counting – from Gentiles and Jews alike. The fact that Gentiles as well as Jews are among those whom he has called and marked out for glory is illustrated by quotations from the prophet Hosea.

For centuries the Gentiles had been looked upon by the chosen people, with but few exceptions, as 'vessels of wrath made for destruction'; and certainly God had 'endured' them 'with much patience'. But now the purpose of his patience was made plain: what he desired was not their doom but their salvation.

And if Israel at present had to such a large extent turned away from God, yet the same pattern of divine action would be reproduced among them too. Here Paul calls on Isaiah as witness to his hope.

In a day of widespread national apostasy Isaiah saw that judgment would fall on Israel and Judah on such a scale that only a handful, the merest 'remnant', would survive. Yet in this remnant he saw the hope of the future embodied; God's purposes and promises to his people Israel, and through them to other nations, would not be frustrated, provided a remnant emerged from the crucible of invasion, defeat and exile, to become the nucleus of a new and purified Israel. The 'saved' remnant would thus be also a 'saving' remnant.

This remnant Paul sees embodied anew in that minority of Jews who, like himself, had acknowledged Jesus as Lord; a minority they might be, but their existence was a guarantee of a wholesale turning to the Lord on a day to come. This hope is developed more fully later (in chapter 11); meanwhile, he turns his attention to another reason for the bestowal of gospel blessings for the present on Gentiles rather than Jews.

7. *'Through Isaac shall your descendants be named.'* A quotation from Genesis 21:12, where God tells Abraham not to oppose Sarah's demand for the expulsion of Hagar and Ishmael, because his descendants are to be reckoned through Isaac, and not through Ishmael – although Ishmael too will be the ancestor of a nation, 'because he is your offspring' (Gn. 21:13).

8. *It is not the children of the flesh who are the children of God, but the children of the promise are reckoned as descendants.* The 'children of the promise' in Paul's exegesis are those who, like Abraham, believe the promise of God and are therefore Abraham's spiritual offspring. Compare 4:11–18, and also the 'allegory' which Paul draws out of the Isaac-Ishmael narrative in Galatians 4:22–31.

9. *'About this time I will return and Sarah shall have a son.'* A quotation from Genesis 18:10, 'I will surely return to you in the spring, and Sarah your wife shall have a son.' This was the 'promise' in accordance with which Isaac was born – the promise which provoked Sarah to laughter (Gn. 18:12; *cf.* 21:6).

11. *Not because of works but because of his call.* Cf. 8:28 for the 'call' which is in accordance with God's purpose.

12. *'The elder will serve the younger.'* From the birth oracle to Rebekah (Gn. 25:23). The prophecy relates not to the individuals Esau and Jacob (for Esau never rendered service to Jacob) but to their descendants; it relates to the long periods during which the Edomites were in servitude to Israel or Judah (*cf.* 2 Sa. 8:14; 1 Ki. 22:47; 2 Ki. 14:7; *etc.*).

13. *'Jacob I loved, but Esau I hated.'* From Malachi 1:2–3, where again the context indicates it is the nations Israel and Edom, rather than their individual ancestors Jacob and Esau, that are in view. The way in which communities can be so freely spoken of in terms of their ancestors is an example of the common oscillation in biblical (and especially Old Testament) thought and speech between individual and corporate personality (*cf.* exposition of 5:12–21, p. 120, n. 1). Israel was the elect nation, and Edom incurred the wrath of God for its unbrotherly conduct towards Israel in the day of Israel's calamity (*cf.* Ps. 137:7; Is. 34:5 ff.; Je. 49:7 ff.; Ezk. 25:12 ff.; 35:1 ff.; Ob. 10 ff.).

15. *'I will have mercy on whom I have mercy, and I will have compassion on whom I have compassion.'* Quoted from Exodus 33:19, where God replies to Moses' request to let him see his glory, after Moses' intercession for the Israelites because of their worship of the golden calf (*cf.* note on verse 3, p. 174). The force of the words is that the mercy and compassion of God cannot be subject to any cause outside his own free grace. (These, incidentally, are the two primary divine attributes in the Qur'ān: 'In the name of God, the Compassionate, the Merciful.')

16. *It depends not upon man's will or exertion, but upon God's mercy.* Again it is emphasized that God's mercy has its cause in himself, and not in human will or activity. 'Exertion' is literally 'running', used of vigorous action, as also in Galatians 2:2; Philippians 2:16, where the reference is to Paul's apostolic energy.

17. *The scripture says to Pharaoh.* 'The scripture' (here Ex. 9:16) is practically personified here as a surrogate for the name of God, who is the actual speaker. *Cf.* Galatians 3:8, 'the scripture . . . preached the gospel beforehand to Abraham' (a reference to the divine promise of Gn. 12:3). The Pharaoh is the Pharaoh of the Exodus (successor to the 'Pharaoh of the oppression' whose death is noted in Ex. 2:23).
'*I have raised you up.* . . .' The Hebrew uses the causative conjugation of the verb '*āmad*, lit. 'I made you stand', which Paul renders by the verb *exegeirō*, 'raise up'. LXX renders 'you were preserved'. The preference may be not only to God's raising up Pharaoh to be king, but to his patience in preserving him alive for so long, in spite of his disobedience.
'. . . *for the very purpose of showing my power in you, so that my name may be proclaimed in all the earth.*' *Cf.* Exodus 15:14–15; Joshua 2:10–11; 9:9; 1 Samuel 4:8, for the effect produced on other nations by the news of the Exodus and attendant events.

18. *So then he has mercy upon whomever he wills, and he hardens the heart of whomever he wills.* The first part of this verse is a further echo of Exodus 33:19 (*cf.* verse 15 above); the second part refers to the occasions on which God is said to 'harden' the hearts of Pharaoh and the Egyptians (Ex. 7:3; 9:12; 14:4, 17).

20. *Will what is moulded say to its moulder, 'Why have you made* *me thus?'* See, in addition to Isaiah 45:9, quoted above (p. 179), Isaiah 29:16:

> 'Shall the potter be regarded as the clay;
> that the thing made should say of its maker,
>   "He did not make me";
> or the thing formed say of him who formed it,
>   "He has no understanding"?'

God is not answerable to us for what he does. Yet he can be relied on to act in consistency with his character, which has been disclosed supremely in Christ. With such a God to trust, why should any of his people question his ways?

21. *One vessel for beauty and another for menial use.* Cf. 2 Timothy 2:20, where, however, the vessels are made of various materials, and those which are for 'ignoble' use are designed for less ornamental (but not necessarily less serviceable) purposes than those which are 'for noble use'. Parallels to Paul's present analogy from the potter's diverse products are found in Wisdom 15:7; Ecclesiasticus 33:10–13.

22. *The vessels of wrath made for destruction.* Not the instruments of his wrath by which he works destruction (*cf.* Is. 13:5; 54:16; Je. 50:25), but objects of his wrath, whose 'end is destruction' (Phil. 3:19).

25–26. *'Those who were not my people I will call "my people", and her who was not beloved I will call "my beloved".'* A free rendering of Hosea 2:23, 'I will have pity on Not pitied, and I will say to Not my people, "You are my people".' The Hosea prophecy came into general use in the early church as a *testimonium* of the Gentile mission; compare the similar application of Hosea 2:23 to Gentile Christians in 1 Peter 2:10.

Hosea learnt to see in the tragedy of his domestic life a parable of the relation between God and Israel. When he married Gomer the daughter of Diblaim and she in due course gave birth to a son, he acknowledged the child as his and named him Jezreel. But her second and third children, he was convinced, were not his, and the names he gave them expressed his disillusionment – Lo-ruhamah ('one for whom no natural affection is felt') and Lo-ammi ('no kin of mine'). These names betokened God's attitude to his people Israel, who had broken their covenant-loyalty to him – Lo-ruhamah ('not the object of my affection, or pity') and Lo-ammi ('not my people'). But, for old time's sake, God will not allow this broken relationship to remain so for ever; he looks forward to a day when those who at present are not his people will once more be his people, and when those who at present have no claim on his kindly feelings will once more be the objects of his compassion.

What Paul does here is to take this promise, which referred to a situation within the frontiers of the chosen people, and extract from it a principle of divine action which in his day was reproducing itself on a world-wide scale. In large measure through Paul's own apostolic ministry, great numbers of Gentiles, who had never been 'the people of God' and had no claim on his covenant mercy, were coming to be enrolled among his people and to be the recipients of his mercy. The scale of the divine action was far wider than in Hosea's day, but the same pattern and principle were recognizable. Through the Gentile mission, in lands where the people of God had once been unrepresented, there were now many believers who were acknowledged as *sons of the living God* (verse 26, quoted from Ho. 1:10).

27. *'Though the number of the sons of Israel be as the sand of the sea, only a remnant of them will be saved.'* Quoted from Isaiah 10:22a. The plain meaning of these words is that, numerous as Israel may be, only a remnant, a small minority, will survive the impending judgment (in which God will use the Assyrians as his agents) and return from exile. But if *only* a remnant will survive, *at least* a remnant will survive and constitute the hope of restoration. Not only will the remnant return from exile, but 'a remnant will return, the remnant of Jacob, to the mighty God' (Is. 10:21). This recurring theme of Isaiah's prophecy was given as a name to his elder son Shear-jashub ('Remnant will return'), who was thus a living 'sign' to the people of the truth of God's message given through his father (Is. 7:3; 8:18). Paul applies the 'remnant doctrine' of Isaiah to the religious situation of his own day here, and again in 11:5.

28. *For the Lord will execute his sentence upon the earth with rigour and dispatch.* An abridgement of Isaiah 10:23, following on from the quotation in the previous verse.

29. *'If the Lord of hosts had not left us children, we would have fared like Sodom and been made like Gomorrah.'* Quoted from Isaiah 1:9. In a time of acute peril for Judah and Jerusalem under the Assyrian invasion, Isaiah uses this language, meaning in effect: 'If God had not spared a remnant among us ("the mere germ of a nation", NEB), we should have been wiped out as completely as Sodom and Gomorrah' (*cf.* Gn. 19:24). Paul, following LXX, says 'the Lord of Sabaoth', leaving Heb. *ṣᵉḇā'ōṯ* ('hosts', 'armies') untranslated (*cf.* Jas. 5:4).

C. HUMAN RESPONSIBILITY (9:30 – 10:21)

1. The stumbling-stone (9:30–33)
Having considered the problem from the standpoint of divine election, Paul now considers it from the standpoint of human responsibility. What, in fact, has happened? The gospel, with its proclamation of the 'righteousness' of God bestowed on believers, came to the Jew first, and also to the Gentile, but (on the whole) it was accepted by the Gentile first. The Gentiles responded gratefully to the message which assured them of their acceptance by God on the ground of faith, and it was 'reckoned to them as righteousness'. The Jews (for the most part) continued to pursue the path of legal righteousness, seeking acceptance with God on the basis of their law-keeping, and yet never attained their goal. The reason was simple: they were following the wrong path. Acceptance by God was assured to faith and not to the works enjoined by the law. It was indeed a hard lesson for them to learn that, in spite of all the privileges which were theirs as Israelites, the divine gift of righteousness could be attained by them only in the same way as it was open to those utter outsiders of Gentiles who had been for ages past

shut out from the knowledge of God and his ways. No wonder the gospel was a stumbling-block to them.

But the very fact of its being a stumbling-block had been foreseen. To establish this Paul quotes from Isaiah again, conflating two oracles which have the common theme of a 'stone' divinely laid in a time of disaster and judgment, which provides refuge for those who entrust themselves to it but proves the downfall of those who stumble against it.

31. *Who pursued the righteousness which is based on law.* Hoping to be justified in God's sight by conformity to the law.

Did not succeed in fulfilling that law. The requirements of the law were not met by those who followed the way of legal righteousness, as they are met by those 'who walk not according to the flesh but according to the Spirit' (8:4).

32. *They have stumbled over the stumbling stone.* In Isaiah 8:13-15 the prophet foretells how the Assyrian invasion will sweep over the land of Israel like the waters of a great flood. But there will be one place of refuge from the overwhelming water: God himself will prove a 'sanctuary' to all who put their trust in him, a rock on which they will stand secure. Those, however, who do not entrust themselves to him but put their confidence in other powers or resources will be swept by the flood against this rock and come to grief upon it; to them, far from being a place of refuge, it will prove a dangerous obstacle – 'a stone of offence and a rock of stumbling'. The passage is later quoted to the same effect in 1 Peter 2:8, where Christ is described as ' "A stone that will make men stumble, a rock that will make them fall"; for they stumble because they disobey the word, as they were destined to do' (destined, that is to say, by the word of God spoken through Isaiah).

33. *'Behold, I am laying in Zion a stone that will make men stumble, a rock that will make them fall.'* In Isaiah 28:16, in the course of a warning about the impending deluge from Assyria which will sweep away the 'refuge of lies' in which king and people are putting their trust, the word of God comes to the prophet: 'Behold, I am laying in Zion for a foundation a stone, a tested stone, a precious cornerstone,[1] of a sure foundation.' This foundation stone appears to be the righteous remnant,[2] the hope of the future, which is embodied personally in the promised Prince of the house of David.[3] This oracle is here conflated with Isaiah 8:14 (referred to in the note on verse 32 above). The combination of the two passages as a prophecy of Christ became commonplace in early Christian apologetic. They are similarly combined in 1 Peter 2:6–8, where they are further linked with a third 'stone' *testimonium* – the rejected stone of Psalm 118:22. (In Luke 20:17–18 the rejected stone of the psalm and the stumbling-stone of Isaiah 8:14 are brought into association with yet another 'stone' *testimonium* – the stone 'cut out by no human hand' of Daniel 2:34–35, which smashed Nebuchadnezzar's dream-image in pieces.)

'*He who believes in him will not be put to shame.*' In the Hebrew text of Isaiah 28:16 this may be the inscription on the stone. The words 'in him' (quoted here and in 10:11) are added in LXX, perhaps reflecting the Messianic interpretation. Those who trust in Christ as the Saviour whom God has provided need never fear that their trust will prove to be ill-founded. God vindicates his people's faith, even when others say, 'He committed his cause to the LORD; let him deliver him, let him rescue him, for he delights in him!' (Ps. 22:8). The Hebrew text of Isaiah 28:16 reads 'He who believes will not be in haste'; that is, one who stands on God's foundation will 'keep his head when all about him are losing theirs and blaming it on him'; he will not panic or fuss or rush around, but will trust in God, confident that his purpose will be accomplished in his own time. The LXX translators possibly read in the Hebrew text before them *lo' yēḇōš* ('will not be ashamed') instead of *lo' yaḥîš* ('will not haste'), but this is not a necessary supposition.

---

[1] *Cf.* Eph. 2:20. See F. F. Bruce, 'The Corner Stone', *ExT* 84 (1972–73), pp. 231–235.

[2] In Qumran literature the Qumran community is identified with this precious cornerstone (*cf.* G. Vermes, *The Dead Sea Scrolls in English*, p. 38).

[3] The Targum of Jonathan interprets the stone of Isaiah 28:16 as the Messiah: 'Behold, I am setting in Zion a king, a mighty king . . .'

2. The two ways of righteousness (10:1–13)

For all that, Paul will not cease praying for Israel's salvation. He understands their state of mind more than most: 'an unenlightened zeal for God' was exactly what he himself had before he met the risen Christ. Of that zeal of his he speaks elsewhere: his zeal for the ancestral traditions of his people impelled him to forge ahead of his contemporaries in his devotion to the study and practice of the Jewish religion, and supplied the motive power in his energetic harrying of the infant church (*cf.* Gal. 1:13–14; Phil. 3:6).

To him the stone laid in position by God had indeed been a 'rock of stumbling' until the scales fell from his eyes and his life was reorientated; now his consuming ambition was to magnify Christ in his life and work and bring others to know him.

If this had happened to him, why could it not happen to his people? True, for the present they did not know God's way of righteousness, but endeavoured to establish a righteousness of their own. Yet, as he himself had found in Christ 'the end of the law', so might his fellow-Jews when they too came to follow the way of faith.

The two ways – the way of law and the way of faith – are illustrated by quotations from the Pentateuch. The conclusion at which he arrives is that God has brought his salvation near to us, in Christ. We do not have to 'climb the heavenly steeps' to procure it; we have no need to 'plumb the lowest deeps' for it, for Christ has risen from the dead to make it secure to us. It is here, present and available; what men and women are called on to do is to accept it by inward faith and to confess Christ publicly as Lord. 'Jesus is Lord' is the earliest, as it remains the sufficient, Christian creed.

2. *I bear them witness.* 'I testify on their behalf.' For another instance of this testimony *cf.* Acts 22:3, 'being zealous for God as you all are this day.'

3. *Being ignorant of the righteousness that comes from God, and seeking to establish their own.* Paul makes the same contrast in Philippians 3:9 between 'a righteousness of my own, based on law' and 'the righteousness from God that depends on faith'.[1]

4. *Christ is the end of the law, that every one who has faith may be justified.* The word 'end' (*telos*) has a double sense: it may mean 'goal' or 'termination'. On the one hand, Christ is the goal at which the law aimed, in that he embodies the perfect righteousness which it prescribes. This is implied in Matthew 5:17, 'Think not that I have come to abolish the law and the prophets; I have come not to abolish them but to fulfil them.' And the law's requirements are fulfilled in the lives of those who are 'in Christ Jesus' (8:3–4; *cf.* 3:31). On the other hand, since Christ is the goal of the law, since in him the law has found its perfect fulfilment, a righteous status before God is available to everyone who believes in him, and that implies the termination of the law's function (real or imagined) as a means of acquiring such a righteous status. In him the old order, to which the law belonged, has been done away, to be replaced by the new order of the Spirit. *Cf.* 2 Corinthians 3:6–18.

The case for understanding *telos* as 'termination' is presented by Käsemann, *ad loc.*; the case for 'goal' by Cranfield, *ad loc.* The two senses are combined by Barrett, *ad loc.*: Christ 'puts an end to the law, not by destroying all that the law stood for but by realizing it'.

5. *The man who practises the righteousness which is based on the law shall live by it.* Quoted from Leviticus 18:5 (*cf.* Lk. 10:28, 'do this, and you will live'), adduced by Paul in Galatians 3:12 to show that 'the law does not rest on faith'; there he contrasts it with Habakkuk 2:4b (*cf.* Rom. 1:17). According to Leviticus 18:5, life – which, for Paul, is interchangeable with justification (*cf.* 5:18, 21; Gal. 3:21) – is assured to one who keeps the divine statutes and ordinances. 'What is wrong with that?' it might be

---

[1] The Jew's relation to the law is carefully studied by E. P. Sanders in *Paul and Palestinian Judaism* (1977), pp. 33–428. He finds that, among Palestinian Jews at least in the period *c.* 200 BC – AD 200, the pattern of religion was what he calls 'covenant nomism' – only impenitent wickedness or apostasy put one outside the covenant, but inside the covenant repentance atoned for breaches of the law, so that all within the covenant might look forward to participation in the world to come. For Paul, the breaking down of the frontiers between Jews and Gentiles ruled out any such reliance on the 'old' covenant.

asked. Just this, Paul would reply, that no-one has succeeded in keeping them perfectly, and therefore no-one has succeeded in gaining life this way. (There is one exception, according to Karl Barth: 'the man' who has perfectly kept the law of God is Christ.[1]) Even if Paul's own earlier career was 'as to righteousness under the law blameless' (Phil. 3:6), he now knew that it was blameless only in the sight of men, but not before God.

6–8. To illustrate the *righteousness based on faith*, Paul goes to another place in the Pentateuch – Deuteronomy 30:11–14, part of Moses' farewell exhortation to Israel. But in its primary setting the sense of Deuteronomy 30:11–14 is almost precisely that of Leviticus 18:5. There the statutes and ordinances of God were enjoined on the people so that they might do them and live. Here God says that his commandment 'is not too hard for you, neither is it far off. It is not in heaven, that you should say, "Who will go up for us to heaven, and bring it to us, that we may hear it *and do it*?" Neither is it beyond the sea, that you should say, "Who will go over the sea for us, and bring it to us, that we may hear it *and do it*?" But the word is very near you; it is in your mouth and in your heart, *so that you can do it.*' (Paul significantly omits the italicized words.) That the doing of the commandment was the way to life in the Deuteronomy context is evident from the words of Moses which follow immediately: 'See, I have set before you this day life and good, death and evil. If you obey the commandments of the LORD your God which I command you this day, by loving the LORD your God, by walking in his ways, and by keeping his commandments and his statutes and his ordinances, then you shall *live* . . .' (Dt. 30:15–16).

Granted that Deuteronomy is suffused with a prophetic, and at times almost evangelical, fervour which is not prominent in Leviticus – granted, too, that there is an inwardness in the language of Deuteronomy 30:11–14 ('in your mouth and in your heart') which anticipates the 'new covenant' oracle of Jeremiah 31:31–34 – yet it is not so easy for us as it was for Paul to draw a distinction between the meaning of Leviticus 18:5 and that of

---

[1] *Cf.* K. Barth, *Church Dogmatics*, E.T. II/2 (1957), p. 245; also Cranfield, *ad loc.*

Deuteronomy 30:11–14. It may be that Paul was familiar with an interpretation of the Deuteronomy passage which facilitated his application of it to the gospel. If, for example, he had been accustomed to see in the passage a reference to wisdom (it is quoted with reference to wisdom in Baruch 3:29–30), then his identification of Christ with the wisdom of God could have led him to his Christian interpretation of Deuteronomy 30:11–14.

Here, then, is his exposition of the language appropriate to 'the righteousness based on faith' (more or less in the *pesher* style now familiar to us from the Qumran biblical commentaries):

Do not say in your heart, 'Who will ascend into heaven?' – that is, to bring Christ down (as though he had never become incarnate and lived on earth).
or 'Who will descend into the abyss?' – that is, to bring him back from the realms of the dead, the nethermost deep (as though he had not already been raised up to newness of life).
No; this is what the good news of justification says:
The word is near you, on your lips and in your heart – that is, the message of faith which we proclaim. It is with the lips and in the heart that the saving response to this message is made.

9. *If you confess with your lips that Jesus is Lord.* It would be better to express the confession in direct speech: 'if on your lips is the confession "Jesus is Lord" ' (NEB). (*Cf.* 1 Cor. 12:3; Phil. 2:11.) Some commentators have thought particularly of the confession of his name before magistrates (*cf.* Lk. 21:12–15; 1 Pet. 3:13–16); but if we are to think of one outstanding occasion for such a confession to be made, we should more probably think of the initial confession made in Christian baptism – 'the pledge of a good conscience towards God' (1 Pet. 3:21, NIV).

And believe in your heart that God raised him from the dead. Saving faith is resurrection faith (*cf.* 1 Cor. 15:17, 'if Christ has not been raised, your faith is futile and you are still in your sins').

10. *Man believes with his heart and so is justified, and he confesses with his lips and so is saved.* The order believing-confessing is the order of both logic and experience. The two clauses say essentially the same thing: believing and confession are inseparable, and justification and salvation – here with an eschatological reference ('unto righteousness . . . unto salvation') – cannot be distinguished.

11. *'No one who believes in him will be put to shame.'* Quoted from Isaiah 28:16 (quoted already in 9:33): those who commit themselves to Christ will never be let down.

12. *There is no distinction.* The righteousness which God imparts is open without distinction to all men and women of faith, whether they are Jews or Gentiles. His saving mercy is lavished with 'undistinguishing regard': all who call on him will receive it. At an earlier stage in the argument of Romans (3:22) the words 'there is no distinction' had a grim sound, because they convicted Jews and Gentiles together of sin against God and incapacity to win his acceptance by personal effort or desert; now the same words have a joyful sound, because they proclaim to Jews and Gentiles together that the gates of God's mercy stand wide open for their entrance, that his free pardon is assured in Christ to all who claim it by faith.

13. *'Every one who calls upon the name of the Lord will be saved.'* Quoted from Joel 2:32, where it relates to the eve of 'the great and terrible day of the LORD' when God's Spirit is to be poured out on 'all flesh'; compare Peter's use of the same scripture (in its context) to explain the events that marked the first Christian Pentecost: 'this is what was spoken by the prophet . . .' (Acts 2:16–21).

3. The world-wide proclamation (10:14–21)
Hence arises the necessity of proclaiming the gospel worldwide. Men and women are urged to call on the name of the Lord and be saved; but they will not call on his name unless they have been moved to believe in him, they cannot believe in him unless they hear about him, they cannot hear about him unless someone brings them the news, and no-one can bring them the news unless he is commissioned to do so. The preacher is an 'apostle' in the primary sense of the word: he is

a herald or ambassador conveying a message from someone who has commissioned him to deliver it. Here Paul magnifies the office of the gospel preachers; it is God's good pleasure by their proclamation of his amnesty to bring his mercy home to those who believe the message. Of one who brings such joyful news the prophet spoke centuries before: 'How beautiful upon the mountains are the feet of him who brings good tidings, who publishes peace, who brings good tidings of good, who publishes salvation' (Is. 52:7). If, in the first instance, the prophet's words referred to the messenger who announced to the desolate city of Zion, 'Your God reigns!' they are now applied, as regularly in the New Testament, to the world-wide preaching of the gospel (see comment on 1:1, p. 68).

But how does this apply to the problem of Jewish unbelief? The message came to the Jews as well as to the Gentiles; indeed, it came to the Jews first. But the Jews (for the most part) did not pay heed to it. Even this, however, was foreseen, as may be gathered from the question of Isaiah 53:1, 'who has believed our message?' The relevance of these words to the gospel arises not only from the general context of Isaiah 40 – 66, but even more so from the particular context of the fourth Servant Song (Is. 52:13 – 53:12), which has made such a notable contribution to the New Testament presentation of the passion and triumph of Jesus. This verse, moreover, is quoted elsewhere in the New Testament as one of a number of Isaianic texts used to account for Israel's unbelief.

But if the disappointed messenger asks, 'Who has believed our message?' it is evident that the message was designed to produce faith. And the message itself rests for its authority on the direct command and commission of Christ.

Perhaps, however (an interested inquirer suggests), the people of Israel did not all hear the message? Indeed they did, Paul replies: the message has been published far and wide; it has been preached in every place where there is a Jewish community.

Well, says our inquirer again, they have heard, it appears, but perhaps they did not understand? No, says Paul, it was not that. They understood well enough, but they refused to obey. They have shown their envy and obstructiveness when Gentiles accepted the message, but they would not believe it themselves. But this too has fulfilled the word of prophecy. The Song of Moses in Deuteronomy 32 contains a sustained indictment of Israel's ingratitude and disobedience throughout her history. Later Christian writers of anti-Judaic apologies, instead of considering whether the same indictment might not have a message for their own community, used it as an arsenal of ammunition against the Jews, regarding it as a strong point in their argument that in this Song Moses himself testifies against them.[1] The Qumran sectarians similarly used the Song in their protest against what they saw as the apostasy of the Jewish nation as a whole.[2] In the Song (Dt. 32:21) God charges his people with idolatry –

'They have stirred me to jealousy with what is no god; they
   have provoked me with their idols' –

and pronounces sentence upon them:

'I will stir them to jealousy with those who are no people;
   I will provoke them with a foolish nation.'

To Paul, 'those who are no people' would readily be interpreted of the Gentiles, to whom he has already applies the phrase 'not my people' in Hosea 1:10. How then does God stir Israel to jealousy by means of the Gentiles? By letting Israel see the blessings which are showered on the Gentiles when they embrace Christ by faith: God no longer speaks of them as 'not my people' but calls them his people. Israel, stirred to jealousy by the sight, asks why these same blessings should not be even more rightfully hers, and is assured that they will indeed be hers on the same basis – faith in Christ. This hope is elaborated by Paul in the next stage of his present argument, but this stage of the argument is summed up in two contrasted texts at the

---

[1] *Cf.* Justin, *Dialogue with Trypho* 20, 119, 130. See J. R. Harris, 'A Factor of Old Testament Influence in the New Testament', *ExT* 37 (1925–26), pp. 6–11; B. Lindars, *New Testament Apologetic* (1961), pp. 244 f., 258, 274.

[2] See the Qumran quotation of Deuteronomy 32:28 against Israel in G. Vermes, *The Dead Sea Scrolls in English*, p. 102.

beginning of Isaiah 65 which are applied respectively to responsive Gentiles and to rebellious Israel.

15. *'How beautiful are the feet of those who preach good news!'* Paul here seems to give his own Greek rendering of the gist of the Hebrew of Isaiah 52:7 instead of reproducing the LXX, which obscures the sense of this verse.

In the New Testament this whole section of the book of Isaiah, from chapter 40 on, is applied to the gospel age. The deliverance from Babylonian exile under Cyrus, like the deliverance from Egyptian servitude in the days of Moses, is treated as the foreshadowing of the greater and perfect deliverance accomplished by Christ. The 'voice' of Isaiah 40:3, which calls for the levelling of a way through the desert by which God may lead his liberated people home to Zion, becomes the voice of John the Baptist, calling together in the wilderness of Judaea a people prepared for the Lord (Mk. 1:3; Lk. 1:17; Jn. 1:23); the 'year of the LORD's favour' (Is. 61:2) is announced by Jesus at the outset of his Galilaean ministry (Lk. 4:18–21); and further examples of the gospel fulfilment of these chapters appear as Paul's argument proceeds.

16. *'Lord, who has believed what he has heard from us?'* The vocative 'Lord' is an addition of the LXX. In Isaiah 53:1 the question is asked by those who hear the announcement of the Suffering Servant's exaltation (*cf.* 15:21, below, for the quotation of Isaiah 52:15, the words immediately preceding those quoted here). 'Who would have believed the announcement we have heard?' they ask in amazement, as they recall the Servant's humiliation. The announcement, now embodied in the gospel message, is still received with incredulity, says Paul – not now by the kings and nations of Isaiah 52:15 so much as by the bulk of the Jewish people. Isaiah 53:1 is quoted in John 12:38 to account for the people's failure to believe in Jesus during his ministry in Jerusalem; it is coupled there with the quotation of Isaiah 6:9–10, also widely current in early Christian times as a *testimonium* predicting Jewish unbelief (*cf.* Rom. 11:8, with note).

17. *Faith comes from what is heard.* 'What is heard' renders the same Greek noun (*akoē*) as 'what he has heard' in verse 16; *cf.* verse 14, 'how are they to believe in him of whom they have never heard?'

What is heard comes by the preaching of Christ. The 'preaching' (*rhēma*, 'utterance', as in verse 8, quoting Dt. 30:14) is the 'word' about Christ, the 'word of faith', so called because it awakens faith in its hearers.

18. '*Their voice has gone out to all the earth, and their words to the ends of the world.*' Quoted from Psalm 19:4 (where LXX *phthongos*, 'voice', presupposed Heb. *qōlām* instead of MT *qawwām*, 'their line'). These words, in their original context, refer to the universal witness of the heavenly bodies. It is unnecessary to suppose that Paul regarded Psalm 19:4 as a regular *prediction* of the world-wide dissemination of the gospel; the dissemination of the gospel, it is implied, is becoming as world-wide as the light of the heavenly bodies. This might seem to be an exaggeration: the gospel had not been carried throughout all the earth, not even to all the lands that were then known to inhabitants of the Graeco-Roman world. Paul was well aware of that; at this very time he was planning the evangelization of Spain, a province where the name of Christ was not yet known (*cf.* 15:18–24). But by now the gospel had been carried to most parts of the Mediterranean area where Jews were to be found; and that is all that the argument requires. For the 'representative universalism' (see p. 210, n. 1) implied in the quotation of Psalm 19:4, *cf.* Colossians 1:5–6 ('the gospel which has come to you, as indeed in the whole word it is bearing fruit and growing') and 23 ('the gospel . . . which has been preached to every creature under heaven').

19. *Moses says.* The quotation from Deuteronomy 32:21 (in the Song of Moses), where Moses represents God as speaking. The Song of Moses furnished early Christians with a remarkable number of *testimonia*, and not exclusively on the subject of Jewish unbelief (*cf.* 1 Cor. 10:20, 22, echoing Dt. 32:16–17; Phil. 2:15, echoing Dt. 32:5; Heb. 1:6, quoting Dt. 32:43, LXX).

'*I will make you jealous of those who are not a nation.*' Because they had provoked God to jealousy by their worship of a 'no-god' (Heb. *lo'-'ēl*), he would provoke *them* to jealousy by means of a 'no-people' (Heb. *lo'-'am*). That is to say, in the course of history God used as the instruments of his judgment on Israel this or that Gentile nation – those whom Israel regarded as being a 'no-people' in the sense that they did not enter nationally into God's electing purpose in the way that Israel did. But in the light of the passages he has already quoted from Hosea (*cf.* 9:25–26) Paul reinterprets these words with reference to the new gospel situation. To one acquainted with the Hebrew Bible, as Paul was, the comparison between Moses' 'no-people' (*lo'-'am*) and Hosea's 'not my people' (*lo'-'ammî*) suggested itself readily (more so than to one who depended exclusively on the LXX). Just how Paul understood the Gentiles' provocation of the Jews to the jealousy is shown below in 11:11.

'*With a foolish nation I will make you angry.*' The Gentiles were 'foolish' from the Jewish viewpoint in that they had not received the knowledge of God (*cf.* 2:20, where the Jew regards himself as 'a corrector of the foolish' – the adjective *aphrōn* there being synonymous with *asynetos* here).

20. *Then Isaiah is so bold as to say.* That is, he goes to the limit of daring, even beyond the point reached by Moses, in his affirmation of the paradox of God's bestowing his covenant mercies on those who were not his people, and had no claim on these mercies.

'*I have been found by those who did not seek me . . .*' In their original context these words from Isaiah 65:1 ('I was ready to be sought by those who did not ask for me . . .') seem to refer to rebellious Israel; but, as in his application of the Hosea prophecy, Paul recognizes here a principle which in the situation of his day is applicable to Gentiles, and the LXX wording (here quoted) lent support to this application. After long centuries of living without the knowledge of the true God, the Gentiles were now turning to seek him.

21. '*All day long I have held out my hands to a disobedient and contrary people.*' These words, quoted from Isaiah 65:2, refer to Israel both in their original context and in Paul's application of them. He finds them as eloquent of the Jews' general refusal of the gospel as he finds Isaiah 65:1 eloquent of the Gentiles' eager acceptance of it.

D. GOD'S PURPOSE FOR ISRAEL (11:1–29)

1. Israel's alienation not final (11:1–12)
A 'disobedient and contrary people' Israel might be, but God had no more written them off now than in earlier days when they rejected his word through Moses and the prophets. 'Those whom he foreknew he also predestined' is a principle not set aside in their case. As in Old Testament times, so in apostolic times God's purpose in choosing his people was safeguarded by his reservation of a faithful 'remnant'. In Elijah's day, when national apostasy had assumed the dimensions of a landslide, there was a loyal minority of seven thousand who refused to worship Baal; so now in Paul's day there was a believing minority of Jews who had not rejected the gospel. Paul ought to know: he was one of them. Of Paul's membership in one of the tribes of Israel there could be no doubt; yet he was a believer in Jesus, as were many more of his kinsfolk 'according to the flesh'. They constituted a faithful remnant, chosen by God's grace, and their existence was in itself proof that God had not abandoned Israel or given up his purpose for them. Even if Israel as a whole had failed to attain his purpose, the elect remnant had attained it. The 'hardening' which affected the majority had been foreseen by God (here three further *testimonia* – from Isaiah, from Deuteronomy and from the Psalter – are adduced, in addition to the composite 'stone' *testimonium* in 9:33). But it was not to be a permanent condition.

Israel had stumbled, but had not fallen so as to rise no more. Through her stumbling the blessings of the gospel had been extended more immediately to the Gentiles. Repeatedly in the Acts of the Apostles it is the refusal of the Jewish community in one place or another to accept the proffered salvation that is the occasion for the missionaries' presenting it directly to the Gentiles. 'It was necessary', said Paul and Barnabas to the Jews of Pisidian Antioch, 'that the word of God should be spoken first to you. Since you thrust it from you, and judge yourselves unworthy of eternal life, behold, we turn to the Gentiles' (Acts 13:46; *cf*. 28:28). Had the Jews accepted the gospel, it would have been their privilege to make it known to the Gentiles; as it was, the Gentiles heard it without their mediation. But if the *stumbling* of Israel had been the occasion of so much blessing to the Gentile word, what would Israel's revival and restoration mean but a veritable resurrection!

1. *Has God rejected his people?* The question (so framed in Greek as to require the answer 'No') and the statement in verse 2, 'God has not rejected his people', echo the LXX wording of Psalm 94:14, 'the LORD will not forsake his people' (*cf*. 1 Sa. 12:22).

A descendant of Abraham. Here the phrase is used primarily in its natural sense (*cf*. 2 Cor. 11:22), but not to the exclusion of its spiritual sense (*cf*. 4:16, above).

A member of the tribe of Benjamin. Cf. Philippians 3:5. It is an 'undesigned coincidence' between Paul's letters and Acts that, while it is only from the former that we learn that Paul belonged to the tribe of Benjamin, it is only the latter that tells us that his Jewish name was Saul. It is not surprising that parents who traced their descent from the tribe of Benjamin and cherished high ambitions for their new-born son should give him the name borne by the most illustrious member of that tribe in the history of Israel – 'Saul the son of Kish, a man of the tribe of Benjamin' (to quote Paul's reference to Israel's first king in Acts 13:21).

2. *Do you not know . . .?* A common expression in Paul (*cf*. 6:16).

What the scripture says. Cf. 9:17. Here the reference is to 1 Kings 19:10, 14, where Elijah is the actual speaker.

Of Elijah. Literally 'in Elijah' – *i.e.* in the section of the books of Kings dealing with Elijah (perhaps 1 Ki. 17:1 – 2 Ki. 2:18). *Cf*. Mark 12:26, where 'in . . . the bush' means 'in the section of the book of Exodus dealing with "The Bush".'

4. *God's reply.* Greek *chrēmatismos*, used of a divine response, like the transitive verb *chrēmatizō*, from which it is derived (*cf*.

Mt. 2:12, 22; Lk. 2:26; Acts 10:22; Heb. 8:5; 11:7; 12:25).

'*I have kept for myself seven thousand men who have not bowed the knee to Baal.*' Quoted from 1 Kings 19:18, in a form closer to the Hebrew text than LXX (which reads '*thou* wilt keep . . .') – although there is nothing in MT or LXX corresponding to 'for myself'. The Hebrew text is best rendered by the future tense: 'Yet I will leave . . .' – the reference being to the small minority which alone would survive the slaughter to be wrought by the swords of Hazael, Jehu and Elisha (1 Ki. 19:17). Paul's point, however, is that now as then there is a believing remnant.

In the Greek text here we find the odd phenomenon of the feminine form of the definite article preceding the masculine noun *Baal*. This reading does not occur in our extant manuscripts of LXX, but it apparently reflects a stage in the transmission of the text where the idolatrous name Baal was marked for replacement (in public reading, at least) by the feminine Hebrew noun *bōšeṯ*, 'shame'.

5. *A remnant, chosen by grace.* Greek *leimma* ('remainder') is found here only in the New Testament, and in the LXX only in 2 Kings 19:4, of 'the remnant that is left' after the Assyrian invasion in Hezekiah's day. The 'remnant' here comprises those who have believed the gospel, but behind their faith lies the divine election. Their forming part of the 'remnant' is thus *no longer on the basis of works* (verse 6).

7. *The rest were hardened.* Greek *pōroō* means 'make hard' or 'render insensitive' (*cf.* the noun *pōrōsis*, 'hardening', in verse 25). In modern English 'blindness' is commonly used to denote this moral or spiritual insensitiveness; hence NEB, 'The rest were made blind to the truth.' If it be asked by whom they were 'hardened', verse 8 seems to provide the answer. Not for the first time in this letter (*cf.* 1:21b; 9:17–18[1]) such inward insensitiveness is divinely inflicted as a judicial penalty for refusal to heed the word of God.

8. '*God gave them a spirit of stupor, eyes that should not see and*

---

[1] A different word (*sklērynō*) is used of the hardening of Pharaoh's heart in 9:18, but the meaning is not greatly different from that of *pōroō* here.

ears that should not hear, down to this very day.' A conflated quotation from Isaiah 29:10 ('the LORD has poured out upon you a spirit of deep sleep, and has closed your eyes . . .') and Deuteronomy 29:4 ('to this day the LORD has not given you a mind to understand, or eyes to see, or ears to hear'). The reference to unseeing eyes and unhearing ears is reminiscent also of Isaiah 6:9–10 ('Hear and hear, but do not understand; see and see, but do not perceive . . .'), used in all four Gospels as a *testimonium* of the failure of Jesus' hearers to pay heed to his message (Mt. 13:14–15; Mk. 4:12; Lk. 8:10; Jn. 12:40; *cf.* also Acts 28:26–27). See comment on 10:16 (p. 196).

The word translated 'stupor' is *katanyxis* (so Is. 29:10, LXX), which literally means 'pricking' or 'stinging', and hence comes to be used of the numbness which results from certain kinds of sting (NEB accordingly renders 'a numbness of spirit').

9–10. *And David says, 'Let their feast become a snare . . .'* Verses 9 and 10 are taken from Psalm 69:22–23 (LXX). This psalm was widely current in the church from earliest days as a *testimonium* of the ministry, and especially the passion, of Christ (*cf.* the quotation of verse 9b in 15:3 below, of verse 9a in Jn. 2:17 and of verse 4 in Jn. 15:25, and the allusion to verse 21 in Mt. 27:34). If the speaker in the psalm is taken to be Christ, those against whom complaints are voiced are interpreted as his enemies (*cf.* the application of verse 25 to Judas Iscariot in Acts 1:20). The emphasis of the present quotation probably lies on the words of verse 10, *'let their eyes be darkened so that they cannot see'* (from Ps. 69:23), which carries on the theme of the composite quotation in verse 8 and is directly relevant to the temporary 'hardening' or 'blindness' that has overtaken all Israel apart from the believing remnant.

11. *Through their trespass salvation has come to the Gentiles, so as to make Israel jealous.* This is Paul's interpretation of the words from the Song of Moses (Dt. 32:21), already quoted in 10:19. It is by the blessing bestowed on those who formerly were a 'no-people' in relation to him, by the salvation which a 'foolish nation' has received through accepting the gospel in faith, that God will stir Israel to jealousy.

12. *How much more will their full inclusion mean!* The 'full inclusion' (*plērōma*, lit. 'fullness') of the Jews is to be understood in the same sense as the 'full number [*plērōma*, 'fullness'] of the Gentiles' in verse 25. The large-scale conversion of the Gentile world is to be followed by the salvation of 'all Israel' (verse 26); this salvation involves their 'full inclusion'.

2. Admonition to Gentile Christians (11:13–24)

Paul now addresses himself more personally to the Gentiles among his readers. He may have been told of a situation in the Roman church which called for such an admonition. In any case, Gentile Christians, on hearing his argument thus far, might be inclined to think patronizingly of their Jewish fellow-believers as refugees, mercifully rescued from the doom about to overtake an apostate nation, and to dismiss from any place in the divine purpose the majority of that nation. 'Jew as I am by birth,' says Paul, 'I am the Gentiles' apostle, and I esteem the honour of my commission very highly. This I do not only for the sake of the Gentiles to whom I carry the gospel, but for the sake of my Jewish brethren as well. I want to stir them to emulation, as they see Gentiles entering into the full enjoyment of gospel blessings. I want to make them say, "Why should the Gentiles have all these blessings? Why should we not have a prior share in them?" Well may they say so, for these blessings are the fulfilment of their own ancestral hope; they are bound up with faith in their own Messiah. And when at last Israel is stimulated to claim the Messiah, with all the blessing he brings, words cannot describe the blessing which Israel's restoration will mean to the world.'

This consummation is not an idle dream, Paul maintains; it is guaranteed by the indefectible purpose of God. The first cake of the batch has already been presented to God, and its consecration means that the whole batch is holy to him. The root of the tree is holy, and the branches necessarily share in its holiness.

This reference to the root and the branches leads Paul on to develop his parable of the olive-tree – a parable which has often been used to show that he was a typical town-dweller, unfamiliar with the most ordinary phenomena of the countryside. For a gardener does not graft a slip from a wild fruit-tree on to a cultivated fruit-tree; it is a shoot or 'scion' from a culti-vated tree that must be grafted on to a stock of the same or an allied species. Sir William Ramsay does, indeed, quote Theobald Fischer to the effect that it was still customary in Palestine at the beginning of the twentieth century 'to reinvigorate an olive-tree which is ceasing to bear fruit, by grafting it with a shoot of the Wild-Olive, so that the sap of the tree ennobles this wild shoot and the tree now again begins to bear fruit'.[1] That a similar process was not unknown in Roman times is evident from Paul's contemporary Columella, according to whom, when an olive-tree produces badly, a slip of a wild-olive is grafted on to it, and this gives new vigour to the tree.[2]

At any rate, Paul's parable is clear. Here are two olive-trees – a cultivated olive and a wild-olive. The latter produced poor fruit which contained little or no oil; the former normally pro-duced good fruit. The cultivated olive is Israel, the people of God; the wild-olive is the Gentile world. But the olive began to grow weak and unproductive; old branches were therefore cut away and a graft was made from the wild-olive. 'The cutting away of the old branches was required to admit air and light to the graft, as well as to prevent the vitality of the tree from being too widely diffused over a large number of branches.'[3] The graft from the wild-olive is the sum-total of Gentile believers, now incorporated into the people of God; the old branches which were cut away are those Jews who declined to accept the gospel.

In such an unusual grafting, it is said, both the graft and the stock on to which it is grafted are affected: the old stock is reinvigorated by the new graft, and the new graft in turn, fed by the sap of the olive stock, is able to bear such fruit as the wild-olive could never produce.

Gentile believers must not yield to the temptation to despise the Jews. But for the grace of God which engrafted them among his people and made them 'fellow citizens with the saints' (Eph. 2:19), Gentiles would have remained for ever lifeless and fruit-less. The new life which enables them to produce fruit for God

---

[1] W. M. Ramsay, *Pauline and Other Studies* (1906), p. 223, citing T. Fischer, *Der Oelbaum* (1904).
[2] Columella, *De re rustica*, 5.9.   [3] Ramsay, *Pauline and Other Studies*, p. 224.

is the life of the old stock of Israel on to which they have been grafted. Israel owes no debt to them; they are indebted to Israel.[1] And if they reply that at least they are better than the *unbelieving* Jews, the branches which were cut off, they are exhorted to learn a salutary lesson from the removal of those old branches. Why were they cut off? Because of unbelief. And if a spirit of pride leads the new graft – the Gentile church – to forget its reliance on divine grace and exchange faith in God for self-confidence, it will suffer the same fate as the old branches; it, too, will be cut off. It is by faith that membership in the true people of God is acquired and maintained; it is by unbelief that it is forfeited. This principle, says Paul, is applied without partiality, to Gentiles as much as to Jews. On the other hand – and here the practical processes of grafting are certainly left behind, for the sake of the spiritual facts which the parable is intended to illustrate – if those Jews, who through unbelief lost their status as members of the true Israel, come at length to faith in Christ, they will be incorporated afresh in the people of God. If old branches which had been cut away from an olive were grafted on to the parent tree once more and began to produce fruit again, that would be an unprecedented miracle in the natural realm. Equally, the reincorporation of the Jewish nation among the people of God when unbelief is replaced by faith would be a miracle in the spiritual realm; but, says Paul, it is a miracle which the grace of God is going to perform.

15. *Life from the dead*. The meaning may be that Israel's conversion will be the immediate precursor of the resurrection, to coincide with the parousia of Christ (see note on 11:26, p. 209).

16. *If the dough offered as first fruits is holy, so is the whole lump*. The allusion is probably to Numbers 15:17–21, where the Israelites are commanded to offer to God a cake from the first ground meal, newly come from the threshing-floor. The presentation of this cake to God (Paul implies) hallows the whole baking. In 1 Corinthians 15:23, 'Christ the first fruits' (*aparchē*, as here), the allusion is rather to the sheaf of the first fruits of

[1] See W. D. Davies, 'Paul and the Gentiles', *Jewish and Pauline Studies* (1984), pp. 153–163.

barley which was to be 'waved' before the Lord on the Sunday following Passover, thus consecrating the whole harvest (Lv. 23:10–11). In the present use of the figure, the 'first fruits' should most probably be understood to comprise those men and women of Jewish birth who had, like Paul, acknowledged Jesus as Messiah and Lord.

And if the root is holy, so are the branches. Changing the figure, Paul now says that since a tree is of the same character throughout (*cf.* Mt. 7:16–20; 12:33; Lk. 6:43–44), the holiness of the root sanctifies the branches. It is natural to take the 'root' here as referring, equally with the 'first fruits' in the preceding figure, to Jewish believers. But it seems inappropriate to call them the 'root', and if the 'root and branch' figure stood by itself, we should think of the patriarchs as constituting the root of the tree whose branches are the Israelites of the Christian era. This interpretation (which, on the whole, is preferable) would be in line with Paul's later reference to contemporary Israel as 'beloved for the sake of their forefathers' (verse 28). Probably there is a transition of thought as Paul passes from the one figure to the other.[1]

17. *You, a wild olive shoot, were grafted in their place.* Perhaps Paul is adapting a Jewish parable in which proselytes are pictured as branches from a wild olive grafted on the good olive tree of Israel.[2] For Israel as an olive tree *cf.* Jeremiah 11:16, 'The LORD once called you, "A green olive tree, fair with goodly fruit".'

20. *You stand fast only through faith.* 'Through faith' is emphatic, as RSV indicates by adding the adverb 'only' (see p. 103 above, with n. 2); 'by faith you hold your place' (NEB). *Cf.* 5:2 (p. 116).

22. *Provided you continue in his kindness; otherwise you too will be cut off.* Throughout the New Testament continuance is the test of reality. The perseverance of the saints is a doctrine firmly

---

[1] It is, of course, possible to take the 'first fruits' of verse 16 as being the patriarchs, but this is a less likely interpretation.

[2] See R. A. Stewart, 'Engrafting', *EQ* 59 (1978), pp. 8–22.

grounded in New Testament (and not least in Pauline) teaching; but its corollary is that it is the saints who persevere. Since 'you stand fast only through faith' (verse 20), it is a healthy exercise to heed Paul's injunction to the Corinthian Christians: 'Examine yourselves, to see whether you are holding to your faith' (2 Cor. 13:5).[1]

24. *Contrary to nature.* Paul may be thought to disarm criticism in advance by showing that he is aware of the unnaturalness of the particular kind of grafting here described. But he need mean no more than that the process of grafting is itself 'contrary to nature' – a view which was commonly taken by the ancients.

3. The restoration of Israel (11:25–29)

Here is unfolded the mystery of God's purpose for Israel – a purpose formerly concealed but now made known. Israel's blindness is only partial (for some Israelites have already been enlightened), and only temporary, with a view to the blessing of the Gentiles. So far as the proclamation of the gospel is concerned, the order is 'To the Jew first'; so far as the reception of the gospel is concerned, the order is 'By the Gentile first, and then by the Jew'. When the full tale of believing Gentiles was made up – a consummation which Paul's own apostleship was bringing nearer – then all Israel, not only a faithful remnant but the nation as a whole, would see the salvation of God. If their temporary stumbling was prophetically foretold, so was their ultimate and permanent restoration. The new covenant will not be complete until it embraces the people of the old covenant. Temporarily alienated for the advantage of the Gentiles, they are eternally the object of God's electing love because his promises, once made to the patriarchs, can never be revoked.

It has been objected here that Paul lets his patriotism override his logic: 'the Jew in himself', it has been said, 'was still too strong.'[2] He has emphasized more than once, even in this letter, that natural descent from the patriarchs is not what matters in God's sight, and now he seems to be saying that, because of

---

[1] See I. H. Marshall, *Kept by the Power of God* (1969).
[2] A. Harnack, *The Date of the Acts and of the Synoptic Gospels*, E.T. (1911), p. 61.

God's promises to the patriarchs, their natural descendants must be restored to covenant relation with him. It might suffice to say, with Pascal, 'the heart has its reasons . . .'; but there is more than that to be said. Paul had a deeper and clearer insight into God's grace than his critics; if God's grace operated in accordance with strict logic, the outlook would be dismal for Jews and Gentiles alike.

One further point: in all that Paul says about the restoration of Israel to God, he says nothing about the restoration of an earthly Davidic kingdom. Without trying to construct an argument from this silence, we may insist that what Paul envisaged for his people was something far better.

25. *Lest you be wise in your own conceits.* Quotation from Proverbs 3:7a.

I want you to understand. Lit. 'I do not want you to be ignorant' (as in 1:13; 1 Cor. 10:1; 12:1; 2 Cor. 1:8; 1 Thes. 4:13).

This mystery. As regularly, Paul uses this word to indicate that he is about to disclose a new revelation which he has received (*cf.* 1 Cor. 15:51; Col. 1:26–27). The remnant principle of verses 1–7 was a subject of ancient prophetic revelation; that 'all Israel' would yet be saved, despite its partial and temporary *hardening*, was a new revelation, conveyed through Paul. He has been accused of trying to eat his cake and have it – of consoling himself with the thought of 'a remnant, chosen by grace', and at the same time insisting on a wholesale restoration of Israel – but if his claim to have received a new revelation be taken seriously, he cannot fairly be blamed. The 'mystery' may indeed have been implicit in the 'revelation of Jesus Christ' which he received on the Damascus road, even if it was in the course of his apostolic ministry to the Gentiles that its full significance came home to him.[1] In Old Testament prophecy the remnant of the old Israel was at the same time the nucleus of the new Israel. So it is here: the existence of the believing remnant is the earnest of the final salvation of 'all Israel'.

Until the full number of the Gentiles come in. 'Full number' is literally 'fullness'. The bringing in of 'the full number of the

---

[1] See S. Kim, *The Origin of Paul's Gospel* (²1984), pp. 83–99.

Gentiles' is to be followed by the 'full inclusion' (lit. 'fullness') of the Jews (verse 12). The bringing in of 'the full number of the Gentiles' is referred to by Paul later on as his 'offering of the Gentiles' (15:16).

26. *And so all Israel will be saved.* It is impossible to entertain an exegesis which understands 'Israel' here in a different sense from 'Israel' in verse 25 ('a hardening has come upon part of Israel'). The connecting words 'and so' (*cf.* 5:12) say more than 'and then': they imply that 'in this way' – by the operation of the divine purpose that the gospel should be received by the Gentile first, and then also by the Jew – the salvation of 'all Israel' will come about. 'All Israel' is a recurring expression in Jewish literature, where it need not mean 'every Jew without a single exception', but 'Israel as a whole'. Thus 'all Israel has a portion in the age to come', says the Mishnah tractate *Sanhedrin* (10.1), and proceeds immediately to name certain Israelites who have no portion therein.

'*The Deliverer will come from Zion, he will banish ungodliness from Jacob.*' Quoted from Isaiah 59:20 ('And he will come to Zion as Redeemer, to those in Jacob who turn from transgression'). Paul's wording conforms with LXX, except that LXX reads 'for Zion's sake' and not 'from Zion' (which is probably taken from Ps. 14:7 or 53:6, 'O that deliverance for Israel would come from Zion!'). The reference is to a manifestation to Israel of her divine Redeemer – a manifestation which Paul may well identify in his mind with the parousia of Christ. See comment on verse 15 (p. 205); *cf.* also Acts 3:19–21. The mention of Zion may suggest further that Jerusalem, for Paul, was not only the place from which the gospel originated (*cf.* 15:19), but would also be the scene of its glorious consummation.

27. '*And this will be my covenant with them when I take away their sins.*' For the first few words Paul continues the quotation from Isaiah 59 (where verse 21 goes on: ' "And as for me, this is my covenant with them", says the LORD'), but then passes into the wording of Isaiah 27:9, LXX ('and this is my blessing of him [Jacob], when I take away his sin'), and the new covenant promise of Jeremiah 31:33–34 ('But this is the covenant which I will make with the house of Israel . . . I will forgive their iniquity, and I will remember their sin no more'). See comments on 7:6 (p. 139); 8:4 (p. 153). This is not a covenant yet to be made, but the fulfilment of one made long before.

28. *As regards the gospel they are enemies of God, for your sake.* The genitive 'of God' is not expressed in the Greek, but it is implied: Israel's present estrangement from God has been the occasion for the Gentiles to embrace the blessings of the gospel and be reconciled to him.

As regards election they are beloved for the sake of their forefathers. This is not a reference to 'the merits of the fathers' (*z^ekût 'ābôt*), the doctrine that the patriarchs' righteousness constitutes a store of merit which is credited to their descendants. The whole argument of this letter is contrary to such a conception of merit (*cf.* 4:2). Paul means that the promises which God made to the patriarchs when he called them are secured to their descendants, not on the ground of merit, but on the ground of God's fidelity to his word of grace, as verse 29 emphasizes.

E. GOD'S PURPOSE FOR THE WORLD (11:30-36)

God's ultimate purpose for the human race is now revealed; it is mercy for both Jew and Gentile. The faithful remnant has not been 'chosen by grace' so that the rest might be consigned to perdition; its election is a token that the divine mercy is to be extended to all without distinction (*cf.* 8:19-21). There is an unmistakable universalism in Paul's language here, even if it be an eschatological universalism and not a present one, or a representative rather than an individual universalism.[1]

Paul has already announced that 'all have sinned and fall short of the glory of God' (3:23). All have been convicted before

---

[1] By an eschatological universalism is meant the hope that ultimately 'the elect will be all the world' (C. H. Spurgeon, quoted in A. C. Benson, *The Life of Edward White Benson,* ii, 1900, p. 276), that 'in the age-long development of the race of men, it will attain at last a complete salvation, and our eyes will be greeted with the glorious spectacle of a saved world' (B. B. Warfield, *Biblical and Theological Studies,* 1952, p. xxx). By a representative universalism is meant that 'there has been a representative acceptance of the Gospel by the various nations' (J. Munck, *Paul and the Salvation of Mankind,* 1959, p. 278).

the tribunal of God; none, whether Jew or Gentile, can lay any claim to his mercy. If there is to be hope for any, it must depend solely on God's grace; but hope is held out in unstinted measure. God's purpose in shutting Jews and Gentiles up together in a situation where their disobedience to his will must be acknowledged and brought to light was that he might lavish his unmerited mercy on Jews and Gentiles together.

Here then is the height of Paul's great argument: here is matter for unending praise to God. The doxology of verses 33–36 does not merely round off chapters 9 – 11; it concludes the whole argument of chapters 1 – 11: 'O the unfathomable wealth of God's wisdom and knowledge! How unsearchable are his decrees! How inscrutable his ways! Well has the prophet asked:

> "Who has grasped the Lord's purpose?
> Who has shared his counsel?
> Who has first given to him,
>   that he should be repaid his gift?"

From him all things proceed; through him all things exist; to him all things return. To him be the glory throughout all ages. Amen.'

32. *That he may have mercy upon all.* That is, on all without distinction rather than all without exception. Paul is not here thinking of those who, like Pharaoh in 9:17, persistently reject the divine mercy. He 'does not intend to make a definite pronouncement about the ultimate destiny of each individual man. But the hope of mankind is more, not less, secure because it is rooted in the truth about God, rather than in a truth about man himself' (C. K. Barrett, *ad loc.*).

33. *Riches and wisdom and knowledge.* Instead of treating these three as separate divine properties (so also NEB), we may take 'wisdom and knowledge' as dependent on 'riches' (so NIV, 'the riches of the wisdom and knowledge of God').

34. *'For who has known the mind of the Lord, or who has been his counsellor?'* An echo of Isaiah 40:13, 'Who has directed the Spirit

211

of the LORD, or as his counsellor has instructed him?' *Cf.* also Jeremiah 23:18; Wisdom 9:13.

35. *'Or who has given a gift to him that he might be repaid?'* *Cf.* God's question in Job 41:11, 'Who has given to me, that I should repay him?'

36. *From him and through him and to him are all things.* The formal resemblance to Marcus Aurelius (*Meditations* 4:23) is often pointed out: 'From thee are all things; in thee are all things; to thee are all things.'

B. The Christian way of life (12:1 – 15:13)

I. THE LIVING SACRIFICE (12:1–2)

In view of all that God has accomplished for his people in Christ, how should his people live? They should present themselves to God as a 'living sacrifice', consecrated to him. The animal sacrifices of an earlier day have been rendered for ever obsolete by Christ's self-offering, but there is always room for the worship rendered by obedient hearts. Instead of living by the standards of a world at discord with God, believers are exhorted to let the renewing of their minds by the power of the Spirit transform their lives into conformity with God's will.

Doctrine is never taught in the Bible simply that it may be known; it is taught in order that it may be translated into practice: 'if you know these things, blessed are you if you do them' (Jn. 13:17). Hence Paul repeatedly follows up an exposition of doctrine with an ethical exhortation, the latter being linked to the former, as here, with the particle 'therefore' (*cf.* Eph. 4:1; Col. 3:5).

It is worthy of note, moreover, that the ethical admonitions of this and other New Testament letters, whether Paul's or not, bear a marked resemblance to the ethical teaching of Christ recorded in the Gospels. They are based, in fact, on what Paul calls 'the law of Christ' (Gal. 6:2; *cf.* 1 Cor. 9:21). In particular, an impressive list of parallels can be drawn up between Romans 12:3 – 13:14 and the Sermon on the Mount. While none of our canonical Gospels existed at this time, the teaching of Christ recorded in them was current among the churches – certainly in oral form, and perhaps also in the form of written summaries.

1. *I appeal to you.* Paul tends to use this verb (*parakaleō*) at turning-points in his argument, especially in introducing an ethical exhortation (*cf.* also 15:30; 16:17); it has a diplomatic flavour about it (and is significantly absent from Galatians).

Present your bodies. Cf. 6:13, 19; the verb there translated 'yield' is the verb used here. Paul now brings out in greater detail what is involved in their presenting themselves to God to be used in his service.

A living sacrifice. The sacrifices of the new order do not consist in taking the lives of others, like the ancient animal sacrifices, but in giving one's own (*cf.* Heb. 13:15–16; 1 Pet. 2:5).

Your spiritual worship. NEB, 'the worship offered by mind and heart.' The noun is *latreia*, used already in 9:4 of the 'worship' ordained for the Israelites. The adjective is *logikos* (from *logos*, 'word', 'reason'), which may mean either 'reasonable' (the service of obedient lives is the only reasonable or logical response to the grace of God)[1] or 'spiritual' (as in 1 Pet. 2:2, 'spiritual milk'). Here 'spiritual worship' is probably set in contrast with the externalities of Israel's temple cult. In the *Testament of Levi* (3:6) the angels are described as 'offering to the Lord a fragrant odour, a spiritual (*logikos*) and bloodless sacrifice'.

2. *Do not be conformed to this world.* This 'world' or 'age' (*aiōn*, as in 1 Cor. 1:20; 2:6; 3:18; 2 Cor. 4:4; Gal. 1:4) is distinguished from the age to come (*cf.* Eph. 1:21). While it is called 'the present evil age' (Gal. 1:4), whose 'god' blinds the minds of unbelievers (2 Cor. 4:4), yet it is possible for people living temporally in this age to conduct themselves as heirs of the age

---

[1] It was well said by Thomas Erskine of Linlathen that 'in the New Testament religion is grace, and ethics is gratitude' (*Letters*, 1877, p. 16). It is not by accident that in Greek one and the same noun (*charis*) does duty for both 'grace' and 'gratitude'.

to come, the age of renewal and resurrection. On them 'the end of the ages has come' (1 Cor. 10:11); for them, because they are a 'new creation' in Christ, 'the old has passed away, behold, the new has come' (2 Cor. 5:17). It is by the power of the indwelling Spirit, the pledge of their inheritance in the world to come, that they can resist the tendency to live according to the standards of 'this world'.

Be transformed. The same verb (*metamorphoō*) is rendered 'transfigured' in the transfiguration narratives of Matthew 17:1–2 and Mark 9:2. The only other place where it occurs in the New Testament is 2 Corinthians 3:18, of believers being 'changed' into the likeness of Christ 'from one degree of glory to another' by the operation of 'the Lord who is the Spirit' – a passage which is a helpful commentary on the present one.

II. THE COMMON LIFE OF CHRISTIANS (12:3–8)

Diversity, not uniformity, is the mark of God's handiwork. It is so in nature; it is equally so in grace, and nowhere more so than in the Christian community. Here are many men and women with the most diverse kinds of parentage, environment, temperament and capacity. Not only so, but since they became Christians they have been endowed by God with a wide variety of spiritual gifts as well. Yet because and by means of that diversity, all can co-operate for the good of the whole. Whatever form of service is to be rendered in the church, let it be rendered heartily and faithfully by those divinely qualified to render it, whether it be prophesying, teaching, admonishing, administering, making material gifts, sick-visiting, or the performance of any other ministry.

To illustrate what he means, Paul uses the figure of a human body, as he had already done in 1 Corinthians 12:12–27. Each part of the body has its own distinctive work to do, yet in a healthy body all the parts function harmoniously and interdependently for the good of the whole body. So should it be in the church, which is the body of Christ.

3. *By the grace given to me*. That is, the 'grace' or spiritual gift of apostleship (*cf.* 1:5; 15:15). According to verse 6, each member of the church has received a special 'grace' in this sense, which is to be exercised for the good of all.

The measure of faith. 'Faith' here has a rather different sense from that which it bears in the earlier part of the letter; here it denotes the spiritual power given to each Christian for the discharge of his or her special responsibility (*cf.* verse 6, 'in proportion to our faith').

5. *One body in Christ.* Compare 1 Corinthians 12:27, 'you are the body of Christ.' In 1 Corinthians and Romans the human body is used as an illustration of the corporate life of Christians, but in Colossians and Ephesians the idea is carried farther. In these later documents emphasis is laid on the relation which the church, as the body, bears to Christ as the head. In them there is no possibility of an ordinary member of the church being compared to the head, or to part of the head (as is done in 1 Cor. 12:16–17, 21); in them, too, the body ceases to be used as a mere simile and becomes rather the most effective term which the apostle can find to express the vital bond which unites the life of believers with the risen life of Christ.[1]

8. *In liberality.* NEB, 'with all your heart.'

He who gives aid. Greek *ho proïstamenos*, understood in a similar sense to the related noun *prostatis*, 'helper', in 16:2. NEB 'if you are a leader' understands the participle in the sense which it bears in 1 Thessalonians 5:12 ('those who . . . are over you').

He who does acts of mercy. NEB, 'if you are helping others in distress.'

III. THE LAW OF CHRIST (12:9–21)

The injunctions in this section to deep, unaffected and practical love are particularly reminiscent of the Sermon on the Mount. Mutual love, sympathy and honour within the brotherhood of

---

[1] See E. Best, *One Body in Christ* (1955).

215

believers are to be expected, but something more is enjoined here – love and forgiveness to those outside the fellowship, and not least to those who persecute them and wish them ill.

9. *Let love be genuine.* Greek *anypokritos*, lit. 'without hypocrisy' (NEB 'in all sincerity').

10. *Outdo one another in showing honour.* Cf. Philippians 2:3, 'count others better than yourselves'; also Ephesians 5:21, 'be subject to one another out of reverence for Christ.'

11. *Be aglow with the Spirit.* The same Greek expression is used in Acts 18:25 of Apollos ('fervent in spirit'); whatever the force of 'spirit' may be there, here the reference is most probably to the Holy Spirit.
Serve the Lord. NEB margin 'meet the demands of the hour' represents an inferior Western reading which replaced the dative *kyriō* ('Lord') by *kairō* ('time', 'opportunity').

14. *Bless those who persecute you; bless and do not curse them.* Cf. Luke 6:28, 'bless those who curse you, pray for those who abuse you.' In the present passage there is some ancient evidence (including that of P46) for the omission of 'you' after 'persecute'; in that case Christians may be exhorted to call down blessings on persecutors, whether they themselves are the victims of the persecution or not. For Paul's own practice in this regard *cf.* 1 Corinthians 4:12b–13a; Acts 28:19b.

15. *Rejoice with those who rejoice, weep with those who weep.* This is no Stoic teaching, according to which an impassive detachment was essential to the good life; it is consistent, however, with the way of Christ.

16. *Live in harmony with one another.* Cf. 15:5–6; see also Philippians 2:2–5, where the injunction to be 'of the same mind' (not the same thing as 'seeing eye to eye') is followed by a statement of the only way in which this is possible in a Christian context: 'Have this mind among yourselves, which is yours in Christ Jesus.'

Do not be haughty. Cf. verse 3; also 11:20, 'do not become proud.'

Associate with the lowly. Or (taking the adjective *tapeinois* as neuter, not masculine) 'give yourselves to humble tasks' (mg.).

Never be conceited. As in 11:25 above, this is a quotation from Proverbs 3:7a.

17. *Repay no one evil for evil.* For the Christian principle of non-retaliation see Matthew 5:38–48. (Cf. 1 Thes. 5:15; 1 Pet. 3:9.)

Take thought for what is noble in the sight of all. 'Let your aims be such as all men count honourable' (NEB). A quotation from Proverbs 3:4 (LXX).

19. *Leave it to the wrath of God.* The genitive 'of God' is implied, but not expressed in the Greek text (cf. 5:9). Make room, the injunction means, for the law of divine retribution to operate whether now or 'on the day of wrath' (2:5).

'Vengeance is mine, I will repay.' A quotation from the Song of Moses: 'Vengeance is mine, and recompense' (Dt. 32:35, MT; LXX has 'in the day of vengeance I will repay'). The present form of the text, found also in Hebrews 10:30, appears in the Aramaic Targums and was probably current in a Greek version not now extant. The point of the quotation here is that, since vengeance and requital are God's prerogative, their exercise should be left to him. So in the Qumran community private vengeance was forbidden on the ground that, according to Nahum 1:2, it is God alone who 'takes vengeance on his adversaries and keeps wrath for his enemies'.[1]

20. *'If your enemy is hungry, feed him; if he is thirsty, give him drink; for by so doing you will heap burning coals upon his head.'* A quotation from Proverbs 25:21–22; Paul omits the concluding clause: 'and the LORD will reward you.' The original force of the admonition may have been :'Treat your enemy kindly, for that will increase his guilt; you will thus ensure for him a more terrible judgment, and for yourself a better reward – from God.' Another view is that the proverb refers to an Egyptian ritual in

---

[1] *Cf.* G. Vermes, *The Dead Sea Scrolls in English,* p. 110.

which a man testified publicly to his penitence by carrying a pan of burning charcoal around on his head. In any case, by placing the proverb in this context and omitting the last clause, Paul gives it a nobler meaning: 'Treat your enemy kindly, for that may make him ashamed and lead to his repentance.' In other words, the best way to get rid of an enemy is to turn him into a friend, and so *overcome evil with good* (verse 21).

21. The series of short clauses which now comes to an end may have been given this form so as to serve as an easily memorized catechesis. *Cf.* 1 Thessalonians 5:14–22.

IV. THE CHRISTIAN AND THE STATE (13:1–7)

When guide-lines are laid down for the behaviour of Christians towards those who are outside the fellowship, it is natural that something should be said about the Christian's relation to the secular authorities – municipal, provincial or imperial. This subject was destined to become specially acute within the decade following the writing of this letter.

So long as the church was mainly Jewish in composition, problems in this sphere were not lacking, but they were not so difficult as they were later to become. The position of Jews within the Roman Empire was regulated by a succession of imperial edicts. Indeed, as a subject nation within the empire, they enjoyed quite exceptional privileges. Jewish communities had the status of *collegia licita* ('permitted associations'). The various practices which marked off Jews from Gentiles were confirmed to them. Those practices might seem absurd and superstitious in Roman eyes, but they were safeguarded none the less by imperial law. They included the sabbath law and food laws and the prohibition of 'graven images'. Imperial policy forbade governors of Judaea to bring military standards, with the emperor's image attached to them, within the walls of the holy city of Jerusalem. If by Jewish law the trespassing of a Gentile within the inner courts of the Jerusalem temple was a sacrilege deserving the death penalty, Rome confirmed Jewish law in this respect even (quite exceptionally) to the point of allowing the execution of the death sentence for such a trespass when the offender was a Roman citizen.

In the first generation after the death of Christ Roman law, when it took cognizance of Christians at all, tended to regard them as a variety of Jews. When the Corinthian Jews in AD 51 or 52 accused Paul before Gallio, proconsul of Achaia, of propagating an illegal religion, Gallio paid little attention to the charge (Acts 18:12–17). To him Paul was as self-evidently a Jew as his accusers were, and the dispute between him and them was in Gallio's eyes a difference of interpretation on points of Jewish law, and he had not come to Achaia to adjudicate on matters of that kind.

Gallio's decision constituted an important precedent; for some ten years thereafter Paul availed himself of the protection which it gave him in his apostolic service, as he continued to propagate the Christian faith not only in the provinces of the Roman Empire but in Rome itself (Acts 28:30–31).

His happy experience of Roman justice is probably reflected in his insistence here that the magistrates, whom he calls 'ministers of God' (verse 6), 'are not a terror to good conduct, but to bad' (verse 3). Yet the principles laid down here were valid even when the authorities were not so benevolent towards Christians as Gallio had been (in effect) towards Paul.

There is another side to the picture of Christianity's relation to the state. Christianity started out with a most serious handicap in the eyes of Roman law, for the sufficient reason that its founder had been convicted and executed on a charge of sedition by the sentence of a Roman judge. The charge was summed up in the inscription attached to his cross: 'The King of the Jews.' Whatever was the nature of the kingship which Jesus claimed, the one record of him known to Roman law was that he had led a movement which challenged the sovereign rights of Caesar. When Tacitus, many years later, wishes his readers to know what kind of people Christians were, he deems it sufficient to say that 'they got their name from Christ, who was executed under the procurator Pontius Pilate when Tiberius was emperor'.[1] That adequately indicated their character.

---

[1] Tacitus, *Annals* 15.44.

When, some seven years before the writing of this letter, Paul's opponents at Thessalonica wished to stir up as much trouble for him and his companions locally as they could, they went to the city magistrates and laid information against them: 'These men who have caused trouble all over the world have now come here. . . . They are all defying Caesar's decrees, saying that there is another king, one called Jesus' (Acts 17:6–7, NIV). This subtle misrepresentation of the truth was calculated to link the missionaries with contemporary fomenters of unrest in Jewish communities throughout the Roman world; it was rendered the more colourable by the fact that Jesus himself had been found guilty before Pilate as an agitator and leader of insurrection.

Nor was Thessalonica the only place where trouble of this kind broke out about the same time. Rome itself remembered the riots of AD 49, stirred up 'at the instigation of Chrestus',[1] which had moved Claudius to expel the Jewish community of the capital; and some of Paul's readers may well have cherished resentment for hardships endured in the course of that expulsion. As for Paul himself, even his best friends could not deny that his arrival in a city was, as often as not, a signal for breaches of the peace. Granted that Paul was not responsible for this, the custodians of law and order would naturally take note of it and draw their own conclusions. It was all the more necessary, therefore, that Christians should be specially careful of their public behaviour and give their traducers no handle against them, but rather pay all due honour and obedience to the authorities. Indeed, Jesus had set them a precedent in this matter, as in so much else, for although his words, 'Render to Caesar the things that are Caesar's, and to God the things that are God's' (Mk. 12:17), referred to a specially delicate issue – the payment of tribute to a pagan ruler by the people of God living in the holy land – they express a principle of more general application.

Paul places the whole question on the highest plane. God is the fount of all authority, and those who exercise authority on earth do so by delegation from him; therefore to disobey them

[1] See pp. 16–17.

is to disobey God. Human government is a divine ordinance, and the powers of coercion and commendation which it exercises have been entrusted to it by God, for the repression of crime and the encouragement of righteousness. Christians of all people, then, ought to obey the laws, pay their taxes and respect the authorities – not because it will be the worse for them if they do not, but because this is one way of serving God.

But what if the authorities themselves are unrighteous? What if Caesar, not content with receiving what is rightfully his, lays claim to 'the things that are God's'? Paul does not deal with this question here, presumably because it had not yet arisen; but it was to be a burning question in the Roman state for generations to come. Caesar could so far exceed the limits of his divinely-given jurisdiction as to claim divine honours for himself and wage war against the saints. Can we recognize Paul's magistrate, the 'minister of God', in John's 'beast from the abyss', who receives his authority from the great red dragon and uses it to enforce universal worship of himself and to exterminate those who withhold worship from him?[1] We can indeed, for Paul himself foresaw precisely such a development when the restraint of law was withdrawn (2 Thes. 2:6–10). 'Without justice', said Augustine, 'what are kingdoms but great gangs of bandits?'[2]

Yet the evidence shows how, in face of gross provocation, Christians maintained their proper loyalty to the state, not least in Rome itself. 'The patience and faith of the saints' wore down the fury of persecution. When the decrees of the civil magistrate conflict with the commandments of God, then, say Christians, 'we must obey God rather than men' (Acts 5:29); when Caesar claims divine honours, Christians must answer 'No'. For then Caesar (whether he takes the form of a dictator or a democracy) is going beyond the authority delegated to him by God, and trespassing on territory which is not his. 'Regarding the State's requirement of worship of Caesar's image,' says Oscar Cullmann, 'Paul would not have spoken otherwise than the author of the Johannine Apocalypse.'[3] But Christians will voice

[1] Rev. 11:7; 13:1–18. [2] *City of God*, 4.4.
[3] *The State in the New Testament* (1957), p. 83.

their 'No' to Caesar's unauthorized demands the more effectively if they have shown themselves ready to say 'Yes' to his
authorized demands.

Some years later, in a document written from Rome on the
eve of a fiery persecution, we hear an echo of these words of
Paul: 'Be subject for the Lord's sake to every human institution,
whether it be to the emperor as supreme, or to governors as
sent by him to punish those who do wrong and to praise those
who do right. . . . Let none of you suffer as a murderer, or a
thief, or a wrongdoer, or a mischief-maker; yet if one suffers as
a Christian, let him not be ashamed, but under that name let
him glorify God' (1 Pet. 2:13–14; 4:15–16).

Later still, in the last years of the first century, a leader in the
Roman church who could remember the outrageous ferocity of
the Neronian persecution thirty years before, and had very
recent experience of Domitian's malevolence, reproduces a
prayer for the rulers who have received 'glory and honour and
power' over earthly things from God, the eternal king, 'that
they may administer with piety, in peace and gentleness, the
authority given to them'.[1] Such language shows how seriously
the Roman church took to heart Paul's injunctions about the
duty of Christians to the powers that be.

1. *Let every person be subject to the governing authorities.* 'The
thirteenth chapter of the Epistle to the Romans', says J. W.
Allen, 'contains what are perhaps the most important words
ever written for the history of political thought. Yet', he
continues, 'it would be a gross mistake to suppose that men,
at any time, took their political opinions from St. Paul.'[2] Some,
however, have made a more deliberate effort to do so than
others.

The question is raised whether the 'governing authorities'
here are angelic powers, or human powers, or both angelic and
human powers.[3] The general biblical view is that secular power

---

[1] 1 Clement 60:2 – 61:2. 'Who would have grudged the Church of Rome her primacy,'
asked J. B. Lightfoot, 'if she had always spoken thus?' (*The Apostolic Fathers*, I.1, [2]1890,
p. 384.

[2] *A History of Political Thought in the Sixteenth Century* (1928), p. 132.

[3] According to O. Cullmann, the 'authorities' here are the *'invisible angelic powers that
stand behind the State government'* (*Christ and Time*, E.T., 1951, p. 195; his italics).

is wielded by 'the host of heaven, in heaven' as well as by 'the kings of the earth, on the earth' (Is. 24:21). It is true, moreover, that the plural of *exousia* ('authority') is freely used by Paul to denote angelic powers (*cf.* 8:38; Eph. 1:21; 3:10; 6:12; Col. 1:16; 2:10, 15). We may compare what he says in 1 Corinthians 2:8 about 'the rulers (*archontes*) of this age' who were responsible for crucifying 'the Lord of glory'; he appears there to have more than human agents in view. Yet in the present context the 'authorities' are best understood as human rulers, who wield 'the sword' for the punishment of wickedness and the protection of the good, who therefore have the right to command and receive obedience, and who are to be paid appropriate taxes and other dues, together with fitting respect and honour. Paul's references elsewhere to angelic powers are very far from suggesting that Christians should be subject to them in any sense; on the contrary, Christians are liberated from their jurisdiction through their union with Christ, for he is the creator and head of all those powers (Col. 1:16; 2:10), and their conqueror when they set themselves in hostility to him and his people (Col. 2:15).

Those that exist have been instituted by God. There is no contradiction between the principle and the argument of 1 Corinthians 6:1–8, where Christians are dissuaded from suing or prosecuting one another in secular law-courts. Recognition of the civil authorities makes no difference to the fact that it is unbecoming for Christians to wash their dirty linen in public. And while civil magistrates or judges are divinely ordained, that ordination carries with it no status in the church: they are 'men who count for nothing in our community' (1 Cor. 6:4, NEB).

2. *Therefore he who resists the authorities resists what God has appointed.* 'Few sayings in the New Testament have suffered as much misuse as this one,' says Oscar Cullmann.[1] He thinks especially of its misuse in justifying uncritical submission to the dictates of totalitarian governments. It is plain from the immediate context, as from the general context of the apostolic writings, that the state can rightly command obedience only

[1] *The State in the New Testament*, pp. 55 f.

within the limits of the purposes for which it has been divinely instituted – in particular, the state not only may but must be resisted when it demands the allegiance due to God alone.

'The obedience which the Christian man owes to the State is never absolute but, at the most, partial and contingent. It follows that the Christian lives always in a tension between two competing claims; that in certain circumstances dis-obedience to the command of the State may be not only a right but also a duty. This has been classical doctrine ever since the apostles declared that they ought to obey God rather than men.'[1]

Those who resist will incur judgment. They 'have themselves to thank for the punishment they will receive' (NEB).

3. *Rulers are not a terror to good conduct, but to bad.* Moffatt's rendering, 'magistrates are no terror to an honest man', is based on the slenderly supported but intrinsically attractive reading *agathoergō* for *agathō ergō*.

Do what is good, and you will receive his approval. Cf. 1 Peter 3:13, 'who is there to harm you if you are zealous for what is right?' (The words immediately following these, in 1 Pet. 3:14, envisage the possibility that the situation might change: 'But even if you do suffer for righteousness' sake . . .')

4. *He does not bear the sword in vain.* The sword was the symbol of a Roman magistrate's *imperium*; cf. Philostratus, *Lives of the Sophists*, 1.25.2: 'a judge bearing the sword.'

The servant of God to execute his wrath on the wrongdoer. The state is thus charged with a function which has been explicitly forbidden to the Christian (12:17a, 19). The Christian state of later days lay, of course, outside the range of Paul's admonition, and no express direction is given by which the Christian ruler or judge may reconcile his duty as a Christian to leave the exacting of vengeance to 'the wrath of God' and his official duty to 'execute his wrath'. This is not to say that he cannot extract

---

[1] Sir T. M. Taylor, *The Heritage of the Reformation* (1961), pp. 8 f. (the closing reference is to Acts 5:29).

principles to guide him from this and similar passages. But it is plain that two distinct spheres of 'service' to God are envisaged.

'The sanction that the Bible, here and elsewhere, gives to the forcible restraint of evil puzzles many modern Christians, because of its apparent contradiction to Christ's way of love and His precept of non-resistance to evil. But this comes from failing to distinguish the preservation of the world from the salvation of the world. The truth is that the Bible affirms both the Law "which worketh wrath" (Rom. 4:15) and the "faith which worketh by love" (Gal. 5:6): both Christ's strange work and His proper work.'[1]

5. *For the sake of conscience.* The Christian has a higher motive for obeying the ruler than the unpleasantness of the consequences of disobedience; the Christian knows that such obedience is in accordance with God's will, and by rendering it will preserve a good conscience in relation to God. For 'conscience' see note on 2:15 (p. 86).

6. *For the same reason you also pay taxes.* RSV is probably right in taking this clause as a statement, not a command; the Greek is ambiguous (the verb may be either imperative or indicative). 'This is your justification for paying taxes to pagan rulers (a matter of conscience for many Jews, and perhaps for some Christians also), because they are carrying out God's service.' Irenaeus, taking issue with a gnostic interpretation, quotes this verse to prove that Paul in this paragraph refers 'not to angelic powers or invisible rulers, as some venture to expound the passage, but to actual human authorities'.[2]

The authorities are ministers of God. The Greek word for 'minister' here is *leitourgos* (not *diakonos*, as in verse 4), a word which in New Testament and early Christian literature is used particularly of religious service. See note on 15:16 (p. 246, n. 2).

7. *Pay all of them their dues.* Possibly an echo of Jesus' direction:

[1] A. R. Vidler, *Christ's Strange Work* (1944), p. 28. See also C. E. B. Cranfield, 'The Christian's Political Responsibility according to the New Testament', *SJT* 15 (1962), pp. 176–192.

[2] *Against Heresies* 5.24.1.

'Render [or 'give back', *apodote*, the same form as here] to Caesar the things that are Caesar's' (Mk. 12:17). But the following verses show that the duty of obedience to secular authorities is a temporary one, lasting only for the present period of 'night' (verse 12); in the 'day' which 'is at hand' a new order of government will be introduced, when 'the saints will judge the world' (1 Cor. 6:2).[1] The state is to wither away (on this Paul and Karl Marx agree); 'the city of God remaineth.'

V. LOVE AND DUTY (13:8–10)

Pay all their dues; let your only outstanding debt be the debt of love, for that debt can never be discharged in full. The quotation of Leviticus 19:18, 'You shall love your neighbour as yourself', as a summary of God's requirements, places Paul right within the tradition of Jesus, who set these words as the second great commandment alongside 'You shall love the LORD your God . . .' (Dt. 6:5), 'the great and first commandment', adding 'On these two commandments depend all the law and the prophets' (Mt. 22:37–40; *cf*. Mk. 12:28–34). Paul mentions the second here and not the first, because the immediate question concerns a Christian's duty to his neighbour – the subject-matter of the commandments in the second table of the Decalogue. These commandments forbid the harming of a neighbour in any way; since love never harms another, love fulfils the law.

8. *He who loves his neighbour has fulfilled the law.* 'His neighbour' is literally 'the other'. It is just possible to translate 'he who loves has fulfilled the other law' – *i.e.* the 'second' commandment of Mark 12:31 or else 'the law of Christ' (*cf*. Gal. 6:2) over and above the law of the state to which obedience has been enjoined in verses 1–7. But the translation in the text is far preferable.

[1] Behind this statement (1 Cor. 6:2) lies Daniel 7:18, 22, 27. But if it is argued that this apocalyptic outlook is incompatible with that of Romans 13:1–7 (*cf*. J. Kallas, 'Romans XIII.1–7: an Interpolation', *NTS* 11, 1964–65, pp. 365–374), let it be borne in mind that, according to that same book of Daniel, pagan monarchs like Nebuchadnezzar owe their authority to the Most High God and are responsible to him for the way in which they exercise it.

9. *'You shall not commit adultery, You shall not kill, You shall not steal, You shall not covet.'* The seventh, sixth, eighth and tenth commandments of the Decalogue (Ex. 20:13-17; Dt. 5:17-21), selected apparently in random order. *Cf.* Mark 10:19.

'You shall love your neighbour as yourself.' The 'second' great commandment, as Jesus called it (Mt. 22:39; Mk. 12:31); in James 2:8 it is designated 'the royal law' ('the sovereign law laid down in scripture', NEB). *Cf.* Galatians 5:14, 'For the whole law is fulfilled in one word, "You shall love your neighbour as yourself." '

10. *Love is the fulfilling of the law.* 'Fulfilling' renders *plērōma*, a word with a wide range of meaning (translated 'full inclusion' in 11:12, 'full number' in 11:25, 'fulness' in 15:29). *Cf.* Augustine, quoted in comment on 6:15 (pp. 133f.).

VI. CHRISTIAN LIFE IN DAYS OF CRISIS (13:11-14)

Paul recognized the critical nature of the times. He was under no illusions about the permanence of his present opportunity of preaching the gospel, but he was determined to exploit it to the full while it lasted. If he no longer uses the apocalyptic imagery of 2 Thessalonians 2:1-12, he knows that the restraint on the submerged forces of darkness and disorder may at any time be removed; Christians should therefore be on the alert. But the prospect should fill them with encouragement, not with despair: 'when these things begin to take place,' Jesus had said, 'look up and raise your heads, because your redemption is drawing near' (Lk. 21:28). And Paul echoes his Master: 'salvation is nearer to us now than when we first believed.' The events of AD 64 and 66 – the beginning of imperial persecution of Christians and the outbreak of the Jewish revolt, which was to end with the collapse of the Second Jewish Commonwealth – were already casting their shadows before. That these events would not be the immediate precursor of the Second Advent and the final salvation of all believers was something which Paul could not have foreseen; if knowledge of that day and hour was withheld even from the Son of man, it was denied *a fortiori* to his servant. But Jesus' words, 'he who endures to the end will be saved' (Mk. 13:13), verified themselves in the experience of his people who passed through these crises, as they have done in other crises since then. With the affliction comes the way of deliverance: 'Here is a call for the endurance and faith of the saints' (Rev. 13:10).

Meanwhile the children of light must live in readiness for the day of visitation, abjuring all the 'works of darkness'. Elsewhere Paul speaks of putting on 'the new man' (Eph. 4:24; Col. 3:10); here, more directly, he bids his readers 'put on the Lord Jesus Christ'. The Christian graces, the 'armour of light', which he exhorts them to display instead of gratifying unworthy desires, what are they but those graces which were displayed in harmonious perfection in their Lord? Paul's knowledge of the historical Jesus and his interest in him were much greater than is allowed by those who misinterpret his words about not knowing Christ 'from a human point of view' (2 Cor. 5:16) to deny such knowledge or interest on Paul's part. For when Paul comes to enumerate in detail the graces which he desires believers in Rome and elsewhere to 'put on', they are the qualities which characterized Christ on earth.

11. *It is full time now for you to wake from sleep.* The duty of spiritual vigilance was constantly enjoined in apostolic teaching; *cf.* 1 Thessalonians 5:4–11.

Salvation is nearer to us now than when we first believed. Salvation is here viewed in its future completeness; it is the 'adoption as sons, the redemption of our bodies', for which believers wait according to 8:23; *cf.* the 'salvation ready to be revealed in the last time' for which, according to 1 Peter 1:5, they are 'guarded through faith'. Its consummation coincides with the manifestation of Christ in glory (*cf.* Heb. 9:28).

12. *The works of darkness . . . the armour of light.* 'Let us therefore throw off the deeds of darkness and put on our armour as soldiers of the light' (NEB). The antithesis between darkness and light is found repeatedly in Paul's writings (*cf.* 2 Cor. 6:14; Eph. 5:8; Col. 1:12–13; 1 Thes. 5:4–5), as well as in John's. It is one of the most obvious points of contact in concept and language between the New Testament and the Qumran texts, where all human beings are governed either by the Prince of Light or by the Angel of Darkness, and the great conflict of the end-time is called 'the war of the sons of light against the sons of darkness'.[1] The 'armour of light' is described in greater detail in 1 Thessalonians 5:8 and Ephesians 6:13–17.

13. *As in the day.* The 'day' is the time for sobriety, for 'those who get drunk are drunk at night' (1 Thes. 5:7).

14. *Put on the Lord Jesus Christ.* A literary parallel to this use of 'put on' is quoted from Dionysius of Halicarnassus, *Roman Antiquities* 11.5, where 'to put on Tarquin' means to play the part of Tarquin.

The practical teaching given to Christian converts in the primitive church (see p. 134) appears to have been arranged, for easy memorization, under various catchwords, of which 'Put on' was one. They were urged to 'put on' Christian virtues as they would put on new clothes (*cf.* Col. 3:12); and as these virtues were all aspects of the new Christian character which they received at conversion, they might be told to 'put on the new man' (Eph. 4:24), or to live as befitted those who had put him on once for all (Col. 3:10). Since this 'new man' was the character of Christ reproduced in his people, it was a simple transition to say, 'as many of you as were baptized into Christ have put on Christ' (Gal. 3:27) or, as here, to exhort believers to 'put on' Christ in the sense of manifesting outwardly what they had already experienced inwardly. While Paul did not know the written Gospels which we have in the New Testament, it is noteworthy that, when he commends to his readers the cultivation of those qualities which the Evangelists ascribe to our Lord, he does so by telling them to 'put on the Lord Jesus Christ'.

And make no provision for the flesh, to gratify its desires. Cf. 6:12. It was the words of verses 13 and 14 that kindled a flame of sacred love in Augustine's heart (see p. 56).

---

[1] *Cf.* G. Vermes, *The Dead Sea Scrolls in English*, pp. 75–78, 122–148.

VII. CHRISTIAN LIBERTY AND CHRISTIAN CHARITY
(14:1 – 15:6)

A. CHRISTIAN LIBERTY (14:1–12)

Paul enjoyed his Christian liberty to the full. Never was a Christian more thoroughly emancipated than he from un-Christian inhibitions and taboos. So completely was he emancipated from spiritual bondage that he was not even in bondage to his emancipation. He conformed to the Jewish way of life when he was in Jewish society as cheerfully as he went along with Gentile ways when he was living with Gentiles. The interests of the gospel and the highest well-being of men and women were paramount considerations with him; to these he subordinated everything else.

But he knew very well that many other Christians were not so completely emancipated as he was, and he insisted that these must be treated gently. A Christian's 'faith' in many respects might be weak, immature and uninstructed; but he must be welcomed warmly as a Christian and not challenged forthwith to a debate about those areas of life in which he is still unemancipated.

Paul mentions two areas of life in which this was liable to happen, and then enlarges on one of them. One was food; the other was the religious observance of certain days. Some Christians (like Paul himself) had no qualms of conscience about taking any kind of food; others had scruples about certain kinds. Some (again like Paul) made no distinction between more and less sacred days, regarding every day as 'holy to the Lord'; others felt that some days were holier than others. What is to be done when Christians of such different convictions find themselves in the same fellowship? Must they start to thrash the matter out, one side determined to convert the other? No, says Paul; let each one be satisfied in his own mind and conscience. Those who enjoy greater liberty must not despise others as being spiritually immature; those who have conscientious scruples must not criticize their fellow-Christians for doing what they themselves would not do. Each Christian is the servant of Christ; it is to Christ that each is accountable, both here and hereafter. Christ died, and is Lord of the dead; Christ lives, and is Lord of the living.

It is not for one Christian to sit in judgment on another – can we hear an echo of our Lord's 'Judge not, that you be not judged' (Mt. 7:1)? – for it is at God's tribunal that all must appear to render account and receive due assessment.

With these words Paul insists uncompromisingly on the principle of Christian liberty. 'A Christian is a most free lord of all, subject to none' (Luther).[1]

1. *Weak in faith.* Not yet mature enough to grasp that all kinds of food are equally *kosher* ('fit'), all days equally holy.

Not for disputes over opinions. 'Without attempting to settle doubtful points' (NEB).

2. *The weak man eats only vegetables.* Perhaps because of vegetarian principles, but more probably in order to avoid eating the flesh of animals that had been sacrificed to pagan deities or not properly slaughtered according to Jewish law (*cf.* Dn. 1:8, 12).

4. *Who are you to pass judgment on the servant of another? It is before his own master that he stands or falls.* Cf. Matthew 7:3-5; Luke 6:37, 41-42; and especially Paul's own words in 1 Corinthians 4:3-5, 'with me it is a very small thing that I should be judged by you or by any human court. . . . It is the Lord who judges me. Therefore do not pronounce judgment before the time, before the Lord comes.' The word rendered 'servant' here is *oiketēs*, 'domestic servant', not *doulos*, 'slave'.

5. *Another man esteems all days alike.* There is no word in the Greek text corresponding to 'alike', although it is added here to complete the sense. It need not mean that 'another man' treats every day as secular; it may mean that he treats every day as equally to be dedicated to the service of God, and this was certainly Paul's attitude.

[1] 'Christianus homo omnium dominus est liberrimus, nulli subiectus' (*On the Liberty of a Christian*, sentence 1).

6. *He who observes the day, observes it in honour of the Lord.* Therefore, 'let no one pass judgment on you . . . with regard to a festival or a new moon or a sabbath' (Col. 2:16). Paul says no more at present about the observance of special days, presumably because this was not a live issue at the time in the Christian community of Rome, as it had been some years before in the churches of Galatia (Gal. 4:10).

He also who eats, eats in honour of the Lord. Therefore, 'let no one pass judgment on you in questions of food and drink' (Col. 2:16).

He who abstains . . . gives thanks to God. That is to say, he says grace for the food that his conscience permits him to eat (not for what he abstains from), just as the Christian with a robust conscience says grace for the indiscriminate food that he takes. In either case the food is sanctified by the thanksgiving (*cf.* 1 Cor. 10:30; 1 Tim. 4:3–5).

7. *None of us lives to himself.* What Paul means, as verse 8 shows, is that each Christian lives out his life in Christ's sight, and as Christ's servant; but a corollary of this is that each Christian's life affects his fellow-Christians and his fellow-men and women in general; therefore he should consider his responsibility to them, and not consult his own interests only.

9. *Christ died and lived again, that he might be Lord . . .* By virtue of his death he is Lord of the dead; by virtue of his resurrection he is Lord of the living. Therefore in life and death alike his people are his; he is Lord of all (Phil. 2:11).

10. *Why do you pass judgment on your brother?* There is no sin to which Christians – especially 'keen' Christians – are more prone than the sin of censoriousness. The apostle's words are seriously intended. 'Should a man not lay his hand upon his mouth before he criticizes his brethren? When we pass swift, uninformed, unloving and ungenerous judgments, surely we have forgotten that if we speak evil of them, at the same time we speak evil of the Lord whose name they bear.'[1]

[1] H. St. John, in *A New Testament Church in 1955*, ed. P. O. Ruoff (1955), p. 91.

We shall all stand before the judgment seat of God. The judgment seat is the *bēma*, or tribunal. There is no difference between this tribunal and the 'judgment seat of Christ' (2 Cor. 5:10). From the earlier part of the second century there has been a tendency to assimilate the reading of our present text to that of 2 Corinthians 5:10 (*cf.* AV).

11. *'As I live, says the Lord, every knee shall bow to me, and every tongue shall give praise to God.'* Quoted from Isaiah 45:23, 'By myself I have sworn, . . . "To me every knee shall bow, every tongue shall swear." ' The same passage is applied in Philippians 2:10–11 to the eventual paying of universal homage to Christ. Here it is designed to emphasize that in the end *each of us shall give account of himself to God* (verse 12).

B. CHRISTIAN CHARITY (14:13–23)

Martin Luther, who begins his treatise *On the Liberty of a Christian* with the words quoted above ('A Christian is a most free lord of all, subject to none'), goes on immediately to say, 'A Christian is a most dutiful servant of all, subject to all.'[1] He was never a more faithful follower of Paul, and of Paul's Master and his, than when he juxtaposed these two affirmations.

Paul, having asserted as plainly as possible the freedom of a Christian, now goes on to show how on occasion that freedom may, and should, be limited – but limited voluntarily. In doing so he enlarges on one of the subjects he has already used to illustrate his assertion of Christian freedom – the subject of food.

The question of what kinds of food might and might not be taken agitated the early church in various ways. One of these affected Jewish Christians more particularly. The Jewish food-laws, which had been observed by the nation from early days, constituted one of the principal features which distinguished Jews from their Gentile neighbours. Not only was the flesh of certain animals absolutely prohibited; the blood of *all* animals

---

[1] 'Christianus homo omnium servus est officiosissimus, omnibus subiectus.'

was absolutely prohibited, and 'clean' animals slaughtered for food had to be killed in such a way that their blood was entirely drained away. Since one could never be sure that meat eaten by non-Jews was free from every suspicion of illegality in one respect or another, it was impossible for a strictly observant Jew to share a meal with a Gentile. Indeed, such a Jew might find it difficult enough to share a meal with a fellow-Jew whom he suspected of laxity in these matters.

Jesus, on one occasion, made a pronouncement about food which, as later reflection on it showed, had the effect of abrogating the Jewish food-laws: 'he declared all foods clean' (Mk. 7:19). Peter, in his noonday vision on the roof of Simon the tanner's house in Joppa, learnt not to count as unclean anything or any one that God has pronounced clean; and thanks to that lesson he was ready to visit the Gentile Cornelius at Caesarea and accept his hospitality. But it was long before the majority of Jewish Christians could think of following his example – if, indeed, the majority of them ever did get around to following it.. On one occasion, some ten years before this letter was written, Peter was resident in Syrian Antioch and enjoying unrestricted fellowship with Gentile Christians there, when visitors from the church of Jerusalem called on him and persuaded him to withdraw from sharing the same table as Gentiles and to eat with Jews only. His example began to have a devastating effect: even so liberal a Christian as Barnabas was disposed to follow it. Paul publicly accused Peter of 'play-acting' – acting a part which did not correspond with his inner convictions (Gal. 2:11–14).

When, shortly afterwards, the Council of Jerusalem agreed that Gentiles should be admitted to church fellowship, like Jews, on the sole ground of faith in Christ, a proviso was added to the effect that Gentile converts should abstain from food which was abhorrent to their brethren of Jewish stock and should conform to the Jewish marriage-laws (Acts 15:20, 29). If Paul went along with this decision (as the narrative of Acts declares he did), he makes no appeal to it in his letters when dealing with the issues which it covered, but bases his argument (as here) on ethical principles.

In any case, while Paul was uncompromising where principles which he counted basic were at stake, he was the most accommodating of men once these were safeguarded. Once the principle had been established that Gentiles were to be accepted as full members of the church on the one sufficient basis of faith in Christ, he himself would have been foremost in reminding his Gentile converts of the wisdom of placing some limitation (voluntary, not dictated) on their freedom in non-essentials for the sake of maintaining fellowship with Jewish Christians, not all of whom could be expected to be so completely emancipated in mind as Paul himself was. If Gentile Christians who lived alongside Jewish Christians charitably refrained from food which the latter would find obnoxious, fellowship between the two groups would be promoted. In fact the food-provisions of the Council of Jerusalem retained their validity in some areas of the church for many generations.

One of the food-provisions of the Council of Jerusalem laid down abstention from the flesh of animals which had been offered in sacrifice to idols. This was a question which was bound to be raised among Christians living in a pagan society. In his correspondence with the Corinthian church Paul dealt with it in some detail, because that church had sent him a letter seeking a ruling from him on the subject.

The buying of butcher-meat in a pagan city presented some Christians with a problem of conscience. Much of the meat sold in the market came from animals which had been sacrificed to a pagan deity. The deity received his token portion; the rest of the carcase would be sold by the temple authorities to the retail merchants. Among resident Christians there would be some with a robust conscience who knew that the meat was neither better nor worse for its association with a pagan deity and who were quite happy to eat it; others were not so happy, feeling that somehow the meat had been 'infected' by its idolatrous association.

In giving his judgment to the Corinthians on this question, Paul ranges himself, on the one hand, with those who knew that there was no substance in the pagan deities, and that a Christian was at perfect liberty to eat meat of this kind. He reminds them, on the other hand, that knowledge is not everything: the claims of love have to be considered. Paul himself was prepared to forgo his liberty if, by insisting on it, he would set a harmful example to a fellow-Christian with a weaker conscience. If a Christian, who thought the eating of idol meat was wrong, was encouraged by the example of his robuster brother to eat some, the resultant damage to his conscience would be debited to the other's lack of charity and consideration.

This does not seem to have been such a burning issue in the Roman church; at least, Paul does not deal with it specifically in Romans as he does in 1 Corinthians. The situation in view here, like the situation addressed by the decree from the Council of Jerusalem, is one in which Jewish and Gentile Christians lived together.

Some of the Christian house-churches in Rome would be mainly Jewish in membership, some would be mainly Gentile, others might be mixed. The problem was not simply that Jewish Christians confined themselves to *kosher* food and continued to observe the sabbath and other holy days, while Gentile Christians practised liberty in both respects. The situation was probably more complex. Many Jewish Christians had become more or less emancipated from the religious obligations of their ancestral law. We may believe that Priscilla and Aquila, with 'the church in their house' (16:5), followed Paul's line in such matters. On the other hand, some Gentile Christians, finding in their Bible (the Greek Old Testament) food-restrictions imposed by divine authority, argued that these restrictions retained their force and should be complied with. As for special days, we know how some Christians of our own time maintain that the seventh day of the week retains the sanctity with which it was invested at the creation and in the law of Sinai and that it should therefore be observed as distinctively holy. That this kind of tendency was not unknown in Gentile Christianity of the apostolic age is evidence from Paul's letter to the Galatians, sent to Gentile converts who were not only keeping the Jewish sacred calendar but even accepting circumcision.

Among the house-churches of Rome, then, we should probably envisage a broad spectrum of varieties in outlook and practice between the firm Jewish retention of the ancestral customs and Gentile remoteness from these customs. Some

Jewish Christians might be found on the liberal side of the
half-way mark between the two extremes and some Gentile
Christians on the 'legalist' side. P. S. Minear has distinguished
five different attitudes in these respects among the Roman
Christians.[1] Variety of this kind can very easily promote a spirit
of division. Paul wishes to safeguard the Roman Christians
against this, encouraging them to treat the variety rather as an
occasion for charity, forbearance and understanding. It is good
to be strong in faith and emancipated in conscience, but Christians are not isolated individuals, but members of a fellowship;
it is therefore the responsibility of all, and especially of those
who are stronger and more mature, to care for the well-being
of the fellowship.

13. *Let us no more pass judgment on one another, but rather decide*
. . . The same Greek verb (*krinō*) does duty for 'pass judgment'
and 'decide'.

Never to put a stumbling block or hindrance in the way of a brother.
That is, never to set an example which might lead another into
sin. A Christian 'stumbles' (*cf.* verse 21) if, imitating the action
of a more emancipated Christian, he does something of which
his own conscience does not approve. It would be better for
the emancipated Christian to help his 'weaker' brother to have
a more enlightened conscience; but this is a process which
cannot be rushed.

14. *I . . . am persuaded in the Lord Jesus that nothing is unclean*
in itself. For Paul all food was *kosher*. He may have been aware
of our Lord's pronouncement on the subject (known to us from
Mk. 7:14–19), but to be 'persuaded in the Lord Jesus' means
more than this: it expresses his conviction as a member of
Christ, as he considers the life and welfare of the believing
fellowship.

But it is unclean for any one who thinks it unclean. This insight,
completely in accord with the teaching of Christ (*cf.* Mk.
7:20–23), has far-reaching implications. Defilement is located in
people's minds, not in material objects. See Titus 1:15.

[1] *The Obedience of Faith* (1971), pp. 8–35. But he has probably demarcated them too
sharply.

15. *Do not let what you eat cause the ruin of one for whom Christ died.* These last words express the divine measure of the worth of a human being.

16. *Do not let what is good to you be spoken of as evil.* 'What for you is a good thing must not become an occasion for slanderous talk' (NEB).

17. *The kingdom of God does not mean food and drink but righteousness and peace and joy.* Cf. Matthew 6:31 and 33. 'Do not be anxious, saying, "What shall we eat?" or "What shall we drink?" . . . But seek first his kingdom and his righteousness.' External commodities like food and drink are ethically neutral compared with the things that matter most. For the sequence 'righteousness . . . peace . . . joy' cf. Romans 5:1–3; also Matthew 5:6, 9 and 12: 'Blessed are those who hunger and thirst for righteousness . . . Blessed are the peacemakers . . . Rejoice and be glad.' A parallel to the construction of the verse is provided by 1 Corinthians 4:20, 'the kingdom of God does not consist in talk but in power' (the power, of course, being the Holy Spirit's).

In the Holy Spirit. As in 8:9–25, the Holy Spirit brings believers here and now into the good of their coming inheritance. For Paul, 'the kingdom of God' (as distinct from the present kingdom of Christ) is the future inheritance of the children of God (*cf.* 1 Cor. 6:9–10; 15:50; Gal. 5:21; Eph. 5:5; 1 Thes. 2:12; 2 Thes. 1:5); but 'in the Holy Spirit' its blessings can be enjoyed already.

18. *He who thus serves Christ.* 'Thus' (*en toutō*, 'in this') probably means 'in the pursuit of righteousness, peace and joy'.

19. *Let us then pursue.* The contextual sense favours the subjunctive *diōkōmen* rather than the indicative *diōkomen*, 'we pursue' (*cf.* 5:1, where the indicative is the more probable reading).

For mutual upbuilding. To 'build up the common life' (NEB).

20. *The work of God.* His inward work of grace is causing the believer's spiritual life to develop. This work, carried out in the individual members, will have a beneficial effect on the growth of the whole community.

21. *It is right not to eat meat or drink wine . . . Cf.* Paul's own policy: 'if food is a cause of my brother's falling, I will never eat meat, lest I cause my brother to fall' (1 Cor. 8:13) – and this despite his persuasion that no food was *per se* impermissible. In food and social customs generally he adapted himself to the company he was in (1 Cor. 9:19–23).

22. *The faith that you have.* 'Faith' in this sense is a firm and intelligent conviction before God that one is doing what is right, the antithesis of feeling self-condemned in what one permits oneself to do.

Happy is he who has no reason to judge himself for what he approves. He, in other words, who has a good (but not insensitive) conscience. *Cf.* Paul's defence in Acts 23:1; 24:16.

23. *He who has doubts is condemned, if he eats.* If he does something about which his conscience is uneasy, he is condemned at heart and incurs a sense of guilt, 'because his action does not arise from his conviction' (NEB). But one who does something knowing it to be not only permissible but positively right does it *from faith.* There is sound sense in the apocryphal incident inserted in *Codex Bezae* after Luke 6:4, which tells how our Lord, 'seeing a man working on the sabbath, said to him, "Man, if indeed you know what you are doing, you are blessed; but if you do not know, you are accursed and a transgressor of the law".'

Whatsoever does not proceed from faith is sin. The implication of this statement appears to be that an action performed against the voice of conscience can never be right.

For evidence that one early edition of Romans came to an end here, see Introduction, pp. 26–29.

C. THE EXAMPLE OF CHRIST (15:1–6)

Paul concludes his words on Christian liberty and Christian charity by adducing the example of Christ. Who was more free from taboos and inhibitions than he? Yet who was more careful to bear with the weaknesses of others? It is so easy for those who are quite clear in conscience about a course of action to snap their fingers at critics and say, 'I'll please myself.' Their right to do so is unquestioned, but that is not the way of Christ. His way is to consider others first, to consult their interests and help them in every possible way. Even 'Christ did not please himself'; if he had done so, we might wonder in what respect his life and ministry would have taken a different course from that which they did take. Christ did not assert his rights; he put the interests of others before his own (*cf.* Phil. 2:5–8). But perhaps Paul means here that he put the will of God first of all: this is suggested by his quotation of Psalm 69:9.

The words that follow this quotation embody a principle which can be traced throughout the New Testament, wherever the Old Testament is cited or referred to. The lessons of endurance which the Old Testament writings inculcate, and the encouragement which they supply to faithfulness, provide a strong incentive to the maintenance of Christian hope. Paul presents them also as a strong incentive to the fostering of brotherly unity, and he prays that the God who teaches his people endurance and provides encouragement for them through the Scriptures may grant them oneness of mind, so that he may be glorified by their united witness.

1. *We who are strong ought to bear with the failings of the weak.* Cf. Galatians 6:1–2, 'if a man is overtaken in any trespass, you who are spiritual should restore him in a spirit of gentleness. . . . Bear one another's burdens, and so fulfil the law of Christ.'

2. *For his good, to edify him.* 'Think what is for his good and will build up the common life' (NEB). Cf. 14:19; also Philippians 2:3–4.

3. *'The reproaches of those who reproached thee fell on me.'* Quoted from Psalm 69:9b. Verse 9a is quoted in John 2:17 with reference to Jesus' cleansing of the temple.[1] Psalm 69, as we have seen (*cf.* comment on 11:9–10, p. 202), was interpreted early in the church's life of Christ's passion and of the retribution to overtake his persecutors. Since the words here quoted (like the greater part of the psalm) are addressed to God, they imply that Jesus' faithfulness to God involved him in reproach and insult which he might have avoided by choosing an easier path.

4. *Whatever was written in former days was written for our instruction.* Compare the statement of the same principle in 1 Corinthians 10:6, 11. The Scriptures (here, of course, the Old Testament Scriptures) provide ample evidence of God's fidelity, especially when they are read in the light of Christ's fulfilment of them; therefore their readers are encouraged to place their hope in the Lord and wait patiently for him.

5. *To live in such harmony with one another, in accord with Christ Jesus.* See comment on 12:16 (p. 216).

6. *That together you may with one voice glorify the God and Father of our Lord Jesus Christ.* If their community life was harmonious, God would be glorified by their united worship and united witness. Such a united witness at the heart of the Roman Empire would be an incomparable factor in the furtherance of the gospel.

VIII. CHRIST AND THE GENTILES (15:7–13)

'So then,' says Paul, 'follow the example of Christ. As he welcomed us without discrimination, so let us make room for one another without discrimination.

'This is what I mean,' he continues. 'Christ came not to receive service but to give it – first, and directly, to the Jews, in order to fulfil the promises which God had made to their

---

[1] *Cf.* C. H. Dodd, *According to the Scriptures* (1952), p. 58.

forefathers, and then also to the Gentiles, that they might rejoice in God's uncovenanted mercy.' But if the bringing of the gospel to the Jews fulfilled the promises to the patriarchs, the evangelization and conversion of the Gentiles were also foretold in the Old Testament. Paul adduces a catena of Old Testament *testimonia* in which the Gentiles are presented as praising the God of Israel and placing their hope in Israel's Messiah.

The manner and extent of the blessing into which God would bring believing Gentiles – their incorporation along with believing Jews in the community of the people of God – might be a mystery concealed from earlier generations until it became a reality through Paul's ministry (Eph. 3:2–6; Col. 1:25–27); but the fact that Gentiles would be blessed by the gospel Paul sees as something clearly predicted in Old Testament times (*cf.* Gal. 3:8). This meant that he viewed his own ministry as God's means towards the fulfilment of his promise to the Gentiles.

A prayer that his readers may abound in joy and peace, faith and hope, concludes this division of the letter in which Paul has presented the Christian way of life.

7. *Welcome one another.* Take your fellow-Christians to your hearts as well as to your homes. If Christ's example is followed, as Paul enjoins, the welcome will be unreserved and God will be glorified by his people's mutual love and kindness. Paul may have in mind especially, though by no means exclusively, the practice of unreserved fellowship between Jewish and Gentile believers.

As Christ has welcomed you. For 'you' (*hymas*) there is, as in many other places, a variant reading 'us' (*hēmas*); *cf.* NEB. 'This is why it is right that they should remain united together, and not despise one another, because Christ despised neither of them'[1] (Calvin, *ad loc.*).

8. *Christ became a servant to the circumcised.* That is, 'of the Jewish people' (NEB). On his own testimony, during his earthly ministry, Jesus was 'sent only to the lost sheep of the house of Israel' (Mt. 15:24). The noun translated 'servant' is *diakonos*;

---

[1] That is, neither Jews nor Gentiles.

compare Jesus' words: 'the Son of man came not to be served (*diakonēthēnai*) but to serve (*diakonēsai*)' (Mk. 10:45), and 'I am among you as one who serves' (*diakonōn*, Lk. 22:27).

To show God's truthfulness. 'By making good his promises to the patriarchs' (NEB) – promises which were fulfilled in Christ.

9. *That the Gentiles might glorify God for his mercy.* Christ's direct ministry to 'the circumcised' was continued by the 'pillar' apostles (Gal. 2:9); the imparting of his blessing to Gentiles was administered pre-eminently by Paul.

'*Therefore I will praise thee among the Gentiles, and sing to thy name.*' A quotation from Psalm 18:49 (2 Sa. 22:50) where David, having incorporated non-Israelite nations in his empire, counts them as now belonging to the heritage of the God of Israel. For the Christian application of this idea *cf.* James's quotation of Amos 9:11–12 (LXX) at the Council of Jerusalem (Acts 15:16–17).

10. '*Rejoice, O Gentiles, with his people.*' A quotation from the Song of Moses (Dt. 32:43). (Compare earlier quotations from the same Song in 10:19; 11:11; 12:19.)

11. '*Praise the Lord, all Gentiles, and let all the peoples praise him.*' A quotation from Psalm 117:1, where the whole world is called upon to praise the God of Israel for his steadfast love and faithfulness.

12. '*The root of Jesse shall come, he who rises to rule the Gentiles: in him shall the Gentiles hope.*' A quotation from Isaiah 11:10, where the 'shoot from the stump of Jesse' (Is. 11:1), *i.e.* the expected Messiah of David's line, 'shall stand as an ensign to the peoples; him shall the nations seek'. The Targum of Jonathan renders the last clause 'to him shall kings render obedience' (*cf.* Gn. 49:10d). For Jesus' Davidic descent see 1:3 with comment (p. 68). Paul finds *testimonia* of the Gentile mission in the Law, the Prophets and the Psalms.

13. *May the God of hope fill you with all joy and peace in believing.* The title 'the God of hope' is perhaps suggested by the mention of 'hope' at the end of the immediatsly preceding quotation from Isaiah 11:10. *Cf.* 14:17, where peace and joy are blessings of the kingdom of God. Because 'the God of hope' gives his children hope in himself, they may enjoy these blessings now.

So that by the power of the Holy Spirit you may abound in hope. Once more, it is the Spirit who enables believers to experience in this life the blessings of the life to come. The grand object of their hope is the glory of God (5:2).

EPILOGUE (15:14 – 16:27)

A. PERSONAL NARRATIVE (15:14–33)

Paul assures the Roman Christians that the teaching in his letter has not been given because he imagined they were incapable of teaching one another. He is well aware of their moral and intellectual quality and what he has written is more by way of a reminder of what they already know than by way of instruction in the elements of Christianity. Moreover, although he is not the founder of their church, he is the apostle to the Gentiles, and it is in that capacity that he has written to them. He views his apostleship as a priestly service and his Gentile converts as the acceptable offering which he presents to God.

For over twenty years now Paul had exercised his apostleship, and although his task was not yet complete, he had no reason, as he looked back over those years, to be dissatisfied with the work that Christ had accomplished through him. From Jerusalem to Illyricum he had preached the gospel: in the principal cities along the main roads of Galatia, Asia, Macedonia and Achaia there were communities of believers in Christ to bear witness to Paul's apostolic activity. His aim had been throughout to preach the gospel where it had not been preached before; and now that he had finished his work in the east he looked to the west and proposed to evangelize Spain. His journey to Spain would afford him an opportunity to realize his long-cherished desire of seeing Rome, and he looked forward to meeting the Christians in the capital and being refreshed by their fellowship.[1]

First, however, he had to pay a visit to Jerusalem. The collection for the Jerusalem church which, for the past two years or so, he had been organizing in his Gentile churches was now ready to be handed over to its recipients, and Paul proposed to accompany the delegates appointed by the churches to deliver their gifts. His presence in the holy city would be for him the occasion to render an account of his stewardship thus far to the Lord who had commissioned him.

Only when his Aegean ministry had been thus 'sealed' would he take his journey to Spain and visit Rome on the way. He has already told the Romans of his eager desire to preach the gospel in their city and see some fruit for his apostolic work there, and now he speaks of his confidence that his visit to them will be attended by great blessing on his preaching. For the present, he asks for their prayers. He was under no illusion about the trouble which he might have to face in Jerusalem. How much he needed their prayers that he might be 'delivered from the unbelievers in Judaea' (verse 31) is clear from the narrative of Acts 21:27 ff. He may even have had misgivings about the welcome which he and his Gentile companions might receive from the Jerusalem church, and the way in which their gift would be accepted (if indeed it was accepted at all); at any rate he asks the Romans to pray that the gift might be acceptable.

Here the narrative of Acts (21:17–25) makes it plain – the more so because we are dealing with a 'we' section – that Paul and the Gentile delegates did meet with a welcome when they visited James and his fellow-elders. But it is equally plain that James and his fellow-elders were anxious about the reaction of the ordinary members of their church – some thousands strong, and zealots for the law – in view of reports that had reached them about Paul's teaching and practice in the lands of the Dispersion. In their anxiety to appease those zealots they suggested to Paul a course of action which, as it turned out, led to his arrest and imprisonment, and to his eventual coming

[1] See J. Knox, 'Romans 15:14–33 and Paul's Conception of his Apostolic Mission', *JBL* 83 (1964), pp. 1–11.

to Rome in circumstances quite different from those he envisaged when he sent this letter.[1]

14. *Able to instruct one another.* As evidently they were doing, unlike the recipients of the letter to the Hebrews, who had to be told, 'by this time you ought to be teachers', whereas in fact they needed to be taught the rudiments of the gospel all over again (Heb. 5:12).

15. *On some points I have written to you very boldly.* 'Very boldly', since the Roman church was not of his planting and he did not feel able to address it with the freedom which he used in writing (say) to the church of Corinth.

The grace given me by God. Cf. 1:5; 12:3.

16. *To be a minister of Christ Jesus to the Gentiles in the priestly service of the gospel of God, so that the offering of the Gentiles may be acceptable.* These clauses are full of the language of worship: Paul is a ministrant (*leitourgos*);[2] his proclamation of the gospel is a 'priestly service' (*hierourgeō*); his Gentile converts are the offering which he presents to God.

Sanctified by the Holy Spirit. There were some, no doubt, who maintained that Paul's Gentile converts were 'unclean', because they were not circumcised. To such cavillers Paul's reply is that his converts are 'clean', having been sanctified by the Holy Spirit who has come to dwell within them (*cf.* verse 19, 'by the power of the Holy Spirit'). 'We are the true circumcision,' he says in another letter, 'who worship God in spirit, and glory in Christ Jesus, and put no confidence in the flesh' (Phil. 3:3). The judaizers, who did glory in the flesh (*i.e.* in the privileges inherent in Jewish birth), were less sanctified than Gentiles who had learnt to glory in Christ alone (*cf.* Rom. 8:8). Similarly, Peter at the Council of Jerusalem reminds his Jewish fellow-believers how, when Gentiles heard the gospel, God gave them

[1] *Cf.* F. F. Bruce, 'The Romans Debate – Continued', *BJRL* 64 (1981–82), pp. 354–359.

[2] *Cf.* 13:6. In the New Testament the word always denotes religious service, and sometimes priestly service, as when Christ is described in Heb. 8:2 as 'a minister (*leitourgos*) in the sanctuary and the true tent'. Compare also verse 17, 'my work for God' (*ta pros ton theon*) with Heb. 2:17, where the same phrase is rendered 'in the service of God' with special reference to Christ's high-priesthood.

'the Holy Spirit just as he did to us; and he made no distinction between us and them, but cleansed their hearts by faith' (Acts 15:8–9).

18. *To win obedience from the Gentiles.* To win their obedience to Christ (*cf.* 1:5), in fulfilment of Old Testament prophecies of the nation's yielding allegiance to the son of David (*cf.* Gn. 49:10, and see comment on verse 12, above).

19. *From Jerusalem.* Paul began his career as a Christian preacher in Damascus and in Nabataean Arabia (Acts 9:19–22; Gal. 1:17). His more extended ministry as apostle to the Gentiles was based at first on Syrian Antioch (Acts 13:1 – 14:28; Gal. 2:11). Why then should he mention Jerusalem here as the starting-point of his ministry? He may conceivably have had some particular occasion in mind, such as the vision described in Acts 22:17–21[1] or (less probably) the conference with the Jerusalem leaders which he relates in Galatians 2:1–10; but it is more likely that he regards Jerusalem as the starting-point and metropolis of the Christian movement as a whole (*cf.* Lk. 24:47; Acts 1:4, 8), substance being thus given to the vision of Isaiah 2:3b and Micah 4:2b.

As far round as Illyricum. The province bordering the Adriatic Sea on the east. Illyricum is not mentioned in Acts or in any of the Pauline letters up to this time. But the interval between the end of Paul's Ephesian ministry and his setting out on his last journey to Jerusalem, while compressed into brief space in Acts 20:1–6, probably covered the best part of two years. At some point during this period Paul appears to have traversed Macedonia from east to west along the Egnatian Way and turned north into Illyricum. To spend some time in a Latin-speaking environment (such as he would find in Illyricum) would be a helpful preparation for his planned campaign in Spain.

I have fully preached the gospel of Christ. 'I have completed the preaching of the gospel of Christ' (NEB). He had done this by preaching it in every province between Judaea and Illyricum

---

[1] *Cf.* O. Betz, 'Die Vision des Paulus im Tempel von Jerusalem', in *Verborum Veritas*, ed. O. Böcher and K. Haacker (1970), pp. 113–123.

(not to every individual), and had thus discharged his apostolic commission in that part of the Gentile world.

20. *Lest I build on another man's foundation*. His practice is stated in 1 Corinthians 3:10, 'like a skilled master builder I laid a foundation, and another man is building upon it.' It is plain that he did not always appreciate the activity of that 'other man', whoever he might be; and he had no desire to incur comparable disapproval himself from other foundation-layers. There is no direct reference here to the Roman church or to its founder.

21. *'They shall see who have never been told of him, and they shall understand who have never heard of him.'* Quoted from Isaiah 52:15 (LXX). The Hebrew text (rendered 'for that which has not been told them they shall see, and that which they have not heard they shall understand') refers to the surprise of nations and their kings when they see the exaltation of the Suffering Servant whom formerly they had despised. The Greek version lends itself well to Paul's statement of his pioneer policy in preaching the gospel. Ample evidence has already been provided in this letter of the use made of Isaiah 40 – 66 as a source of gospel *testimonia* (see pp. 68, 196).

22. *I have so often been hindered*. Cf. 1:13.

23. *I have longed for many years to come to you*. It was not just recently that Paul had a vision of the part which the Roman church could play in the expansion of the gospel, in fellowship with (and, eventually, in continuation of) his apostolic service. See pp. 14–15.

24. *And to be sped on my journey there by you*. Without saying so expressly, Paul hopes that the Roman church will provide a base for his advance into Spain.

25. *With aid for the saints*. The members of the church of Jerusalem are 'the saints' *par excellence* (*cf.* verse 31; 1 Cor. 16:1; 2 Cor. 8:4; 9:1, 12). But Paul's converts and other Gentile Christians have become their 'fellow citizens' (Eph. 2:19), so he makes a point of regularly referring to them also as 'saints', the holy people of God (see note on 1:7). The phrase 'with aid' renders the present participle of the verb *diakoneō*, 'serve' (*cf.* 12:7; 15:8; 16:1).

Further details about this 'aid' are supplied in 1 Corinthians 16:1–4 and 2 Corinthians 8:1 – 9:15. Paul speaks more freely about it to the Roman Christians, because they were not directly involved in it. The contributing churches were those which Paul himself had planted, and it is evident that the enterprise was one to which he attached the highest importance.

For one thing, as he tells the Romans, it was a means of bringing home to the Gentile Christians their indebtedness to Jerusalem. It was from Jerusalem that the gospel had spread, first into the provinces adjoining Judaea (such as Syria, with its capital Antioch on the Orontes) and then to more distant territories (such as those which Paul had been evangelizing for the past ten years). It was a small return on the part of the Gentile churches if they were invited to contribute to the material need of the mother-church of Christendom.

For another thing, Paul envisaged it as a means of cementing the fellowship that ought to be maintained between Jerusalem and the Gentile churches. He knew that many of the stricter brethren in Jerusalem looked with grave suspicion on his Gentile mission. Some of them, indeed, thought it their duty to win his converts over from his teaching to a conception of Christian faith and life more in keeping with that which obtained among the rank and file of Jerusalem believers. Even when matters were not pushed to such an extreme, a cleavage between Jerusalem and the Gentile mission could do no good to the cause of Christ. Nothing could hope to overcome such a cleavage but a generous gesture of brotherly love.

The collection for Jerusalem marked no innovation in policy on Paul's part. A decade earlier he and Barnabas had brought a similar gift from the Christians in Syrian Antioch to the Jerusalem church in time of famine (Acts 11:30; 12:25). When the Jerusalem leaders gave Paul and Barnabas their blessing for the work of Gentile evangelization to which they had manifestly been called, they urged them to go on remembering 'the poor' (see comment on verse 26 below) – 'which very thing', says Paul as he relates the incident, 'I was eager to do' (Gal. 2:10).

But was the sending of gifts to 'the poor' in the Jerusalem church understood by both sides in the same sense? For Paul, it was a spontaneous gesture of brotherly love, a token of grateful response on the Gentiles' part to the grace of God which had brought them salvation. In the eyes of the Jerusalem leaders, however, it may have been a form of tribute, a duty owed by the daughter-churches to their mother (comparable, perhaps, to the half-shekel paid annually by Jews throughout the world for the maintenance of the Jerusalem temple and its services).

In Paul's eyes it was not only his Gentile converts' recognition of their spiritual indebtedness to Jerusalem; it was not only calculated to forge a bond of fellowship and brotherly love. It was, in addition, the climax of Paul's Aegean ministry, an act of worship and dedication before he set out for his new field of ministry in the west. It was indeed the outward and visible sign of that 'offering of the Gentiles' which crowned his priestly service thus far. The presence in Jerusalem of Gentile believers bearing gifts was a token that Paul's apostleship thus far had not been exercised in vain – a token not only to the Jerusalem church but in the sight of God. Paul perhaps planned to consummate his thanksgiving for the past and his dedication for the future by an act of worship at that very place in the temple where the Lord had once appeared to him and sent him 'far away to the Gentiles' (Acts 22:21).

26. *Macedonia and Achaia have been pleased*. Paul mentions these two provinces probably because he had been in close touch with the churches there for several months past. According to 1 Corinthians 16:1 he had organized a similar contribution in the churches of Galatia, and the presence of Tychicus and Trophimus with him on the journey to Jerusalem (Acts 20:4; *cf.* 21:29) indicates that the churches of Ephesus and other cities of proconsular Asia also had a share in this ministry.

The poor among the saints at Jerusalem. The Jerusalem believers apparently referred to themselves as 'the poor' (*cf.* Gal. 2:10, where the same word, *ptōchoi*, is used as here), and the designation, in its Hebrew form *'ebyōnîm*, survived among those

Jewish Christians of later date who were known as Ebionites. It is unnecessary to suppose, with K. Holl,[1] that Paul uses the expression to conceal his embarrassment over the fact that the collection was destined for the Jerusalem church as a whole; his repeated reference to 'the contribution for the saints' or the like suggests that he felt no embarrassment on this score.

27. *Indeed they are in debt to them.* The contribution was a voluntary gesture on the part of the Gentile churches (except that Paul kept them at it when their zeal faltered); yet it was the acknowledgment of a debt – a moral debt, not a legal one.

They ought also to be of service to them in material blessings. The view that this was not simply a charitable act, but a tribute which the mother-church had every right to expect from Gentile Christians,[2] may represent well enough the attitude of the Jerusalem church, but it was not Paul's attitude. He insists that it is an act of grace and not of formal obligation on the part of the contributing churches (*cf.* 2 Cor. 8:6–9). Perhaps, too, by this material token of the grace of God among the Gentiles he hoped more particularly to stimulate that salutary 'jealousy' of which he speaks in 11:14.[3] The verb 'be of service' here is *leitourgeō* (*cf.* the noun *leitourgos* in verse 16, with note; also 2 Cor. 9:12, where the contribution is called a *leitourgia*, 'service').

28. *And have delivered to them what has been raised.* Lit. 'and have sealed to them this fruit'. Paul uses a formal business expression; *cf.* NEB, 'delivered the proceeds under my own seal.' Perhaps, however, it is not Paul's own seal that is in view, but the seal of the Spirit; here is conclusive evidence of his work among the Gentiles (*cf.* verse 16).

29. *The fulness of the blessing of Christ.* This blessing (*eulogia*, used of the Gentiles' contribution in 2 Cor. 9:5) would be shared by Paul with the Roman Christians, and communicated through them to others (*cf.* 1:11–15).

---

[1] *Gesammalte Aufsätze*, ii (1928), pp. 58–62.

[2] K. Holl, *Gesammelte Aufsätze*, ii, pp. 44–67.

[3] *Cf.* J. Munck, *Paul and the Salvation of Mankind*, p. 303.

30. *By the love of the Spirit.* That is, the love which the Spirit imparts and maintains (*cf.* 5:5).

Strive together with me. 'Be my allies in the fight' (NEB). Perhaps he seeks their co-operation not only in prayer regarding the delicate situation awaiting him in Jerusalem, but also in his wider ministry.

33. *The God of peace be with you all. Amen.* The title 'the God of peace' recurs in 16:20 (*cf.* Phil. 4:9; 1 Thes. 5:23; also Heb. 13:20; and 2 Cor. 13:11, 'the God of love and peace'). For the possibility that one early edition of the letter came to an end with this benediction, see p. 28.

B. COMMENDATION OF PHOEBE (16:1–2)

The letter, when completed, was evidently taken to its destination by Phoebe, a Christian lady of substance who was making the journey on her own account. Paul takes the opportunity to commend her to the hospitality of the Christians to whom he writes.

1. *Our sister Phoebe, a deaconess of the church at Cenchreae.* Cenchreae, situated on the Saronic Gulf, was one of the two seaports of Corinth (*cf.* Acts 18:18). The church there was probably a daughter of the metropolitan church of Corinth. She was a *diakonos*, 'a fellow-Christian who holds office in the congregation at Cenchreae' (NEB); in a church context the word should be rendered 'deacon', whether masculine or feminine. That the duties of a deacon could be performed by either men or women is suggested by 1 Timothy 3:11, where 'the women' are to be understood as 'deacons' (like the men of verses 3–10).

2. *Receive her in the Lord.* That is, as a fellow-Christian; but, if there is any distinction here between 'in the Lord' and 'in Christ',[1] the meaning of the phrase may be conveyed more fully in the following words, 'as befits the saints.' Travelling

[1] On 'in the Lord' (7 times) and 'in Christ' (4 times) in this chapter see C. F. D. Moule, *The Origin of Christology* (1977), p. 59.

Christians could always be sure of finding hospitality with fellow-Christians wherever any were to be found (*cf.* 15:7).

A helper of many and of myself as well. The feminine noun rendered 'helper' (*prostatis*, 'patroness') is related to the participle *proïstamenos* ('he who gives aid') in 12:8. Phoebe was evidently to Cenchreae what Lydia was to Philippi (*cf.* Acts 16:15). What kind of help she gave to Paul we can only surmise.

C. GREETINGS TO VARIOUS FRIENDS (16:3–16)

Phoebe's commendation is followed by a series of personal greetings to people mentioned by name.

From this series of greetings it has been widely argued that Romans 16 was intended not for Rome but for Ephesus – that it was for Ephesus that Phoebe was bound and (more particularly) that the friends to whom Paul sends greetings lived in Ephesus.

That a separate letter to the church in Ephesus has somehow been tacked on to a letter addressed to Rome is highly improbable. The idea of an ancient letter consisting almost entirely of greetings is not such a monstrosity as was once thought by H. Lietzmann. But if chapter 16 is regarded as a separate letter of commendation, it must be recognized that greetings were habitually absent from such letters.[1] This consideration would not weigh so heavily, indeed, against the view that Paul sent a copy of Romans 1 – 15 to his friends at Ephesus,[2] and appended to it a note of commendation and a number of personal greetings.

However, 'possession is nine points of the law', and since this chapter comes at the end of a letter which was manifestly addressed to the Christians of Rome, it is natural to suppose that this chapter was equally addressed to them, unless very weighty reasons to the contrary can be adduced.

What then are the principal arguments for postulating an Ephesian destination for Romans 16?

[1] See H. Gamble, *The Textual History of the Letter to the Romans* (1977), pp. 47, 87, 91.
[2] See p. 20 with n. 4.

i. In this chapter Paul sends personal greetings to twenty-six individuals and five households or 'house-churches'. Is it probable that he knew so many people in a city which he had never visited? We should think rather of one of the cities with which he was well acquainted. Corinth can be ruled out, because the letter (including, in particular, chapter 16) was written from Corinth; but Ephesus (where he had recently spent between two and three years) is clearly indicated, especially for the two following reasons.

ii. The first persons to whom Paul sends greetings here are Prisca (Priscilla) and Aquila (verse 3). When we last heard of them, either in Acts (18:26) or in Paul's correspondence (1 Cor. 16:19), they were resident in Ephesus, where they had a church in their house, as they have here. In the absence of any hint to the contrary, we may presume they were still in Ephesus.[1]

iii. The next person to be greeted by name is Epaenetus, 'the first convert in Asia for Christ' (verse 5). Paul's first convert in the province of Asia would naturally be looked for in Ephesus, not in Rome.

iv. In addition to these personal greetings, the admonitory passage in verses 17–20 has also been thought to point to an Ephesian destination. It is unlike the rest of the letter in substance and style. In it Paul seems to depart from his policy of not addressing the Roman church with the note of apostolic authority which he used when writing to churches which he had founded himself. Besides, the dissensions referred to in this paragraph do not correspond to anything in the life of the Roman church which could be gathered from other parts of the letter. Elsewhere in the letter the only possibility of tension within the church that is hinted at is that which might arise if the Gentile members began to adopt an air of superiority over their Jewish brethren (11:13–24). On the other hand, the present admonition has points of affinity with Paul's words of exhortation and foreboding to the elders of the Ephesian church in Acts 20:28–31. We may compare the dissensions and false teaching at Ephesus mentioned in the two letters to Timothy – not to speak of the heresy which, according to the letter to

---

[1] In 2 Tim. 4:19 they appear to be in Ephesus, but at what time is uncertain.

the Colossians, was finding an entrance among Christians in another region of the province of Asia.

What now can be said in favour of the Roman destination of this chapter, over and above the initial presumption that it was sent to the same people as the rest of the letter to which it is appended?

i. Such a list of greetings would be exceptional in a letter written to a church with which Paul was well acquainted. If this chapter was intended for Ephesus, we can envisage the meeting of the church at which it was read aloud. Those present would hear Paul's greetings read out to twenty-six of their number by name. But Paul certainly knew more than twenty-six members of a church in whose midst he had spent such a long time. What would the others think? Each of them would ask, 'Why leave *me* out?' But in a letter written to a church in which he was personally unknown Paul might well send greetings to friends whom he had met elsewhere in the course of his apostolic service, and who were now resident in Rome. If he mentioned them by name, the others would not feel aggrieved at being omitted, because they would not expect to be included. In the letter to the Colossians, which was also written to a church which Paul had never visited, similar greetings are sent to a few individuals – only a few, because it did not lie on a main road and was not nearly such an important place as Rome. But Rome was the capital of the world: all roads led to Rome, and it is not surprising that many people whom Paul had come to know in other places should in the mean time have made their way to Rome. In particular, the death of the Emperor Claudius in October, AD 54, probably meant for all practical purposes the lapsing of his edict of five years earlier, expelling the Jews from Rome. If there was a general return of Jews to Rome about this time, Jewish Christians would certainly be among them. Prisca and Aquila, who had been compelled to leave Rome by the edict of AD 49 (Acts 18:2), would have gone back in AD 54 or shortly afterwards, leaving managers, perhaps, in charge of the Corinthian and Ephesian branches of their business (as they may have left one in charge of their Roman branch when they had to leave the capital). Tradespeople like them led very mobile lives in those days, and there is nothing improbable or unnatural about their moving back and forth in this way between Rome, Corinth and Ephesus.[1]

Epaenetus may well have attached himself to Prisca and Aquila and gone with them when they returned to Rome. On their return to Rome, they would keep in touch with Paul and, in particular, let him know how the Christian cause was faring there.

ii. A number of the names in verses 7–15 are better attested at Rome than at Ephesus.[2] This is largely because many more inscriptions are available from Rome than from Ephesus; and in any case it is for the most part the names and not the persons that are attested. Details are given in the notes below; readers can weigh the evidence for themselves. Perhaps the strongest case can be made out for members of 'the family of Narcissus' in verse 11; we know of a 'family of Narcissus' in Rome at this very time. Rufus (verse 13) was a commoner name at Rome than at Ephesus, but if this Rufus was the Rufus of Mark 15:21, it was probably in neither of these cities that he received his name. Yet the Rufus of Mark 15:21 seems to have been well known by name in the Roman church; we cannot say that there was not a Rufus in the Ephesian church, but we do not know that there was one. On the whole, a study of these names inclines the balance of probability in favour of Rome.

iii. 'All the churches of Christ' which send their greetings in

---

[1] The Cemetery of Priscilla, a very early Christian burying-place in Rome, situated on the Via Salaria, provides no evidence that Priscilla and Aquila spent their closing days in Rome. It was presumably called after the owner of the land, but there is no reason to identify her with the New Testament Priscilla. All that can be said is that the two ladies probably belonged to the same family (the *gens Prisca*). This cemetery contains a crypt belonging to the noble Roman family of the Acilii Glabriones. But the *nomen gentile* Acilius (Aquilius) is not to be associated with the name Aquila; our Aquila, a Pontic Jew by birth, was certainly not a member of the Roman nobility. One Acilius Glabrio was among the people executed by the Emperor Domitian about AD 95 on a charge involving a mixture of 'atheism' with addiction to Jewish ways, which has often been taken to imply Christianity (*cf.* Dio Cassius, *History, Epitome* 67.14).

[2] The evidence is presented conveniently by J. B. Lightfoot in *The Epistle to the Philippians* (1868), pp. 171–178, in his excursus on 'Caesar's Household'. Accepting the Roman provenance of Philippians, Lightfoot collected such evidence as he could find, from Rom. 16:8–15 and extra-biblical literary and epigraphic material, with a possible bearing on the identity of some of the 'saints . . . of Caesar's household' mentioned in Phil. 4:22. In so far as this evidence is relevant to Romans 16, it is summarized for what it is worth in the comments on verses 8–15 below.

verse 16 would be the Gentile churches whose delegates were joining Paul at this time to convey their churches' contributions to the Jerusalem relief fund.[1] It would be a particularly happy thought to send these churches' greetings to Rome. It might indeed be said that it would be a happy thought to send their greetings to Ephesus, but since Ephesus was one of the churches represented – by Trophimus and possibly Tychicus (Acts 20:4) – there would not be the same point in sending their greetings there.

iv. As for the admonition of verses 17–20, it would not be surprising if, after long self-restraint in addressing a church not of his own foundation, Paul broke out at last in an urgent warning against certain trouble-makers of a type with which he was only too familiar in his own mission-field. It would be too much to expect that they would not visit Rome (if they had not already done so) and try to win acceptance for their teaching there. Paul would regard it as his plain duty to put the Roman Christians on their guard against such people; moreover, his own reception in Rome could be placed in jeopardy if they preceded him there and gained a favourable hearing.[2]

3. *Greet Prisca and Aquila.* Paul says 'Prisca' (*cf.* 1 Cor. 16:19; 2 Tim. 4:19), while Luke uses the more familiar form of her name, Priscilla. 'Luke regularly uses the language of conversation, in which the diminutive forms were usual; and so he speaks of Priscilla, Sopatros and Silas always, though Paul speaks of Prisca, Sosipatros and Silvanus.'[3] Both Paul and Luke generally name Prisca (Priscilla) before her husband; perhaps hers was the more impressive personality. Paul first met them in Corinth, soon after their enforced departure from Rome (Acts

---

[1] The churches mentioned in Acts 20:4 are Beroea, Thessalonica, Derbe (or, according to the western text, Doberus in Macedonia), and the churches of Asia. Philippi was perhaps represented by Luke.

[2] The argument for the Ephesian destination of Romans 16 is presented most cogently by T. W. Manson, *Studies in the Gospels and Epistles* (1962), pp. 234–241; that for its Roman destination by C. H. Dodd, *The Epistle to the Romans* (1932), pp. xvii–xxiv. On the integrity of this chapter with the body of the letter see also K. P. Donfried, 'A Short Note on Romans 16', in *The Romans Debate*, ed. K. P. Donfried (1977), pp. 50–60.

[3] W. M. Ramsay, *St. Paul the Traveller and the Roman Citizen* (1920), p. 268.

18:2); they were probably Christians already, for Paul nowhere implies that they were converts of his.

4. *Who risked their necks for my life.* One can only speculate when and where this happened; it may have been during one of the critical phases of Paul's ministry at Ephesus.

5. *Epaenetus, . . . the first convert in Asia for Christ.* Lit. 'the first-fruits of Asia for Christ' (*cf.* 1 Cor. 16:15, where Stephanas and his family are similarly called 'the first converts of Achaia'). On Epaenetus in Rome, see p. 256.

6. *Mary, who has worked hard among you.* This has been thought to point to an Ephesian destination. Paul would know who did outstanding service in Ephesus; how could he know who had 'worked hard' among the Roman Christians? He certainly had some sources of information about the Roman church (*cf.* 1:8–9): Prisca and Aquila could tell him about its earlier days and now, since their return to Rome, they were probably in regular communication with him. Beyond that we can but speculate; we have no other reference to this Mary (one of six bearers of that name in the New Testament).

7. *Andronicus and Junias.* The second of these names might be either masculine (Junias, a shorter form of Junianus) or feminine (Junia, as in AV). But, since there seems to be no certain occurrence of the form Junias, the feminine Junia is to be preferred. This couple (perhaps husband and wife) were Jewish by birth (Paul calls them his 'kinsfolk'); they had shared one of Paul's frequent imprisonments (*cf.* 2 Cor. 11:23), possibly in Ephesus. Moreover, they were 'of note among the apostles', which probably means that they were not merely well known to the apostles but were apostles themselves (in the wider, Pauline, sense of the word), and eminent ones at that. They had been Christians from a very early date, since before Paul's own conversion. They may have been among the Hellenists of Acts 6:1 (their names suggest that they were Hellenists rather than 'Hebrews'); their title to apostleship was probably based on their having seen the risen Christ (*cf.* 1 Cor. 15:7, 'all the apostles').

8. *Ampliatus.* The name is common in Roman inscriptions of the period, and is found repeatedly as borne by members of the imperial household. A branch of the *gens Aurelia* bore this cognomen. Christian members of this branch of the family are buried in the Cemetery of Domitilla on the Via Ardeatina, one of the oldest Christian burying-places in Rome, the beginnings of which go back to the end of the first century (see comment on verse 15, p. 262). One tomb in that cemetery, decorated with paintings in a very early style, bears the inscription AMPLIAT in uncials of the late first or early second century.

9. *Urbanus.* This name, which means 'belonging to the *urbs*' or 'city' (*i.e.* Rome), is by its very nature specially common in Rome. But it was not in Rome that Urbanus served as Paul's *fellow worker in Christ*, unless the point is that he served the same Lord in Rome as Paul served elsewhere.

Stachys. This name, meaning 'ear' (of grain), is not common; one or two of its occurrences are in association with the imperial household.

10. *Apelles.* A name sufficiently common among the Jews of Rome for Horace to use it as a typical Jewish name: '*credat Iudaeus Apella.*'[1] One notable bearer of the name was a tragic actor from Ascalon to whom at one time the Emperor Gaius showed signal marks of favour.[2] It is found in Roman inscriptions, both in relation to the imperial household and otherwise.

Those who belong to the family of Aristobulus. Who this Aristobulus was cannot be determined with certainty. Lightfoot suggests his identification with a brother of Herod Agrippa I, who lived in Rome as a private citizen and, like his brother, enjoyed the friendship of Claudius. If he bequeathed his property to the emperor (a far from improbable supposition), his slaves and freedmen would have been distinguished from other members of the imperial household as *Aristobuliani* (the Latin equivalent of Paul's *hoi ek tōn Aristoboulou*). In the light of this suggested identification of Aristobulus with a member of the

---

[1] *Satire* 1.5.100.   [2] Philo, *Legation to Gaius,* 203–206.

Herod family, is it a coincidence that the next name in Paul's list is Herodion?

11. *My kinsman Herodion.* 'My kinsman' probably indicates that he was of Jewish birth (*cf.* verse 7).

The family of Narcissus. Calvin (*ad loc.*) and others have identified this Narcissus with Tiberius Claudius Narcissus, a wealthy freedman of the Emperor Tiberius, who exercised great influence under Claudius but was executed by order of Nero's mother Agrippina soon after Nero's accession in AD 54.[1] His goods being confiscated, his slaves would become imperial property and would be distinguished from other groups in the imperial household by the designation *Narcissiani.* If the identification is sustained, this greeting would be addressed to Christians among those *Narcissiani.*

12. *Tryphaena and Tryphosa.* Probably near relatives or sisters, and quite possibly twins, to whom it was not uncommon to give names derived from the same root. Of the two names Tryphosa is the more frequently found, but both occur in Roman inscriptions in connection with the imperial household and otherwise. The names, however, have Anatolian associations: Tryphaena appears in the apocryphal second-century *Acts of Paul* (chapters 27 – 43) as the name of a queen who showed kindness to Thecla at Pisidian Antioch (there was a historical Queen Tryphaena, related to the Emperor Claudius, mother of Polemon II who, at the time when this letter was written, was king of Pontus and Cilicia).

Persis. This name (meaning 'Persian woman') appears in Greek and Latin inscriptions at Rome and elsewhere as that of a slave or freedwoman, but not in connection with the imperial household.

13. *Rufus.* This name (meaning 'red', 'red-haired'), a word of Italic rather than Latin origin, was so common in Rome and Italy that there would be little point in discussing it were it not for two points of interest: first, the mention of Rufus in Mark

---

[1] Tacitus, *Annals* 13.1.4; Dio Cassius, *History, Epitome* 60.34.

15:21 as one of the two sons of Simon of Cyrene, and second, the present reference to the mother of this Rufus as being (in Paul's words) *his mother and mine*. Mark, writing his Gospel in the first instance for Christians in Rome,[1] identifies Simon of Cyrene for his readers a generation after the incident in which Simon figures as cross-bearer by saying in effect: 'You will know which Simon I mean if I tell you that he was the father of Alexander and Rufus.' He thus implies that there was a Rufus well known in Roman Christian circles in the sixties, and it is tempting to identify him with Paul's *Rufus, eminent in the Lord* (Gk. *eklektos*, 'chosen', naturally acquires the meaning 'choice' and hence 'eminent', 'outstanding').

But if this Rufus was the son of Simon of Cyrene, when did his mother prove a mother to Paul? One might hazard the guess that it was when Barnabas fetched Paul from Tarsus to become his colleague in the ministry at Syrian Antioch (Acts 11:25–26). Simeon surnamed Niger ('dark-skinned'), one of the other teachers of the church there (Acts 13:1), has been identified with Simon of Cyrene; if Paul lodged with him we can well envisage the wife of Simeon (or Simon) playing the part of a mother to their disinherited guest.

14. *Hermes*. As the name of the god of good luck this was exceptionally common as a slave-name.

Patrobas. Abbreviated from Patrobius, a name borne by a wealthy freedman of Nero. Lightfoot (*Philippians*, p. 179) suggested that Paul's Patrobas 'might well have been a dependant of this powerful freedman'.

Hermas. An abbreviation of some such name as Hermagoras, Hermodorus or Hermogenes, and a very common name. A couple of generations later it was borne by the Roman Christian (a slave) who wrote the popular allegory entitled *The Shepherd*.

15. *Philologus, Julia, Nereus and his sister*. One should render literally (with AV, RV, NEB) 'Philologus and Julia, Nereus and his sister', which might suggest that Julia was sister to Philologus as Nereus's sister was to him. Another possibility is that Julia was

---

[1] See F. F. Bruce, 'The Date and Character of Mark', in *Jesus and the Politics of His Day*, ed. E. Bammel and C. F. D. Moule (1984), pp. 69–89.

Philologus's wife; her name implies some kind of association with the imperial household. The name Philologus appears more than once in association with the imperial household.

Nereus. Roman ecclesiastical tradition from the fourth century associates Nereus (and his companion Achilleus) with Flavia Domitilla, a Christian lady of noble birth who was exiled by her uncle Domitian in AD 95 to the island of Pandateria, off the Campanian coast, but released after his death in the following year. It is from her that the Cemetery of Domitilla (see comment on verse 8, p. 259) takes its name.

Olympas. An abbreviated form of Olympiodorus.

16. *Greet one another with a holy kiss.* Cf. 1 Corinthians 16:20; 1 Thessalonians 5:26 (in 1 Pet. 5:14 it is called 'the kiss of love'). The 'kiss of peace', which plays a part to this day in the liturgy of the Eastern Church, is first mentioned as a regular feature of Christian worship in Justin Martyr's *First Apology*, 65 ('when we have ceased from our prayers, we greet one another with a kiss').

The name of Peter is conspicuously absent from those to whom greetings are sent. If these greetings were sent to Rome, the absence of his name suggests that he was not in Rome at this time.

All the churches of Christ salute you. A reference, probably, to those Gentile churches whose representatives were about to set out with Paul for Jerusalem and were with him at the time of writing (see pp. 256f.). Some of those representatives are named in Acts 20:4. At a time when one very important phase of Paul's ministry was being concluded, he might well send greetings from all the churches associated with that phase of his ministry to a church which not only occupied a unique position in the world (as the Roman church did) but also, in Paul's intention, was to play a crucial part as he embarked on a new phase.[1]

---

[1] See K. Holl, *Gesammelte Aufsätze*, ii, p. 47, n. 2.

D. FINAL EXHORTATION (16:17–20)

On the relation of this warning against subversive intruders to the letter as a whole, see pp. 254, 257. Those intruders partake of the character of the workers of iniquity against whom Paul warns other churches (*cf.* 2 Cor. 11:12–15; Phil. 3:2, 18–19). The reputation which the Roman church enjoyed for fidelity to the gospel was such, however, that a brief admonition against such sowers of discord would be sufficient. Discord was the work of Satan, and these men were servants of Satan (2 Cor. 11:14); but if the Roman Christians kept them and their teaching at a distance, God, who is the God of peace, not of discord (*cf.* 1 Cor. 14:33), would give them the victory over Satan and all his works.

17. *I appeal to you, brethren.* Cf. 12:1; 15:30; and see note on 12:1 for the 'diplomatic' flavour of *parakaleō*. There is nothing peremptory about this admonition.

Dissensions and difficulties. 'Dissensions' (*dichostasiai*) are included among the 'works of the flesh' in Galatians 5:20. 'Difficulties' (*skandala*) are obstacles in the way. One such obstacle or 'hindrance' has been mentioned in 14:13, and it may be included among those in view here.

In opposition to the doctrine which you have been taught. 'Or to the standard of teaching to which you were committed' (6:17; the same word, *didachē*, is translated 'teaching' there and 'doctrine' here). Paul is confident that the teaching which the Roman church has received is on the same lines as that which he imparted to his own churches; indeed, if the Romans pay heed to what he has said to them in 14:1 – 15:7, they will be safeguarded against the propaganda of the intruders to whom he now refers.

18. *Such persons . . . serve . . . their own appetites.* Literally, 'their own belly' (*koilia*); cf. Philippians 3:19, 'their god is the belly.' If this implies (among other things) laying down the law about food, Paul's earlier words would be apposite: 'Do not, for the sake of food, destroy the work of God' (14:20). It is impossible to be sure about the particular form of teaching against which Paul's present warning is given.

19. *I would have you wise as to what is good and guileless as to what is evil* – not so 'simple-minded' as to swallow whatever is offered (verse 17). Cf. 1 Corinthians 14:20, 'do not be children in your thinking; be babes in evil, but in thinking be mature'; also Matthew 10:16b, 'be wise as serpents and innocent [*akeraioi*, translated 'guileless' here] as doves.'

20. *The God of peace.* The title is repeated from the benediction of 15:33. It is specially apposite here, since Satan is the author of discord.

Will soon crush Satan under your feet. An echo of Genesis 3:15, where the seed of the woman is to bruise the serpent's head. The people of Christ share in his victory. Cf. Psalm 91:13.

The grace of our Lord Jesus Christ be with you. P46 and some other early witnesses omit 'Christ'; the western text omits the whole benediction, postponing it to verse 24 (see p. 266).

E. GREETINGS FROM PAUL'S COMPANIONS (16:21–23 (24))

Paul sends greetings from various friends who are with him at the time of writing.

21. *Timothy.* A native of Lystra, a convert of Paul's, whom he chose as assistant and colleague in his ministry (Acts 16:1–3). In him Paul found a peculiarly like-minded companion, a *fidus Achates*, who (he said) 'as a son with a father . . . has served with me in the gospel' (Phil. 2:22). According to Acts 20:4, he was in Paul's company along with others on the eve of his setting out for Jerusalem.

Lucius. If 'my kinsmen' applies to all three who have just been mentioned, Lucius would be a Jewish Christian. An identification with Lucius of Cyrene (Acts 13:1) cannot be made out. What of A. Deissmann's view that he was Luke the physician?[1] It is plain from the record of Acts 20:5 – 21:18 that the narrator accompanied Paul to Jerusalem, but he includes no Lucius among Paul's fellow-travellers. Luke the physician was a

---

[1] *Light from the Ancient East*, E. T. (1927), pp. 437 f.

Gentile Christian (this is indicated by Col. 4:14 in the light of Col. 4:10, and is borne out by the internal evidence of Luke-Acts). Here it would be possible, but unnatural, to punctuate after 'Lucius' so as to leave only Jason and Sosipater to be described as Paul's 'kinsmen'. There is evidence that Lucas was used as an equivalent of Lucius, but Paul elsewhere refers to the physician as Luke (Gk. *Loukas*, Lat. *Lucas*); why should he change his usage and call him Lucius?

Jason. Perhaps the Jason who was Paul's host on his first visit to Thessalonica (Acts 17:6–7, 9); he is not listed, however, as a Thessalonian delegate among Paul's companions in Acts 20:4.

Sosipater. Probably 'Sopater of Beroea, the son of Pyrrhus' who, according to Acts 20:4, was also in Paul's company at this time. On Paul's preference for formal names see comment on verse 3 (p. 257).

22. *I Tertius, the writer of this letter, greet you.* Paul regularly employed amanuenses to write his letters, but Tertius is the only one known to us by name. Whether he sent his greetings personally on his own initiative or at Paul's suggestion, Paul would certainly approve of his sending them. Perhaps he was a professional amanuensis; he was evidently a Christian, since he sends his greetings *in the Lord*.

At this point Tertius may have handed the pen to Paul. The sender of a letter in antiquity, after dictating most of it, frequently wrote the last few words in his own hand. Such an autograph (not necessarily, and indeed not usually, his signature) was Paul's authenticating mark in all his letters (2 Thes. 3:17). We may, then, envisage Paul writing the remainder of the letter himself, perhaps in the 'large letters' to which he draws attention in Galatians 6:11.

23. *Gaius, who is host to me and to the whole church.* There is much to be said for the identification of Gaius with Titius Justus, who extended the hospitality of his house to Paul and his hearers when they were expelled from the synagogue next door (Acts 18:7). 'Gaius Titius Justus' would then be his full designation (praenomen, nomen gentile, and cognomen) as a Roman citizen (a citizen of the Roman colony of Corinth).[1] Gaius was, in any case, one of Paul's first converts in Corinth (1 Cor. 1:14).

Erastus, the city treasurer. He has been identified with the civic official of that name mentioned in a Latin inscription on a marble paving-block discovered at Corinth in 1929 by members of the American School at Athens: 'ERASTVS. PRO. AED. S. P. STRAVIT' ('Erastus, in return for his aedileship, laid this pavement at his own expense'). The aedile ('commissioner for public works') was a responsible magistrate in a Roman city. The office of *oikonomos*, perhaps 'clerk of works' rather than 'city treasurer', was a much humbler one (Lat. *arcarius*). Since the pavement seems to belong to a later part of the first century, it might be inferred that Erastus acquitted himself so satisfactorily in the inferior office that he was promoted to the higher magistracy, and showed his appreciation of the honour thus done him by presenting the city with a marble pavement. He need not be identified with the Erastus of Acts 19:22 or 2 Timothy 4:20; the name was common enough.

Our brother Quartus. He is otherwise unknown. RSV assumes (like NEB and NIV) that 'brother' means 'brother in the Lord'; in that case why is he singled out to receive a designation which was common to all those mentioned? If the word means 'brother in the flesh', whose brother was he? Erastus's, since his name immediately precedes? Or, since *Quartus* is Latin for 'fourth', and *Tertius* for 'third', would it be excessively far-fetched to think of him as Tertius's brother, born next after him?

(24). At this point, as RSV margin says, 'Other ancient authorities insert verse 24, *The grace of our Lord Jesus Christ be with you all. Amen.*' The western text, which lacked the doxology (verses 25–27), brought the letter to an end with this benediction (omitting that in verse 20b). The Byzantine text (followed by the Received Text and AV) took over the western benediction here as well as the earlier one in verse 20b. A few witnesses (codices P 33 104 365 436, with the Syriac Peshitta and Armenian versions, and Ambrosiaster's Latin text) put this benediction

---

[1] See W. M. Ramsay, *Pictures of the Apostolic Church* (1910), p. 205; E. J. Goodspeed, 'Gaius Titius Justus', *JBL* 69 (1950), pp. 382 f.

after the doxology (as verse 28) and not before it (as verse 24). In its present position the benediction should not be too readily dismissed as unauthentic; if the doxology is not original (either absolutely or in its position at the end of chapter 16), the benediction forms a very fitting conclusion to the letter.[1]

F. DOXOLOGY (16:25-27)

The varying positions of the doxology in our witnesses to the text of Romans have been discussed in the Introduction (pp. 26-28). But its original position is not the only question which has been raised regarding it. Harnack argued that, as it now stands, it represents an orthodox expansion of a shorter Marcionite doxology:

'Now to him who is able to strengthen you according to my gospel, according to the revelation of the mystery which was kept secret for long ages, but is now disclosed to all the nations, according to the command of the eternal God, to bring about the obedience of faith; to the only wise God be glory for evermore through Jesus Christ! Amen.'[2]

This, he supposed (and others have followed him),[3] was a paragraph added by the followers of Marcion as a conclusion to their master's truncated text of the letter.

We have, indeed, no MS or other objective evidence for such a shorter text of the doxology. It has been argued, however, that those phrases which, on Harnack's hypothesis, are orthodox additions to the original wording are awkwardly attached,[4] especially the reference to the 'prophetic writings' in verse 26. This reference would certainly have to be recognized as an orthodox addition, if the doxology were originally Marcionite; the 'prophetic writings' played no part in the Marcionite scheme

---

[1] See H. Gamble, *The Textual History of the Letter to the Romans* (1977), pp. 129-132.

[2] In *Sitzungsbericht der preussischen Akademie der Wissenschaften* (1919), pp. 531 ff., reprinted in *Studien zur Geschichte des Neuen Testaments und der Alten Kirche* (1931), pp. 184 ff.

[3] *Cf.* G. Zuntz, *The Text of the Epistles* (1954), pp. 227 f.

[4] 'Paul has made a long period by introducing many ideas into a single sentence, and has complicated this period by a grammatical rearrangement' (Calvin, *ad loc.*).

of things. But in the absence of independent evidence for a shorter text of the doxology, the burden of proof rests on Harnack's hypothesis. If the doxology were originally Marcionite, it could not be ascribed to Marcion himself; Origen, as we have seen (p. 27), says explicitly that Marcion's edition of the letter lacked the doxology (together with everything else that comes after 14:23).

The doxology was most probably orthodox from the start. It may have been composed as a suitable conclusion for the letter in the truncated form which the western editors took over (in their innocence) from Marcion: it is based to some extent on the wording of the opening salutation. The mention of the 'prophetic writings' echoes 'which he promised beforehand through his prophets in the holy scriptures' (1:2) and 'made known to all nations, . . . to bring about the obedience of faith' is practically a repetition of 'to bring about the obedience of faith . . . among all the nations' (1:5). Cranfield, while noting that '16.25-27 makes . . . a rather un-Pauline impression', considers the passage 'to form a not unworthy, even if non-Pauline, doxological appendix to Paul's most weighty epistle' (*Romans*, pp. 7, 809).

25. *According to my gospel. Cf.* 2:16 (and 2 Tim. 2:8).

And the preaching of Jesus Christ. This phrase is essentially synonymous with 'my gospel': 'preaching' represents *kērygma*, the message proclaimed (as in 1 Cor. 1:21), and Jesus Christ is its subject-matter and substance.

According to the revelation of the mystery. For 'mystery' (a secret once kept dark but now divulged) *cf.* 11:25 (with comment); here the 'mystery' is the gospel, made known to Paul himself (at least *in nuce*) on the Damascus road for proclamation to the Gentiles (Gal. 1:12, 15-16) – the 'mystery of Christ', on account of which he was shortly to be imprisoned (Col. 4:3).

Kept secret for long ages. Cf. Ephesians 3:9; Colossians 1:26.

26. *Is now disclosed and . . . made known to all nations.* Better, 'to all the nations' (the article is expressed, as in 1:5). The 'mystery' of Ephesians 3:3-11 and Colossians 1:26-27 has special reference to Paul's apostleship to the Gentiles, through which

Gentile believers (as joint-heirs of the divine promises with Jewish believers) have been incorporated into Christ – an outpouring of blessing on a scale not contemplated in the Old Testament.

Through the prophetic writings. Harnack regarded this phrase as an orthodox addition to a Marcionite doxology, and an inept addition at that, for if the mystery was 'kept secret for long ages' and manifested only now, how could it be known through the prophetic writings? Harnack was not the only one to recognize this problem, but his solution is not the only possible one. 'Although the prophets had formerly taught all that Christ and the apostles have explained, yet they taught with so much obscurity, when compared with the shining clarity of the light of the gospel, that we need not be surprised if these things which are now revealed are said to have been hidden' (Calvin, *ad loc.*). Paul and his fellow-apostles used the 'prophetic writings' copiously in their gospel preaching; but it was only in the light of the new revelation in Christ that they were able to understand and expound those writings (*cf.* 1 Pet. 1:10–12).

27. *To the only wise God be glory for evermore through Jesus Christ! Amen.* This rendering is smoother than the Greek text which, by inserting 'to whom' before 'be glory', presents the doxology without a principal clause. The awkwardness of the construction is reproduced in RV: '. . . to the only wise God, through Jesus Christ, to whom be the glory for ever. Amen.'

William Tyndale's prologue to Romans ends with this admonition:

'Now go to, reader, and according to the order of Paul's writing, even so do thou. First behold thyself diligently in the law of God, and see there thy just damnation. Secondarily turn thine eyes to Christ, and see there the exceeding mercy of thy most kind and loving Father. Thirdly remember that Christ made not this atonement that thou shouldest anger God again: neither cleansed he thee, that thou shouldest return (as a swine) unto thine old puddle again: but that thou

269

shouldest be a new creature and live a new life after the will of God and not of the flesh. And be diligent lest through thine own negligence and unthankfulness thou lose this favour and mercy again.'

SELECT BIBLIOGRAPHY

I. COMMENTARIES

Barrett, C. K., *The Epistle to the Romans*. Black's New Testament Commentaries (London, 1957).

Barth, K., *The Epistle to the Romans*, E.T. from 6th German edition (Oxford, 1933).

Best, E., *The Letter of Paul to the Romans*. Cambridge Bible Commentary on the NEB (Cambridge, 1967).

Black, M., *Romans*. New Century Bible (London, 1973).

Brunner, E., *The Letter to the Romans: A Commentary*, E.T. (London, 1959).

Calvin, J., *The Epistles of Paul the Apostle to the Romans and to the Thessalonians*, E.T. from 1st Latin edition, Strasbourg, 1540 (Edinburgh, 1961).

Cranfield, C. E. B., *The Epistle to the Romans*. International Critical Commentary. 2 vols. (Edinburgh, 1975, 1979). On the Greek text.

Denney, J., 'St. Paul's Epistle to the Romans', *Expositor's Greek Testament*, II (London, 1900), pp. 555–725. On the Greek text.

Dodd, C. H., *The Epistle of Paul to the Romans*. Moffatt New Testament Commentary (London, 1932; reprinted in Fontana Books, 1959).

Godet, F., *The Epistle to the Romans*, E.T. (Edinburgh, 1880–81; reprinted Grand Rapids, 1956).

Haldane, R., *Exposition of the Epistle to the Romans* (Edinburgh, 1835–39; reprinted London, 1959).

Harrisville, R. A., *Romans*. Augsburg Commentary (Minneapolis, 1980).

Hendriksen, W., *New Testament Commentary: Romans* (Grand Rapids, 1982).

Hodge, C., *Commentary on the Epistle to the Romans* (Philadelphia, ²1864; reprinted Grand Rapids, 1951).

Hunter, A. M., *The Epistle to the Romans*. Torch Commentaries (London, 1955).

Käsemann, E., *Commentary on Romans*, E.T. (Grand Rapids, 1980).

Knox, J., 'The Epistle to the Romans', *Interpreter's Bible*, IX (New York/Nashville, 1954), pp. 355–668.

Kuss, O., *Der Römerbrief*, 3 parts, unfinished (Regensburg, 1957–78).

Leenhardt, F. J., *The Epistle to the Romans*, E.T. (London, 1961).

Lightfoot, J. B., 'The Epistle to the Romans: Analysis and Commentary (Chapters i-vii)', *Notes on the Epistles of St. Paul* (London, 1895), pp. 237–305. On the Greek text.

Luther, M., *Lectures on Romans*. Library of Christian Classics. E. T. from the Weimar edition, Vol. 56 (1908), based on Luther's Latin autograph of 1515–16 (London, 1961).

Luther, M., *Commentary on the Epistle to the Romans*, abridged E.T. from Weimar edition (Grand Rapids, 1954).

Manson, T. W., 'Romans', *Peake's Commentary on the Bible* (London, ²1962), pp. 940–953.

Michel. O., *Der Brief an die Römer*. Meyer Kommentar (Göttingen, ⁴1966). On the Greek text.

Moule, H. C. G., *The Epistle of St. Paul to the Romans*. Expositor's Bible (London, 1893).

Murray, J., *The Epistle to the Romans*. New International Commentary on the New Testament. 2 vols. (Grand Rapids, 1960, 1965). One-volume edition (Grand Rapids, 1968).

Nygren, A., *Commentary on Romans*, E.T. (London, 1952).

Parry, R. St. J., *The Epistle of Paul the Apostle to the Romans*. Cambridge Greek Testament (Cambridge, 1912). On the Greek text.

Schlier, H., *Der Römerbrief*. Herders Theologischer Kommentar zum Neuen Testament (Freiburg, 1977).

Taylor, V., *The Epistle to the Romans*. Epworth Preacher's Commentaries (London, 1956).

Vaughan, C. J., *St. Paul's Epistle to the Romans* (London, ⁵1880). On the Greek text.

Vine, W. E., *The Epistle to the Romans* (London, 1957).
Wilckens, U., *Der Brief an die Römer*. Evangelisch-Katholischer Kommentar zum Neuen Testament. 3 parts (Zurich/Neukirchen-Vluyn, 1978–82).

II. OTHER WORKS

Barrett, C. K., *Reading Through Romans* (London, 1963).
Beker, J. C., *Paul the Apostle* (Edinburgh, 1980).
Bruce, F. F., *Paul: Apostle of the Free Spirit* (Exeter, 1977).
Chadwick, H., 'The Circle and the Ellipse', *History and Thought of the Early Church* (London, 1983).
Davies, W. D., *Paul and Rabbinic Judaism* (London, 1980).
Davies, W. D., *Jewish and Pauline Studies* (London, 1984).
Deissmann, G. A., *Paul: A Study in Social and Religious History*, E.T. (London, ²1926).
Dibelius, M., and Kümmel, W. G., *Paul*, E.T. (London, 1953).
Dodd, C. H., 'The Mind of Paul', *New Testament Studies* (Manchester, 1953), pp. 67–128.
Donfried, K. P. (ed.), *The Romans Debate* (Minneapolis, 1977).
Drane, J. W., *Paul: Libertine or Legalist?* (London, 1975).
Ellis, E. E., *Paul's Use of the Old Testament* (Grand Rapids, ²1981).
Furnish, V. P., *Theology and Ethics in Paul* (Nashville, 1968).
Gamble, H., *The Textual History of the Letter to the Romans* (Grand Rapids, 1977).
Hanson, A. T., *Studies in Paul's Technique and Theology* (London, 1974).
Hort, F. J. A., *Prolegomena to St. Paul's Epistles to the Romans and the Ephesians* (London, 1895).
Hübner, H., *Law in Paul's Thought*, E.T. (Edinburgh, 1985).
Hunter, A. M., *Paul and his Predecessors* (London, ²1961).
Kim, S., *The Origin of Paul's Gospel* (Grand Rapids, ²1984).
Knox, J., *Chapters in a Life of Paul* (London, 1954).
Knox, W. L., *St. Paul and the Church of Jerusalem* (Cambridge, 1925).
Knox, W. L., *St. Paul and the Church of the Gentiles* (Cambridge, 1939).
Lake, K., *The Earlier Epistles of St. Paul* (London, 1911).

Liddon, H. P., *An Explanatory Analysis of St. Paul's Epistle to the Romans* (London, 1893).

Lightfoot, J. B., 'The Structure and Destination of the Epistle to the Romans', *Biblical Essays* (London, 1893), pp. 285–374 (including a critique of Lightfoot by Hort, and Lightfoot's reply).

Longenecker, R. N., *Paul, Apostle of Liberty* (New York, 1964).

Machen, J. G., *The Origin of Paul's Religion* (New York, 1921).

Munck, J., *Paul and the Salvation of Mankind*, E.T. (London, 1959).

Räisänen, H., *Paul and the Law* (Tübingen, 1983).

Ridderbos, H. N., *Paul: An Outline of his Theology*, E.T. (Grand Rapids, 1975).

Sanders, E. P., *Paul and Palestinian Judaism* (London, 1977).

Sanders, E. P., *Paul, the Law, and the Jewish People* (Philadelphia, 1983).

Schnackenburg, R., *Baptism in the Thought of St. Paul*, E.T. (Oxford, 1964).

Schoeps, H. J., *Paul: The Theology of the Apostle in the Light of Jewish Religious History*, E.T. (London, 1961).

Schweitzer, A., *The Mysticism of Paul the Apostle*, E.T. (London, 1931).

Scott, C. A. A., *Christianity according to St. Paul* (Cambridge, 1927).

Stendahl, K., *Paul among Jews and Gentiles* (Philadelphia, 1976).

Vos, G., *The Pauline Eschatology* (Grand Rapids, 1952).

Wagner, G., *Pauline Baptism and the Pagan Mysteries*, E.T. (Edinburgh/London, 1967).

Whiteley, D. E. H., *The Theology of St. Paul* (Oxford, 1964).

Ziesler, J. A., *The Meaning of Righteousness in Paul* (Cambridge, 1972).